MORROW PAPERBACK EDITIONS $2.95

MAN AND HIS UNIVERSE

What We Know About Our Own Solar System
and What We Are Searching for in the
Great Depths of Space

by Zdeněk Kopal

Man and His Universe

BY THE SAME AUTHOR

An Introduction to the Study of Eclipsing Variables
Numerical Analysis
Close Binary Systems
The Moon
Telescopes in Space
Exploration of the Moon by Spacecraft
Widening Horizons
New Photographic Atlas of the Moon

MAN AND HIS UNIVERSE

Zdeněk Kopal

William Morrow & Company, Inc., New York   1972

Published in the United States in 1972.
Copyright © 1971 by Zdeněk Kopak
Published in Great Britain in 1971.

All rights reserved. No part of this book may be reproduced or utilized in any form or by any means, electronic or mechanical, including photocopying, recording or by any information storage and retrieval system, without permission in writing from the Publisher. Inquiries should be addressed to William Morrow and Company, Inc., 105 Madison Ave., New York, N.Y. 10016.

Printed in the United States of America.
Library of Congress Catalog Card Number 74–166343

Preface

Perhaps many of you who open this book had once thought of becoming an astronomer; possessing a large telescope such as you often see featured in magazines; sitting at night at its end in the dark dome of an observatory; observing distant worlds and—eventually—making a great discovery that would make you famous all over the world. If, however, each of us who ever nursed such a thought also came to realize it, there would probably be more astronomers on this Earth than engineers, businessmen or farmers. For who is not enthralled by the starry sky at night, and does not long to fathom the depths of space with a large telescope? And yet engineers or farmers are very much more numerous than astronomers, which suggests that to become an astronomer may not perhaps be as easy as it may seem.

But, of course, one does not have to be an astronomer to have an interest in the stars. There are a great many more people who have been interested in the stars and other celestial objects since childhood, who read astronomical books and magazines, who may be members of astronomical associations, and observe the sky through telescopes which they have made with their hands. These are amateur astronomers, whose love of the subject is in no way diminished because they may not have realized their youthful plans to make a study of the stars their lifetime profession. On the contrary, most professional astronomers were recruited to their careers from the ranks of the amateurs; for if they had not truly loved their subject they would not be suited for their job.

The present book is addressed primarily to that large majority of our fellow-inhabitants of this Earth in whom the cares of daily life have not blunted—have maybe even stimulated—an interest in the Universe around us, and who may be able to spare some hours of their leisure time to join us in a guided tour of the sky and its wonders which we propose to unfold in the pages of this book.

As the reader can gather by a glance at the table of contents, the subject matter of the present book has been divided into three main parts. The first will be concerned with a class of celestial objects commonly called 'the stars', which deserve primacy in our narrative because they constitute the fundamental type of building blocks with which the mass of our Universe has been organized. Why is this so? How far away are the stars from us and how luminous are they? What makes the stars shine, and for how long? How are they formed, and how long do they last? These are some questions which we shall attempt to answer as far as our present knowledge permits. And, appropriately enough, we shall commence our story by first making an acquaintance with the nearest star to us in space—our Sun, to which we owe our daylight, whose moderate heat tempers our (cosmic) climate; and whose beneficial rays gave a chance for life to develop on our planet.

A minute inspection of the immediate cosmic neighbourhood of many stars like the Sun might show them to be surrounded with a family of another class of astronomical bodies, much smaller in mass, which because of that do not shine with a light of their own and are commonly called 'the planets'. Since their size is small and their brightness borrowed from their central luminaries, planets of other stars are very difficult to discover in close proximity to their stars; and, so far, the only indications of their existence have been detected in our neighbourhood. One such planetary family we know, however, rather well: namely, the planetary system surrounding our Sun, of which our Earth—the cosmic cradle of us all—represents only one fairly insignificant member. What is the origin, age and evolution of the solar system, and what has transpired so far from the direct exploration by spacecraft of its members which are nearest to us? In particular, what could have been the origin of life—of which we appear to be the crowning achievement—and why did life develop on the Earth alone? Some answers to these questions may be found in the second part of this book.

Its third and last part will be devoted to the 'sociology' of the stars at large. What kind of associations do they form, and how are they organized on a large scale? This will lead us to the concept of stellar systems commonly called 'galaxies'—of which our own Milky Way happens to be but one—which Nature has mass-produced in high numbers according to a certain general pattern. These 'island-universes' and their clusters represent the largest organized formations which we have so far been able to recognize; and their exploration will take us to the limit of the observable Universe. What does the present momentary glimpse of its structure disclose about the past and the future of this Universe—is it eternal or evolving? And if it evolves, in which way and to what distant goals?

Such questions as these are—in turn—bound to give rise to other fundamental questions, no less enthralling even though their scope may lie beyond the boundaries of 'legitimate' science. What is Man's place in the physical Universe, as seen in the perspective of our entire human knowledge accumulated up to the last third of the 20th century? How far can astronomical exploration be carried forward in the centuries and millenia to come? How long can Man continue to evolve in his terrestrial cradle, and how far can he leave it? Is there life elsewhere in the Universe, and what are the prospects of mutual communication? What is Man's astronomical future in the Universe, and his ultimate significance?

These are, in brief, the questions which will occupy us on many pages of this book; and the reader can judge for himself as to the extent to which we, in doing so, depart from any previous conventional astronomical 'textbook'. In another sense it will not deserve the title of a textbook; for it will not cover all the topics that one could expect to find mentioned in a textbook. We will omit any that do not prove to be associated closely enough with the central theme of our narrative. A large majority of the questions which we propose to raise, and attempt to answer, will be concerned not so much with 'How', but 'Why?'.

Some may say that a too rational approach to natural phenomena on the Earth, as well as in the sky, tends to dispel their lure for the uninitiated. I do not believe so. Why should phenomena of nature appear any less interesting merely because we succeed in understanding their cause? Is the beauty of the blue sky on a spring day—or of the golden glare of the setting Sun—diminished by our knowledge that the first phenomenon is due to the scattering of sunlight on air molecules; and the second, to its absorption by water vapour?

Instead, let the Sun set and night spread its wings unveiling the fathomless depths of the glacial lake of the stars. Perhaps it is one of those enchanted evenings in the spring when we do not walk under the stars with head bent down; and when stars may appear to us as flowers of the sky giving off the scent of jasmine and lilac which pervades the air around us. Is the view any less entrancing because we know that all stars are but distant suns of which we may not even recall a single name?

Astronomy—like any other science—can be compared to an ever-growing edifice to which new floors and fixtures are constantly being added by each successive generation. In order to make this possible a growing throng of diligent workers and craftsmen have had to surround the edifice itself with scaffolding—equivalent to the technical tools of our science—which is indispensable for further progress; and may sometimes make some of us unable to see the building behind it. This pitfall we shall earnestly try to avoid. Our aim will be to help the reader contemplate the magnificent edifice of astronomical science at some distance, as if its scaffolding were not there. It is true that, in so doing, we may lose sight at times of the signs 'men at work—pass at your own risk' which conscientious workers on top floors often post at their stations. Nevertheless, what we may perhaps lose in detail by disregard of the scaffolding that still protects our current theories or working hypotheses, we more than gain in general perspective.

In the meantime, we travel through the world, read books, listen to music, admire nature—the glaciers of its mountains and the flowers of its meadows; all because we wish to enjoy to the full what life can offer. Let us now turn to look above—not only with our eyes, but in our thoughts—at the Universe around us and all that it contains, both near and far. Our own horizon will increase immeasurably; and the treasure-chest of our knowledge, impressions, and understanding will be enriched by new diamonds of transcending beauty, not to be found anywhere on the Earth.

Zdeněk Kopal

Table of Contents

	Page
PREFACE	5
LIST OF ILLUSTRATIONS	13
GLOSSARY OF ASTRONOMICAL TERMS	15

Part One

The Building Blocks of the Universe—The Stars

CHAPTER I:	THE NEAREST STAR—OUR SUN	23
	1. The Interior of the Sun	27
	2. Sources of Solar Energy	34
CHAPTER II:	OUR STELLAR NEIGHBOURHOOD AND ITS POPULATION	43
	1. Vital Statistics of the Stars	45
	2. The Story of Starlight	54
	3. Heavenly Twins	61
CHAPTER III:	ORIGIN AND EVOLUTION OF THE STARS	74
	1. Interstellar Substrate	75
	2. The Life and Death of a Star	86
	3. Inquest by Observations	101

Part Two

The Solar Family and our Terrestrial Cradle

CHAPTER IV:	MAJOR PLANETS OF THE SOLAR SYSTEM	118

		Page
CHAPTER V:	OUR EARTH—ITS ORIGIN, STRUCTURE AND EVOLUTION	124
	1. The Anatomy of the Earth and its Composition	128
	2. The Surface of the Earth and its Evolution	137
CHAPTER VI:	LIFE ON THE EARTH	157
	1. The Evolution of Man on the Earth	168
CHAPTER VII:	OUR NEAREST CELESTIAL NEIGHBOUR—THE MOON	175
	1. Some Facts and Figures	177
	2. Lunar Landscape and its Formations	188
	3. Structure and Composition of the Lunar Surface	194
CHAPTER VIII:	OTHER TERRESTRIAL PLANETS	208
	1. Venus	208
	2. Mars	218
	3. Mercury and Pluto	225
CHAPTER IX:	COMETS AND METEORS	228
CHAPTER X:	THE SOLAR SYSTEM—ITS ORIGIN AND GRAND DESIGN	236

Part Three
The Universe at Large

CHAPTER XI:	THE COMMUNITY OF THE STARS AND OUR GALAXY	251
CHAPTER XII:	THE REALM OF EXTERNAL GALAXIES	264
CHAPTER XIII:	THE STRUCTURE AND EVOLUTION OF OUR UNIVERSE	274
	1. The Size of the Universe	274
	2. The Expansion of the Universe and its Age	284
CHAPTER XIV:	LIFE IN THE UNIVERSE?	300
INDEX		309

List of Illustrations

Between pages 160 and 161

1. A star called the Sun.
2. The great nebula in Orion.
3. Reflection nebulae surrounding the principal stars of the Pleiades cluster.
4. A 'Hole in the Sky'.
5. The 'Horsehead' dark nebula just south of Zeta Orionis.
6. Star clouds in the Milky Way.
7. Spectra of distant stars showing positions of interstellar absorption lines with their fine structure.
8. The Crab Nebula in the constellation of Taurus.
9. The planet Jupiter.
10. The planet Saturn.
11. The Earth taken from an Apollo spacecraft in July 1969.
12. Man on the lunar surface.
13. Views of the lunar crater Copernicus.
14. Lunar terrain view.
15. Man's footprint on the Moon.
16. (top) Far-encounter picture of Mars. (bottom) Near-encounter picture of Mars.
17. Halley's comet of 1910.
18. A young association of bright stars in the Perseus arm of our Galaxy.
19. The globular cluster Messier 3 in the constellation of Canes Venatici.
20. The Magellanic Clouds in the southern sky.
21. The Great Nebula in Andromeda with its companions.
22. The spiral nebula Messier 33—NGC 598 in the constellation of Triangulum.

23 The central part of the Great Nebula in Andromeda with its nucleus and dark lanes surrounding the centre.
24 (left) The Andromeda Nebula photographed in blue light. (right) NGC 205, companion of the Andromeda Nebula, photographed in yellow light.
25 The spiral nebula M51 in the constellation of Canes Venatici.
26 The spiral nebula M81 in Ursa Major.
27 The spiral nebula NGC 4565 in the constellation of Coma Berenices.
28 A cluster of external galaxies in the constellation of Coma Berenices.
29 The cluster of external galaxies in the constellation of Hercules.
30 A cluster of external galaxies in the constellation of Hydra.
31 Photographs of different types of external galaxies.
32 Relation between red-shift and distance for extragalactic nebulae.

Figures

	Page
1. The principle of the stellar parallax	46
2. Hertzsprung-Russell diagram for nearby stars	60
3. The Hertzsprung-Russell diagram for stellar population in our galactic neighbourhood	88
4. Mass-luminosity relation for Main Sequence stars	91
5. A schematic cross-section of the interior of the Earth	131
6. The Milky Way	256
7. The Hertzsprung-Russell diagram of Population II stars in the globular cluster Messier 3	262

Glossary of Terms

Aeon—a unit of time sometimes used for a time-span of thousand million (i.e., billion) years.

Astronomical Unit—the planetary unit of length equal to the mean distance between the Sun and the Earth. It is now known to be equal to 149,597,892 km, with an uncertainty of only ± 5 km.

Black Hole—the final stage of the evolution of a massive star, which on continuing contraction becomes so dense that space will close around it, and gravitational potential will prevent the escape of light from its fold.

Cepheid Variables—a class of stars in advanced evolutionary stage —called after their prototype of δ Cephei—exhibiting characteristic light variations of clock-like regularity. Their periods are, moreover, closely correlated with their absolute brightness by a 'period-luminosity relation', which has been of fundamental importance for measuring great distances in the Universe. The cepheids with periods of less than one day are frequently referred to as 'cluster-type variables', because of their occurrence in large numbers among stars of the globular clusters.

Cosmic Rays—elementary charged particles (mainly protons and electrons) accelerated in stellar and interstellar magnetic fields to relativistic velocities.

Degenerate Stars—stellar configurations compressed by contraction to such an extent that the temperature of their material will no longer respond to compression, and their density depends on the pressure alone.

Doppler Effect—a systematic shift in frequency of sound or light, caused by the relative motion of approach or recession of the emitting source.

Ecliptic—the plane in which our Earth orbits around the Sun.

Faraday Rotation—twist in the polarization plane of radiation passing through a magnetic field.

Greenhouse Effect—storage mechanism for heat absorbed by solid surface protected by an atmosphere which is transparent to incident light, but opaque to that re-emitted by the surface in longer wavelengths.

HR-Diagram—a plot of the absolute magnitude (luminosity) of the stars against their spectra (i.e., temperature), which reflects the evolutionary trends of the stellar population at large. For stars at the same distance (for instance, members of remote star clusters) the same role can be played by their 'magnitude-colour diagrams'.

Hubble's Law—an (apparently) linear relation between the red shifts of the spectral lines of extragalactic objects indicative of recession and their distance. The constant of proportionality ('Hubble's constant') in this relation corresponds to a mean velocity of expansion between 60–100 km/sec per megaparsec.

Laser—acronym for 'light amplifier with stimulated emission of radiation'; a term used to describe coherent light in which all waves oscillate in the same phase.

Light Year—a unit of length equal to the distance traversed by light in the course of one year (of 31,558,150 seconds). As light travels through empty space at a velocity of 299,793 km/sec, the length of one light-year is equal to $9 \cdot 46 \times 10^{12}$ kms or $0 \cdot 3169$ parsecs.

Magnitude (*stellar*)—a logarithmic measure of the brightness (apparent or absolute) of a star, having nothing to do with its size, and defined so that a difference of one magnitude corresponds to a ratio of $(100)^{1/5}$ or $2 \cdot 512$ in their intensity. Accordingly, a star shining a hundred times more intensively will be five magnitudes brighter. Absolute magnitude of a star is equal to its apparent brightness at a standard distance of 10 parsecs.

Main Sequence—the locus along which most stars aggregate in the HR-diagram. The reason is the fact that stars situated on the Main Sequence derive their light from a gradual conversion of their hydrogen into helium—i.e., using their most abundant and longest-lasting fuel. This is why most stars seen at any time are caught in that stage.

Glossary of Terms 17

Mascons—acronym for 'mass-condensations'—is a term used to refer to gravitational anomalies on the Moon, caused by anomalously dense material strongly localized at shallow depth below the surface.

Nova—or 'temporary star'—a term applied to recurrent flare-ups of the stars at advanced evolutionary stages, during which the respective star may temporarily increase its brightness several thousand times; and thus stars previously invisible may suddenly appear in the sky (hence their name).

Olbers' Paradox—the fact that in a supposedly infinite Universe filled everywhere with stars the sky does not appear uniformly bright in all directions.

Optical (Radio) Window—a term referring to the relative transparency of our atmosphere to visible light at wavelengths between 0.3–0.8 microns ('optical window'), and again at wavelengths in excess of 1 mm in the radio-domain of the spectrum. To light of other wavelengths the terrestrial atmosphere is almost completely opaque.

Parallax of a Star—the range of the apparent motion of a star in the sky, arising from the annual motion of the Earth around the Sun, which can be used to triangulate the distance of the respective object from us in terms of the Sun–Earth distance taken as the unit.

Parsec—the distance at which the annual parallax of the star would be equal to one second of arc. It is equal to 206,265 planetary 'astronomical units'; or to 3.262 light years.

Plasma—a microscopically neutral assembly of charged elementary particles, obtained by ionization of the elements. In ordinary plasma ('koino-plasma') particles of positive charge (like protons or other atomic nuclei) are systematically more massive than the corresponding negative particles (electrons); but in a primordial (hypothetical) 'ambi-plasma' particles of opposite polarity are encountered at all mass levels.

Pulsar—a 'pygmy star' some 100 km in size, extremely dense and representing the remnant of a supernova collapse.

Quasar—acronym for 'quasi-stellar radio source' in the sky—extragalactic objects of extreme luminosity but of enigmatic nature.

Red Shift—displacement towards longer wavelengths of spectral lines emitted by a source of light receding along the line of sight due to the radial velocity of the respective object, to systematic recession connected with the expansion of the Universe ('cosmological' red shifts), or to the presence of intensive gravitational field ('gravitational' red shifts, required by the general theory of relativity).

Regolith—fragmented stony layer covering the surface of the Moon (and other small terrestrial planets), due to cosmic abrasion of planetary surfaces unprotected by any atmosphere.

Supernova—an explosion of an ageing star of above-average mass, which eventually collapses into a pygmy star (pulsar) amidst spectacular light phenomena which lift it temporarily amongst the brightest objects in the Universe (with possible exception of the quasars); but at a loss of almost its entire mass (that gets dispersed into space).

Zeeman Effect—a splitting of spectral lines of certain elements in two or more components in strong magnetic fields.

PART ONE

The Building Blocks of the Universe

The Stars

IN OPENING up this story of man's quest to understand the Universe in which he lives, we should for modesty's sake roll up the curtain on the Universe first, and postpone man's entrance onto the stage till we can place his celestial home in proper perspective. That man and his works are not very important from the point of view of the Universe will transpire in the course of our story which, in this respect, may not be very flattering to our terrestrial egos. Yet, in a way we are important—far beyond our share in the Universe by mass and size—by being aware of its existence, and because we can contemplate its existence, and our own, with understanding. This is more than a star or even a galaxy can do on its own.

Physically speaking, however, the fundamental building blocks of the Universe—the macroscopic units in which the bulk of its mass is organized—are the stars, of which our Sun—the nearest star to us on the Earth—is only one. Such stars possess many properties in common, and differ in others, as we shall recount in the first part in this book; but basically they consist of a huge number of the more elementary particles which we call atoms, or indivisible particles—which they are not; for if they were, no star would shine very long. Our Sun consists, for example, of some 10^{57} such atoms—a number too large to be imagined, or even to be written down in full. A man weighing 150 pounds consists of about 5×10^{27} atoms of the kind most abundant in the Sun—which places him, on the mass scale, almost half-way between an atom and a star.

By and large, however, human beings are well suited by their mass and size, as well as their cosmic station, to explore the world of the stars and atoms without prejudice, and to investigate the connection between them. This connection will, in fact, provide a leading motive for the subject-matter of most of this book; and while our main attention will be directed to the macroscopic world, its understanding would be impossible without some knowledge of the microscopic structure and composition of the material of which celestial bodies consist. And while a quest for this understanding will take us—in Part III—to the most distant parts of the Universe accessible to our telescopes, the beginning of our story should commence nearer home—with our Sun.

CHAPTER I

The Nearest Star—Our Sun

'WHICH is more useful, the Sun or the Moon?' asked Kuzma Prutkov, a Russian philosopher created by the imagination of Alexei Tolstoy, and he answered after some reflection, 'The Moon, because it shines at night, when it is dark; while the Sun shines only in daytime.'

Of course, all of us know from elementary school-age that moonlight is but reflected light from the Sun. But how many of us can answer the question as to the real origin of sunlight? And this should be a very important question for every inhabitant of the Earth, whether he is an astronomer or not; for not only now, but since time immemorial, there has hardly been any phenomenon on the Earth whose cause cannot be traced back—directly or indirectly —to the energy radiated by the Sun. It is not only the suntan we acquire when basking on the beach that we owe to the Sun, or the greenery which adorns our springtime. All motion of air or water which we observe around us—from clouds overhead and the winds which propel them, to the brooks and rivers carrying rainwater back to the sea—and indeed all ocean currents at or below the surface represent but different aspects of a thermal engine constantly propelled by absorption of sunlight. And more: just as the wood we burn in our fireplace represents deposits of sunlight accumulated during its period of growth, the coal we burn in a furnace gives proof that the same Sun whose light makes our forests grow shone above the weird forests of ferns and lepidodendrons in the Carboniferous era some three hundred million years before our time; and whenever we step on the accelerator of our car we burn gas extracted from oil deposits left behind by the extinct life of bygone ages once flourishing in sunlight. In fact, whichever source of energy we consider—from windmills to hydroelectric power, from burning wood or coal to combustion of gas or oil—all this is stored sunlight, contemporary or fossil. Power due to nuclear disintegration represents the only source of energy tapped recently by human hand which may not be of solar origin, and whose sources may antedate the birth of the Sun; but even of this we are not yet sure.

Radiation is, moreover, not the only blessing which we receive from our central luminary. The mass of the Sun, which binds us to it by its attraction, sees to it that we on the Earth do not get lost in cold interstellar space, but accompanies the Sun on its journey through space at a safe distance for enjoying our relatively mild climate. The Sun is responsible for the alteration of our days and nights, for the seasons of the year, even for the fluctuations of paleo-climates across geological intervals of time; and, last but not least, for the emergence of life on this planet.

How did our Sun come into being, what keeps it shining, and what will be its ultimate destiny? Let us first describe the Sun as we see it today, and measure its present vital statistics before we enquire into its ageing process. And the clue to all this, the indispensable datum which we must establish before we can take the absolute measure of our daily star, is the distance separating us from it.

How far is it to the Sun? This question baffled the astronomers of antiquity, and even Galileo and Kepler were still ignorant of it at the beginning of the seventeenth century. The first realistic estimate was not obtained till towards the end of that century—during Newton's time—as a result of a triangulation undertaken by the scientists of the French Academy. The value then obtained—138 million kilometres—was still an underestimate; and in the course of the next 250 years astronomers improved upon it by many ingenious devices. Today, we mensurate the solar system (an effort of which a determination of the Sun-Earth distance is only a part) by timing the return of radar echoes of short pulses sent out by terrestrial transmitters—akin to the way in which the control towers of our airports keep track of incoming aircraft. This method, developed to perfection in the last ten years, made obsolete the results of previous triangulation; and disclosed that the mean distance from the Earth to the Sun is equal to $A = 149,597,892$ km, with an uncertainty of less than 5 km. Such is the precision with which we know this distance—we shall call it an 'astronomical unit'—today; light will traverse it in just under 500 seconds. It is a long way to the Sun, indeed; but the distance is not incomparably large; the cumulative yearly mileage of all the carriages on the underground systems in New York or London would exceed this 'astronomical unit' by a considerable margin.

How large is the Sun? Its apparent diameter in the sky subtends an angle of about half a degree (or, more precisely, 1919 seconds of arc), which at the mean distance of the Sun from us corresponds to an absolute radius of $R=695,700$ km, or about 109 times as large as the Earth. The distance between the two is therefore equal to approximately 214 solar radii.

How heavy is the Sun? The mass which it contains can be determined—as for all celestial bodies—by the effects of attraction which it exerts at a given distance; or, more specifically, from the length of time which it will take to swing another body—such as a planet—around it. If we employ our Earth for this exercise, we know the length of this swing to be equal to one astronomical unit or, as we have seen, $1 \cdot 496 \times 10^{13}$ cms; and at this distance the Earth will take one (sidereal) year of $31 \cdot 56$ million seconds to circumnavigate the Sun. If so, it follows from a simple rule (which astronomers call 'Kepler's third law') that the central mass whose attraction is just sufficient to perform this feat is equal to $1 \cdot 987 \times 10^{33}$ grams or just under 2000 quadrillion tons. If we were to write this number in full, the leading digit of two would be followed by 27 zeros. In the face of so long a number one could almost be tempted to think one does not have to count these zeros too accurately. But Nature does count them off exactly —a feat for which we should be grateful; for if there were only one too many, all life on the Earth would be scorched to cinders; while if one were missing, all our oceans would freeze and atmospheric gases would liquefy. For the time being, we shall defer to Chapter III-2 the question how Nature counts these zeros.

Since the mass of our Earth is (*cf.* Chapter V-1) known to be equal to $5 \cdot 978 \times 10^{27}$ grams, the mass of the Sun proves to be 328,900 times as large as that of the Earth; but since the latter is 109^3 or $1 \cdot 295$ million times less voluminous, it follows that the mean density of the solar globe is considerably smaller than that of the Earth: in fact, it comes out to be equal to $1 \cdot 408$ grams per cubic centimetre, or almost 41% higher than that of ordinary water.

The most conspicuous physical characteristic of the Sun is its output of radiation determining its brightness. Not all sunlight reaches us on the surface of the Earth, as its flux is quite severely filtered by our atmosphere. In particular, all ultraviolet just short of visible light is completely gobbled up by atmospheric oxygen (molecular or atomic) down to the domain of X-rays and beyond; while the infrared part of sunlight is very largely (though not completely) blotted out for us by oxygen compounds (mainly water vapour and carbon dioxide). Such light would not be visible to the human eye even if it could penetrate the atmosphere; but is nevertheless as real as the light you see. Light from an infrared lamp can burn your skin or, in greater intensity, blind you by causing damage to the retina of your eyes; while ultraviolet light (carrying more energy) can do the same with even greater ease— as mountaineers, who deprive themselves progressively of atmospheric protection at high altitudes, can testify from experience.

However, the bulk of the sunlight is emitted at intermediate wavelengths which do penetrate through our atmosphere without ill effects; and illuminates our landscape with light which used to be called 'white' before Newton first decomposed it into a spectrum. Moreover, its 'missing wings' behind the atmospheric curtain on each side of its 'optical window' of transparency between the red and the violet can now be recorded—and their relative contributions to total sunlight measured—with the aid of suitable detectors carried as a matter of routine beyond the confines of the terrestrial atmosphere by sounding rockets or artificial satellites.

Taking into account all contributions to sunlight emitted—both visible and invisible to the human eye—over the entire span of the spectrum, the total flux of radiant energy reaching the Earth from the Sun amounts to just about 2.00 ± 0.04 calories cm^{-1} min^{-1} —meaning that if a cubic centimetre of water were exposed normally to total incident sunlight, its temperature would rise by about 2 degrees centigrade each minute. Astronomers used to call this important value the 'solar constant'. The physicists accustomed to work in absolute units would express this as a flux of 1.39×10^6 ergs per square centimetre per second (an erg, equivalent to 2.37×10^{-8} of a calorie, constitutes the unit of energy possessed by a gram of mass moving at a speed of one centimetre per second).

We have already learned that the mean distance A of the Earth from the Sun is equal to 149.6 million kilometres (i.e., 1.496×10^{13} cm); and if each square centimetre of the surface ($4\pi A^2$) of a sphere described around the Sun with this radius is to receive an equal amount of heat, the total energy emission of the Sun must be equal to $3 \cdot 93 \times 10^{33}$ ergs/sec.* This is a truly stupendous level of energy output; the largest hydroelectric (or nuclear) power plants on the Earth are incapable of sustained energy production of more than some 10^{10} watts; and the total power consumption of all the industrial nations on the Earth at present does not exceed 10^{19} ergs/sec. The solar production exceeds our pygmy efforts by a factor of the order of 10^{14}—a number which would possess fourteen zeros if fully spelled out as a decimal number.

In order to trace this almost unimaginably large outflow of solar energy to its source, let us recall that the radius R of the Sun is known to be equal to 695,700 km; and, therefore, the visible surface of the Sun covers $4\pi \times (6 \cdot 957 \times 10^{10} \text{cm})^2 = 6 \cdot 08 \times 10^{22} \text{cm}^2$. A comparison of this latter figure with the surface of a sphere with the radius of one astronomical unit discloses that, in order to account for the value of the 'solar constant' 2·00 calories per sq cm per minute or $1 \cdot 39 \times 10^6$ ergs/cm²sec observed on the Earth, a flux of energy streaming constantly through each square centimetre of the visible solar surface must be equal to $1 \cdot 39 \times 10^6 (A/R)^2 = 6 \cdot 46 \times 10^{10}$ ergs/sec.

The Sun does not send out $6 \cdot 46$ ergs/cm²sec of radiant energy because its surface is very hot (5,800°K); rather, the surface is maintained at this temperature because a flux of $6 \cdot 46 \times 10^{10}$ ergs of radiant energy is streaming each second through each square centimetre of it from the 'engine room' of the Sun below its visible surface, where temperatures much higher still can be expected to prevail; and from which radiant energy flows out impelled by negative temperature gradient. If, therefore, we wish to discover the true sources of the tremendous solar power, we must work our way 'upstream' of the flow of the radiation carrying it outwards—deep into the interior of the Sun which is the true seat of its power.

I–1: The Interior of the Sun

How can we hope to penetrate the internal structure of the Sun and discover the secrets of its 'engine room'? The tremendous barrier of mass guarding it from direct view has already been

---

*$3 \cdot 93 \times 10^{33}$ ergs/sec $= 1 \cdot 39 \times 10^6$ ergs/cm² sec $\times 4\pi (1 \cdot 496 \times 10^{13} \text{cm})^2$.

estimated in the preceding section; and its sheer magnitude would seem to render our task hopeless from the outset. Surely no fairy-tale princess was guarded by more formidable dragons than those which would seem to stand between us and the deep interior of the Sun. Nevertheless, scientists of the past fifty years, undaunted by the task, have emerged triumphant from the protracted struggle with the dragons of ignorance, using irresistible weapons called 'laws of nature'. The laws of nature can be forged into swords sharper than Excalibur; and their use by skilful hands can force Nature to reveal its most closely guarded secrets.

The principal laws of nature which the astrophysicist who sets out to force his way into the interior of the Sun—or of any star—must employ are the three famous 'principles of conservation': namely, the conservation of mass, energy and momentum. These are principles of great generality, governing the physical world on the Earth as well as in the heavens; and their consequences can be expressed in terms of mathematical equations whose solution contains the answer to each particular problem. Our present problem can, in turn, be formulated as follows: Does an agglomeration of matter equal to the Sun's mass have to occupy the volume of a sphere of the solar radius and emit the light which we observe (corresponding to a flux of $3 \cdot 9 \times 10^{33}$ ergs of radiant energy per second)?

The problem confronting the astronomer in this connection bears a close comparison with the task of a terrestrial architect or engineer at the design stage of a new building or an aircraft fuselage. In order to find out whether the projected building will not collapse, or the aircraft disintegrate when exposed to the expected stresses, the engineer does not have to build the structure first and see what happens. He can predict the outcome from known properties of the materials and their response to anticipated stresses, which are governed by differential equations deduced from the conservation laws.

The 'astrophysical engineer' concerned with a reconstruction of the internal structure of the Sun does likewise; and, in some respects, enjoys advantages which should fill his terrestrial colleagues with envy. The latter are frequently called upon to deal with the properties of materials in a solid state, which are notoriously difficult to coerce under a mathematical harness. On the other hand, stellar astrophysicists deal exclusively with proper-

The Nearest Star—Our Sun

ties of matter in the gaseous state—and, moreover, at such high temperatures that differences between properties of different kinds of matter (i.e., different chemical elements) are largely obliterated. The mathematical equations governing the internal structure of the Sun are simple in comparison with those controlling the stability of ferro-concrete skyscrapers or supersonic aircraft.

What are the more specific requirements which the internal structure of the Sun must satisfy in order to account for the observed properties of our luminary? First, the principle of the conservation of momentum requires that the total pressure of gas (and radiation) anywhere inside the Sun must be adequate to support the weight of the overlying mass—so that the whole structure neither expands, nor shrinks—and at the centre must attain the maximum value due to self-compression by the entire mass. An elementary application of the hydrostatic principle discloses that the pressure at the centre of the Sun must be of the order of magnitude of the quantity Gm^2/R^4, where m and R denote, as before, the solar mass and radius while G stands for the value of the 'gravitational constant'. Since the latter is known (see Chapter V) to be equal to $6 \cdot 67 \times 10^{-8} \text{cm}^3/\text{g sec}^2$, and $m = 1 \cdot 99 \times 10^{33}$g while $R = 6 \cdot 96 \times 10^{10}$cm, this central pressure should be about ten billion atmospheres. The pressure resulting from a self-compression of solar mass into the volume which it occupies is thus enormous! We may add that the more exact value of this pressure (resulting from an integration of the detailed appropriate equations) is 17 billion atmospheres.

The conservation of mass is likewise enforced in the Sun by the very high degree of self-attraction generated by its mass; so that only a very minute trickle of it can dissipate through the solar corona to give rise to a semi-permanent 'solar wind'; and the same is true of that fraction of the solar mass which can dissolve into radiation and escape as nimble-footed photons with the velocity of light, thumbing their noses at gravity.

The principle of the conservation of energy leads to somewhat more complicated consequences for the regulation of heat flow inside the Sun, which we shall attempt to explain with the aid of a terrestrial analogy. Suppose that the room in which I write or you read enjoys the blessings of a central heating system, the furnace of which, located in the basement, constitutes a source of heat which is transported through piping by steam or water into the 'radiator' in our proximity. In what way does this proximity benefit us? The central heating plant should maintain our radiator at a temperature considerably above that of the room, as we can verify by placing our hand upon it. But it is not only our hand which can derive some benefit from heat thus imported to our room. The air around the radiator gets heated as well, expands as a result and rises to the ceiling—making room for cooler air near the ceiling to take its place. This, in turn, sets up a system of air circulation inside the room which re-distributes temperature between the heating element and any other place by a process which physicists call 'convection'; and our room is in 'convective equilibrium', which may remain in 'steady state' (with the temperature remaining everywhere constant—though not necessarily the same) until we disturb it by opening a window or shutting off the radiator. In addition, a certain (small) amount of heat will reach us from the radiator directly by conduction through the air; though in gaseous media—not only in our room—convective transport of heat by material currents is very much more effective than that provided by conduction.

Suppose, however, that we annihilate both convection as well as conduction by enclosing the radiator of the central heating in a container which we evacuate and thus deprive of any contact with the air around it. Do we derive any heating benefit from it under these conditions? The answer is in the affirmative; for our heating element also radiates light whose absorption can produce a sensation of heat as well. The radiative properties of such an element should approximate closely to those of what physicists call a 'black body'; and from Planck's law we know that the amount of total radiation emitted by it increases with the fourth power of its absolute temperature. Suppose that our heating plant maintains the radiator at a temperature of 80°C. At this temperature, the bulk of black body radiation is emitted in the deep infrared to which our eyes are insensitive. However, some of it would no doubt be absorbed by outstretched hands; and although it would not warm them much, its intensity could be recorded by appropriate instruments.

At temperatures as low as 80°C radiative transport of heat is very much less effective than that which takes place by convection; and, therefore, we could describe our room as being in 'convective equilibrium'. This would not, however, be the opinion of a steel worker in front of an open blast furnace, because molten iron at a temperature of 1,800°K emits 700 times as much radiation as the central heating element in our room; nor is radiative transfer of heat which we receive through the walls of a vacuum valve from its incandescent filament inside negligible. Every physical system transports heat by all means available to it for this purpose—conduction, convection, or radiation—but it may happen in particular cases that one of these proves so much more effective for its task than the others that it alone can be considered as the sole vehicle of energy transport; the exclusion of others would make no significant difference. In such cases we may speak of a 'radiative equilibrium' or 'convective equilibrium' of a given physical system, referring to the prevalent process of energy transport; though all others are operative as well and contribute what they can.

Which type of energy transport prevails in the Sun? We know now that, throughout most parts of the solar interior, energy flows outwards predominantly in the form of radiation; other methods of transport are relatively insignificant, except in the outermost fringe of the Sun—at levels accessible to direct observation—where the phenomenon of 'solar granulation' (a transient net of surface structure giving it an appearance of boiling rice) is unmistakably caused by convection. The individual short-lived 'granulae', which form and dissolve on the time scale of a few minutes, represent the tops of convective columns in the solar atmosphere (analogous to the cumulus 'clouds of good weather' on the Earth). Occasionally, the solar good weather gets broken by local cyclones and electrical storms which the astronomers call 'sunspots' (see Plate 1); and such storms may sometimes hover in the same locality for up to two or three months. Whatever hazards such spots may offer to solar weather forecasting, one prediction will be true at all times: namely, the weather will invariably be 'very hot'—about 5,800 degrees!

The convective columns in the outer layers of the Sun—whose symptom is photospheric granulation—do not reach to very great depth; only down to about one per cent of the total radius of the Sun. Below that level, the temperature keeps steadily increasing inwards; but its gradient causes convection to cease and radiative equilibrium is established almost to the Sun's centre. Whether or not the 'deep interior' of the Sun is compressed sufficiently to enable it to develop a small convective core near the centre remains still an open question; but such a core—if it exists—could occupy only a very small space.

When the equations governing solar structure are integrated for the appropriate type of equilibrium, it transpires that the density of solar material—which is equal to only about 10^{-4}g/cm^3 at the base of its atmosphere where we can penetrate with our observations—near the centre attains an incredibly high value of some 90 g/cm^3, which is approximately five times that of solid gold. No material of comparable density can be produced in terrestrial laboratories. More accurate computations disclose that the central temperature of the Sun should be close to 13,700,000 degrees; and that its internal temperature should be between one and ten million degrees throughout most of its mass.

These computations imply that the solar material behaves like a perfect gas. Is such an assumption legitimate in view of the high densities to which such material is compressed? The answer to this question turns out to be in the affirmative; and the clue to it is the high degree of ionization of matter which should be expected under these circumstances.

In the gases of the atmosphere of the Sun—the composition of which can be determined by an analysis of the solar spectrum—the predominant constituents are hydrogen (75 per cent by weight) and helium (24 per cent); followed by heavier elements present in amounts so small that they could be almost described as impurities. Moreover, virtually all these elements are present in the neutral state—meaning that their atoms could, in the prevailing climate, retain the full complements of their electrons. As the pressure and temperature rise inwards, however, increasing ionization will take place which will deprive all but the heaviest nuclei of the greater part of their elaborate electron cloaks, and convert the originally neutral gas into a plasma which is susceptible to a much greater degree of compression.

The physical state prevalent in the neutral gas can be compared with a ballroom of bygone days in which ladies were attired in crinolines—analogous to the complete electron shells of neutral atoms. Obviously, under such circumstances, only a limited number of pairs could move freely in a ballroom of a given size—like particles of matter in a gaseous state. If more and more couples force their way to the parquet, however, the crinolines are soon bound to be crushed by mutual collisions between individual couples, which may sometimes lead even to a temporary separation of partners. The dance can still go on; though the ladies' attire will soon resemble more modern fashions; and increasing temperature will transform the gentlemen's starched shirts into limp rags. In the Sun, according to the laws of physics governing atomic structure, it is possible to prove that ionization of matter brought about by increasing compression will so diminish the specific volume of the ions that their mobility will enable them to behave like gas particles at densities of $100 \text{g}/\text{cm}^3$ or even higher.

Just as a dance hall so congested that partners would only occasionally get hold of each other would not be a very comfortable place of amusement, the interior of the Sun constitutes a veritable inferno which would have completely defeated the imagination of Dante or any other poet; and to describe it properly calls for the pen of a scientist. Listen to the account of its scenery outlined by the late Sir Arthur Eddington, one of the knights for whom stellar interiors were their second habitats, in his delightful lectures on *Stars and Atoms**.

'Dishevelled atoms tear along at 50 miles a second with only a few tatters left of their elaborate cloaks of electrons torn from them in the scrimmage. The lost electrons are speeding a hundred times faster to find new resting-places. Look out! there is nearly a collision as an electron approaches an atomic nucleus; but putting on speed it weeps round it in a sharp curve. A thousand narrow shaves happen to the electron in 10^{-10} of a second; sometimes there is a sideslip at the curve, but the electron still goes on with increased or decreased energy. Then comes a worse slip than usual; the electron is fairly caught and attached to the atom, and its career of freedom is at an end. But only for an instant. Barely has the atom arranged the new scalp on its girdle when a quantum of light runs into it. With a great explosion the electron sucks up the energy of the ray and darts off again for further adventures. Elsewhere two of the atoms are meeting full tilt and rebounding, with further disaster to their scanty remains of vesture.

'As we watch the scene we ask ourselves, can this be the stately drama of stellar evolution? It is more like the jolly, crockery-smashing turn of a music hall, or the hair-breadth

*Oxford University Press (1930).

escapades on the films. The knock-about comedy of atomic physics is not very considerate to our aesthetic ideals, and this "music of the spheres" has almost a suggestion of—jazz. But it is all a question of time-scale. The motions of the electrons in stellar interiors are as harmonious as those of the stars but in a different scale of space and time, and the music of the spheres is being played on a keyboard 50 octaves higher....

'And what is the result of all this bustle? Very little. The atoms and electrons for all their hurry never get anywhere; they only change places. Just as many electrons are repaired as they are smashed; just as many bundles of light are sent out as they are absorbed; just as many electrons are captured as are exploded away. The light waves are the only part of the population which do actually accomplish something. Although apparently darting in all directions indiscriminately, they do on the average make a slow progress outwards. There is no outward progress of the atoms and electrons; gravitation sees to that. But the encaged light wave leaks out slowly as through a sieve. It hurries from one atom to another, forwards, backwards, now absorbed, now flung out again in a new direction, losing its identity, but living again in its successor. It changes at the lower temperature from X-rays to light-rays, being altered a little at each re-birth. It will thread the maze for hundreds of years, until, at last, it finds itself so near the boundary that it can dart outside and travel forward in peace.'

And perhaps, we may add, it will be intercepted on its way through space by a tiny solid speck known as the Earth, to tell its inhabitants that the Sun is shining.

I–2: Sources of Solar Energy

The light we receive from the Sun represents the most direct link with our central luminary; but its source remains yet to be accounted for. In the preceding section we attempted to reconstruct from the observed mass and size of the Sun the physical properties of its interior. Does it follow from these properties that matter exposed to them is bound to emit light, in amounts adequate to account for the observed brightness of the Sun?

In the first section of this chapter we mentioned that the Sun emits into space an amount of radiant energy equal to $3 \cdot 9 \times 10^{33}$

ergs per second. A globe of coal of solar mass could give off so much heat for only about 6,000 years before getting completely burned out; and although this time scale would have satisfied Archbishop Ussher (or, for that matter, Isaac Newton) as being compatible with biblical tradition, it is far too short to accommodate the evolution of the observed features of the surface of the Earth. By the middle of the nineteenth century, the physicists Helmholtz and Kelvin pointed out that if the Sun shrank in the past to its present size from a state of infinite distension, a conversion of the gravitational energy thus lost into heat would provide a source to defray the present solar energy output for about 50 million years. This period, while about ten times as long as that provided by chemical burning, proved to be impossibly short in comparison with the age of solid rocks, computation of which has been established since the commencement of this century from the progress of spontaneous decay of certain radioactive trace elements. The age of the oldest rocks found on the Earth is approximately $3 \cdot 5$ aeons or thousand million years; and that, moreover, their structure and stratification show clearly the effects of wind and water. If, however, liquid water existed on the Earth's surface that long ago, the mean temperature on the surface of our globe maintained by the heat from the Sun could not have been very different then than it is now. Therefore, it follows that the Sun must have possessed in its interior an energy store capable of releasing, in the course of the time, radiant energy equal to its present output times $3 \cdot 5 \times 10^9$ years or $1 \cdot 1 \times 10^{17}$ seconds; and $3 \cdot 9 \times 10^{33}$ ergs/sec times $1 \cdot 1 \times 10^{17}$ seconds leads to a tremendous quantity of 4×10^{50} ergs which the Sun should have expended in the past. Where does it come from?

It has become evident within the past 30–40 years that the only possible source equal to the required demand is subatomic energy, stored in the structure of atomic nuclei; and the investigations of the past quarter of a century have enabled us to establish its identity. In order to do so, it will be necessary to consider what kind of nuclear fuel is likely to be available in the requisite abundance—i.e., the chemical composition of the solar interior—a question which so far we have largely been able to keep in abeyance. Computations of the pressure or density prevailing inside the Sun depend on the chemical composition of its material; but in not too sensitive a manner. Chemical composition affects the mean molecular weight of the material, intervening in a relation between pressure and temperature; but on account of high ionization the range within which molecular weight of solar plasma can vary throughout the interior is very small almost regardless of composition.

This composition affects somewhat more sensitively the absorption of light by solar plasma, which impedes the energy flow in radiative zones. This plasma is, in effect, so opaque that if we could —by some kind of a physical miracle—find ourselves in the midst of it, we could barely see more than a foot or so ahead; and in denser parts of the deep interior we could scarcely see the noses in front of our faces; so opaque is solar matter in its ionized state. Heavy elements contained in it are such voracious devourers of radiation that a small admixture of them may affect the energy flow to an appreciable extent.

The only part of the Sun which can be analyzed for chemical composition of the material is the semi-transparent outer fringe open to spectroscopic analysis; and we have mentioned already that its predominant constituent is hydrogen. The same turns out to be true in the Sun's interior as well—recent computations indicate that hydrogen forms not less than three-quarters of its mass. At temperatures prevalent in the solar interior all hydrogen is completely ionized—i.e., its constituent nuclei (protons and electrons) are divorced into an ionized gas whose characteristics were described by Arthur Eddington in the preceding section. Is it, however, possible for Nature to squeeze out of it the requisite amount of light, and in what manner?

In order to answer this question, let us consider the most common phenomenon which can occur in solar plasma: namely, an encounter of two of its protons—the electrons, although equally numerous or more (through ionization of heavier elements), cannot matter much because of their minute mass. As they encounter each other in innumerable cases, do they always have to swing by, or can they sometimes get stuck? Under the conditions prevailing in the solar interior (approximating closely to the conditions which physicists call a 'thermodynamic equilibrium') the velocities of all particles are controlled solely by the temperature of the plasma; and at 14 million degrees—a temperature prevalent near the Sun's centre—the average velocity of its constituent protons should be close to 600 km/sec.

It does not follow that all particles—even of the same kind—move with the same velocity (just as not all dancers in a packed hall move about with the same speed). In thermodynamic equilibrium, the distribution of their velocities is governed by Maxwell's law, which admits the simultaneous existence of particles of any speed, but only in certain proportions which depend again on the temperature. For example, while 600 km/sec represents the average velocity of protons in the deep interior of the Sun, about 4·4% of the mixture can be expected to move twice as fast; while the proportion of those moving five times as fast is only 6×10^{-15} of the whole; and Maxwell's law can be invoked to describe similarly the proportion of particles endowed with any other excess speed.

If, as a result of their endless 'random walk' through the solar interior, two protons happen to run against each other at high speed, under what conditions can they manage to 'stick'? A formidable obstacle to such an event is the mutual electrostatic repulsion of two particles carrying equal charge—an obstacle to which the physicists refer as the 'Coulomb barrier'. The strength of this barrier is tremendous, and yields only to a nuclear artillery-fire of a most exceptional kind. The physicists assess the energy necessary to penetrate this barrier at about a million 'electron volts'.* This energy becomes, however, equal to that of a proton projectile moving at a speed of almost 20,000 km/sec—i.e., more than 30 times as fast as the average velocity of particles in a hydrogen plasma at 14 million degrees; and Maxwell's law makes it evident that the number of the protons possessing the requisite energy in the solar plasma in thermodynamic equilibrium will be minute. The physicists estimate that any particular pair of its protons is likely to undergo this experience only once every 10^{10} years, or 10 aeons of cosmic time.

On the other hand, this does not mean that this extremely low probability of a single event of this kind should make them rare in the solar interior as a whole. Far from it; for the actual number of the protons in the solar interior is again tremendously large. We have already mentioned in the first section of this chapter that the total mass of the Sun is equal to 2×10^{33} grams, of which not

---

*An electron-volt (eV)—a unit of energy frequently used in atomic physics—represents the gain in energy of an electron traversing a potential difference of one volt. In absolute units, $1 \text{ eV} = 1 \cdot 591 \times 10^{-12}$ ergs.

less than three-quarters represents hydrogen. The mass of a single proton has been measured in the laboratory to be equal to $1 \cdot 67 \times 10^{-24}$ of a gram. A division of these two numbers discloses that the solar interior contains about 10^{57} protons. Therefore, in spite of the fact that any pair of them is likely to collide with energy sufficient for penetration of their respective Coulomb barriers only once in ten billion years or 10^{17} seconds, some $10^{57-17} = 10^{40}$ of them are likely to react in this manner each second; and the outcome is the production, from two protons, of the nucleus of a 'heavy hydrogen' or deuteron, accompanied by the emission of a positron and a neutrino. The positron will, however, almost instantly react with one of the ubiquitous free electrons of the plasma and disappear in the flash of gamma-radiation which represents the first instalment of the production of light in this manner; while the neutrino (an elementary particle of mass comparable with that of the electron, but possessing no charge) reacts with matter so weakly that it may escape from the Sun into space without contributing in any way to its luminosity. Untold numbers of such solar neutrinos may, in fact, be passing through your body as you sit reading these words.

To describe these events in less technical and more picturesque terms, any proton of solar plasma in the deep interior of the Sun can be compared to a knight-errant constantly jumping on his charger at high speed and presenting a target to the continuous bombardment by the bullets and arrows from other knights in the melée. Most of them will find the armour he wears—equivalent to the Coulomb barrier of our proton—impermeable; and their bullets will bounce off his breastplate like peas shot from a child's catapult. However, very rarely a bullet arrives at such speed as to penetrate the armour and sink into the knight's flesh. If and when this occurs, a wonderful transformation will take place inside the armour which will change the identity of its inhabitant; for as we lift the visor of his helmet, we no longer find the former proton there, but a new and heavier version of our knight—Sir Deuteron.

Sir Deuteron will, of course, continue his aimless prance in the lists and expose his breast to the incoming shots of lesser breeds who pursue him wherever he turns. His armour is, however, no longer the same as it was; and its inhabitant becomes almost instantly the prey of another proton, leading to the production of a nucleus of 'light helium', accompanied by the emission of another flash of gamma-rays. This destruction of the deuteron is almost instantaneous; for whereas any two protons may wait 10^{10} years for a chance to procreate a deuteron, their offspring is likely to lead an independent existence, under the same conditions, for only about 10 seconds before giving birth to light helium.

At this stage, a continuation of this process by further proton capture becomes no longer possible. Instead, by far the likeliest sequel is a reaction between two light helium nuclei leading to the production of the nucleus of ordinary helium (i.e. an alpha-particle) which—under solar conditions—is entirely immune to any further proton bombardment, and returning two protons into the fray.

The net result of the irreversible cycle of reactions, representing a nuclear fire burning hydrogen 'fuel' into helium 'ashes', results in the production of one alpha-particle, two positrons and two neutrinos from four protons. The two positrons, once formed, will perish almost immediately by annihilation with two electrons to give birth to the requisite quanta of gamma-radiation; and the latter will be rapidly transformed by absorption into local thermal energy.

But the formation of an alpha-particle from four protons constitutes by itself an exothermic process par excellence—and one of the most effective which we shall meet in our Universe. For the atomic weight of a proton is known from accurate laboratory measurements to be equal to 1·008131; and that of an alpha-particle, 4·00386; hence, the mass-defect m of our cycle in grams is equal to 0·02866 times $1·673 \times 10^{-24}$ g, corresponding to an energy $E=mc^2$ where $c=2·99 \times 10^{10}$ cm/sec is the velocity of light. Accordingly, the energy released by the formation of any single alpha-particle by our proton-proton cycle is equal to $E = 4·32 \times 10^{-5}$ ergs; and since (as we have seen) there are some 10^{40} protons in the Sun which could enter the cycle each second, its energy production estimated on this basis should be about $4·3 \times 10^{-5} \times 10^{40} = 4 \times 10^{35}$ ergs/sec—i.e., a hundred times as large as the solar luminosity actually observed.

Two conclusions follow from this comparison. First, that nuclear burning of hydrogen into helium in the solar interior will provide a more than adequate source of energy to keep the Sun shining, at its present rate, for a very long time. If the entire mass of the Sun represents hydrogen potentially convertible to helium, its total

energy store available for re-radiation is equal to $5 \cdot 3 \times 10^{51}$ ergs*
which at the present rate of expenditure of $3 \cdot 9 \times 10^{33}$ ergs/sec
would not be expended till $4 \cdot 5 \times 10^{10}$ years have passed—a time
interval about ten times as long as the age of the oldest lumps of
solid matter—terrestrial or cosmic—now in our hands.

Secondly, the fact that the observed output of radiant energy
of the Sun proves to be only about one-hundredth of that which
could be squeezed out of its mass under conditions prevailing in
the solar interior, makes us realize that hydrogen can burn into
helium in a relatively small part of the Sun's mass; only in its
central regions where conditions are sufficiently extreme for nuclear
burning to occur at an appreciable rate. It is indeed only the central
regions of the deep interior—containing no more than a few per
cent of the Sun's total mass—which constitute a 'lukewarm' and
slowly burning (or, rather, smouldering) thermonuclear reactor that
is responsible for generating the entire energy which makes—and is
bound to make—the Sun shine. The rest—more than nine-tenths
of the entire mass of the Sun, in which the temperature drops
below ten million degrees—is already 'cold' from the nuclear point
of view, and constitutes only the 'casing' or walls of the reactor.
This 'casing' fulfills several eminently useful roles. The weight of
the overlying material prevents the central reactor from flying
apart, and (by its low rate of energy transmission) keeps it thermostated to run at a correct and steady rate. In addition, its absorption
properties are such that light born in the deep interior, in the form
of moderately hard gamma-rays, is gradually transformed into
thermal X-rays and radiation of gradually increasing wavelengths
—until the light actually leaving its surface has lost its earlier
virulence which would make exposure to it too dangerous.

A gradual burning of hydrogen into helium in the deep interior
of the Sun constitutes, moreover, a process that is irreversible and
proceeds at a controlled rate. Therefore, the hydrogen/helium ratio
obtaining at any particular time could be used, in principle, to
estimate the age necessary to establish it, as well as the future still
remaining before all hydrogen becomes converted to helium and
the flow of energy (due to this cause) ceases. At the present time,
the solar mass consists of approximately 75% hydrogen, and 24%
helium; while all elements heavier than helium add up to no more

*$1 \cdot 98 \times 10^{33} \times 0 \cdot 02866 \times c^2$.

than 1% of the Sun's mass. What can these proportions tell us about the Sun's past and the future?

Astrophysicists studying these problems conclude that, as time goes on and the hydrogen depletion results in the accumulation of helium 'ashes', the luminosity of the Sun will gradually increase. If, furthermore, the bulk of the present 24% helium content of the Sun has been the result of nuclear burning in the past, the present age of the Sun should be between 4–5 aeons (i.e., four to five thousand million years); the more exact value depending on the amount of helium which the mass of the Sun may already have contained at the time of its birth. Moreover, the new-born Sun should have been about 40% less luminous then than it is now; though as to whether or not it was any different in size, opinions still differ.

In the future, the Sun will grow gradually brighter—in advanced stages of its evolution becoming several times brighter than we see it today without losing more than 0.8% of its mass by radiation. This, eventually, is bound to spell doom to all life on the Earth—our oceans will evaporate, and the atmosphere dissipate into space; while surface rocks will be brought to red heat. However, these dire events—while inevitable eventually—will not take place too soon; for the evolution of the Sun is a very slow process. Its remaining hydrogen content guarantees that the solar future will be much longer than its past; and that not five, but many aeons of time are still bound to elapse before the solar symptoms of old age will make our terrestrial abode uncomfortable. At present the Sun is, in fact, still in the prime of its life.

Moreover, the rate of its evolution is too slow for us to take any note of. The Sun which illuminates our own days is indistinguishable from Napoleon's 'sun of Austerlitz'; or from the bright disc worshipped at Stonehenge or by the Egyptian pyramid-builders. And more; it is the same Sun which saw our distant ancestors descend from the trees to practise walking erect, or the dinosaurs feed in the Jurassic steppes. It was the heat of this Sun which nurtured the growth of the cryptogamic jungles of the Carboniferous period, now petrified as coal which we burn in our fireplaces. It is possible that sunlight was a bit dimmer than today when the first trilobites crawled on to the dry land from the Cambrian puddles some 500 million years ago; and the days were probably a good deal less bright at the time when the first symptoms of terrestrial life flickered in the shallow waters of the Earth some 2–3 aeons ago.

Yet, throughout this time, the beneficial rays of the Sun have never ceased to lovingly nurture those strange creatures on the Earth. Modern science has dispelled a good deal of the mystery surrounding the brilliant disc of the Sun—worshipped by our ancestors since time immemorial as the giver of life and ruler of the seasons. Science has helped us to understand not only its present manifestations but also its past and its future far more completely than any visions of the ancient priests or poets could have done; and our new knowledge should fill us with far greater reverence for the Sun than could be felt by Akhen-aten on the eastern bank of the Nile more than three thousand years ago.

CHAPTER II

Our Stellar Neighbourhood and Its Population

IN THE previous chapter we have been concerned with the principal properties of our daily star—the Sun. This Sun is the most important celestial body for us, even though it may only shine in daytime! Besides, if the Sun sets for us, it still dispenses its light and heat to the antipodes; and regular alternation of day and night sees to it that no part of the Earth's surface will be cut off from sunlight for too long.

If we watch the brilliant disc of our central luminary slowly setting below the horizon, descending darkness gradually unveils the stars above our heads. What are they—these stars who watch with ageless enigmatic eyes from afar the teeming humanity on Earth preparing after each sunset for its daily rest? In this case, we cannot quote the authorities of old Greece to enlighten us; because for them stars were just individual lights suspended from the celestial sphere since the time of their creation, and moved about by angels in their appointed immutable courses. In Christian times the Fathers of the Church, realizing the compatibility of such a picture with the story of the Creation according to the Old Testament (a story going back to pre-Greek times), adopted it as their own; and in the Middle Ages Dante Alighieri, by basing the structure of his *Comedia Divina* upon it, secured poetical immortality for it.

The idea that the Sun is a star—and differs in brightness from the multitude of others we see at night only on account of its nearness to us—represents one of the great discoveries of the human mind which we cannot credit to the ancients; for the first inkling of it did not emerge till the time of the Renaissance. In the middle of the fifteenth century, Nicholas de Cusa (1401–1464), Cardinal of the Roman Church, entertained at least a germ of this idea which—160 years later—was to bring Giordano Bruno (1548–1600) to the sacrificial pyre. The idea that the Sun is a star flickered briefly on the pages of the famous Diaries by Leonardo da Vinci (1452–1519); but the consequences of this hypothetical identity were not drawn for centuries to come. The great Dutch scientist Christiaan Huyghens (1629–1695)—a senior contemporary of Newton—was the first man who attempted to estimate the distance to the stars by a comparison of their apparent brightness with that of the Sun (on the basis of the knowledge—discovered by Kepler in 1604—that the intensity of a light source in empty space falls off with an inverse square of its distance). However, it was not till much later—in 1837, in fact—that the distance of the first stars was actually measured in terms of the Sun–Earth distance used as a basis of triangulation; and since that time the hypothesis that our Sun is but one of the stars we see in the sky—and none too conspicuous a one—has been established beyond any doubt.

But how about the other stars which look down upon us each night from the sky? At the first glance, it might seem that their number is infinite. Appearances are, however, often deceptive; if we attempt to enumerate the stars visible to the naked eye in any given part of the sky, we find it to be not too difficult a task; and an extension of the same counting procedure to the whole sky discloses that the number of stars is about six thousand, of which less than half can be seen at any one place and time. Telescopes disclose a great many more than can be seen with the unaided human eye; and about a million of them have already been catalogued or charted by astronomers in various ways. Moreover, photographic plates (and other means of impersonal observation) have already disclosed the existence of more than 100 million individual stars in the sky; and yet—as we shall detail in the last part of this book—their total number in our Universe is vastly greater still.

The stars appear to be the most common product of natural processes, and constitute the commonest units in which the mass of the Universe seems at present to be organized. The aim of this chapter will be to explain why this is so, and what kind of stellar specimens we encounter among them. We shall begin with a survey of the stellar population which we find in our neighbourhood. We shall attempt first to identify these neighbours, establish their distance, and compare their various physical properties with those of our Sun. Having established the statistical properties of the stars in our neighbourhood, we shall ask ourselves: why are they such as we see now, and how did they get that way? In other words, we shall not be concerned only with the description of a momentary glimpse at our stellar neighbourhood as it looks to us now, but—as we did for our Sun—shall inquire about its past history, as well as its future evolution. The stars may be the most important building blocks of the Universe in which we live, but they are not eternal. How do they originate, how long will they continue to adorn our sky; and how will they meet their end? The aim of the sections which follow will be to provide at least some answers to these questions, based on the present state of our knowledge.

II–1: Vital Statistics of the Stars

As we have already found out in connection with our Sun, the clue to the physical properties of any celestial body is a knowledge of its *distance;* and for the stars in our neighbourhood this distance must be determined by triangulation. As the Earth revolves around the Sun, the positions of all stars should exhibit an apparent periodic motion on the celestial sphere—called a 'yearly parallax' —as the respective objects are viewed from different vantage points in different parts of each year. The principle of this method— which does not differ from the one employed by geodesists to triangulate the altitude and distance of inaccessible mountain peaks on the Earth—is graphically illustrated in the accompanying Figure 1.

Human efforts to bridge the gap which separates us from the stars by angular measurements of this kind have long remained unavailing—not only throughout the entire era of pre-telescopic astronomy, but long after the discovery of the telescope. The distance of the stars seemed immeasurable—until 1837, when not one, but three stars surrendered a knowledge of their parallaxes, namely, α Centauri—the third brightest star of the heavens—whose yearly parallactic displacement proved to possess an amplitude of $\pi = 0''.76$; Vega—one of the brightest stars of the northern hemisphere with $\pi = 0''.123$; while the third was an inconspicuous little star from the constellation of the Swan—known as 61 Cygni—which was selected for the effort because its position among the stars was gradually shifting, a fact suggesting its proximity to us. At the hands

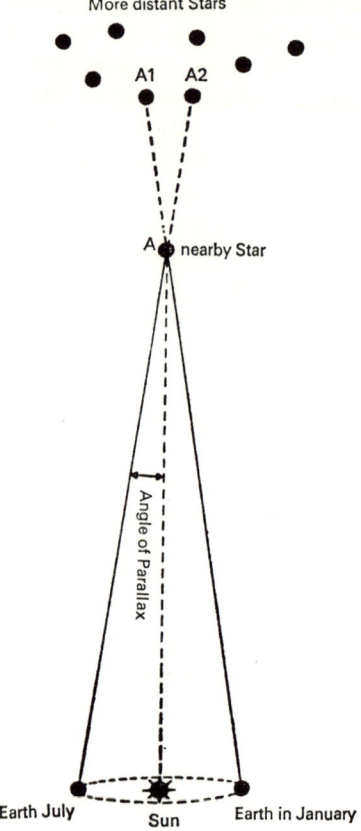

Figure 1 The principle of the stellar parallax.

of F. G. W. Bessel, its parallax proved to be 0″.314 (a value differing but little from its modern value of 0″.293).

The parallax of 0″.293 for 61 Cygni or 0″.123 for Vega signifies that, from their distance, the radius of the terrestrial orbit around the Sun would be seen at that angle: in other words, their distance is $206{,}265/\pi''$ astronomical units if the parallax π'' is expressed in seconds of arc. For α Centauri, 61 Cygni, or α Lyrae (Vega), these distances result as 271,000, 703,000 and 1,670,000 astronomical units, respectively; for more distant stars the corresponding values would grow in inverse proportion of their diminishing trigonometric parallaxes. Such numbers would obviously be much

Our Stellar Neighbourhood and Its Population 47

too large for extensive use in practice. Therefore, astronomers have long adopted another unit of length more appropriate for expressing the distance to the stars: namely, a *parsec*—which signifies a distance at which one astronomical unit would appear at an angle of one second of arc (i.e., to have a parallax $\pi = 1''$). In other words, the distance of one parsec is equal to 206,265 astronomical units (this numerical factor denoting the reciprocal value of one second of arc expressed in radians).

In terms of this unit, 61 Cygni turns out to be 3·41 parsecs away from us; and Vega, 8·1 parsecs; while α Centauri—the nearest of the three and the nearest star (or, rather, stellar system) to us in space—is at a distance of a mere 1·32 parsecs. Light travelling at 299,860 km/sec would need 3·26 years to traverse the distance of one parsec. Therefore, 61 Cygni is 11·1 light years away from us; Vega, 27 light years; and α Centauri, 4·3 light years. Compare these times with 499 seconds (8 min and 19 sec) which light takes to traverse the distance of one astronomical unit, with a little more than an hour necessary to reach Saturn (the farthermost planet known to the ancients); or with some $5\frac{1}{2}$ hours to Pluto—the outermost sentinel of the solar system. The disparity between 5·5 hours and 4·3 years is an eloquent indication of the width of the gravitational no-man's land which separates our solar system from the nearest stars. Nevertheless, since 1837 this gap has been bridged with increasing frequency by astronomical triangulation using the dimensions of the terrestrial orbit around the Sun as our baseline; and by now a few thousand individual stars have had their distance from us measured in this manner. The accompanying Table II–1 contains a list of such objects—eleven in number (in addition to the Sun)—which have been found to be less than ten light years away from us; while Table II–2 contains a similar list of the brightest stars of our sky, in which their parallaxes (in seconds of arc) and distances (in parsecs) are listed.

On account of the smallness of the parallactic displacements, to measure the distance of any star from us by triangulation using the Sun-Earth distance as a baseline represents always an arduous task requiring a high amount of skill and perseverance. Another characteristic of each individual star—and easier by far to measure than the distance—is the star's apparent brightness in the sky. Since time immemorial, watchers of the sky have been accustomed to describe these in so-called 'stellar magnitudes'—a concept repre-

TABLE II-1

The Nearest Stars

Star	Apparent Vis. Magnitude	Parallax (in secs of arc)	Distance (in light years)	Luminosity (in solar units)	Spectrum
Sun	−26·8	—	0·0000158	1	G1
α Centauri A	0·1	0″·760	4·3	1·1	G0
,, B	1·7	0·760	4·3	0·28	K5
,, C	11	0·760	4·3	0·000 052	M5e
Barnard's star*	9·5	0·545	6·0	0·000 40	M5
Wolf 359	13·5	0·421	7·7	0·000 017	M6e
Luyten 726-8, A	12·5	0·410	7·9	0·000 04	M6e
,, B	13·0	0·410	7·9	0·000 03	M6e
Lalande 21185*	7·5	0·398	8·2	0·004 8	M2
Sirius A	−1·6	0·375	8·7	23	A0
,, B	7·1	0·375	8·7	0·008	White Dwarf
Ross 154	10·6	0·351	9·3	0·000 36	M5e

*Attended by unseen companion

TABLE II-2
First Magnitude Stars

Star	Name	Vis. Magn.	Parallax	Distance (in light years)	Luminosity (in solar units)	Spectrum
α Canis Maioris	Sirius	−1·58	0″·375	8·7	23	A0
α Carinae	Canopus	−0·86	0·018	180	5 200	F0
α Centauri		+0·06	0·760	4·3	1·1	G0
α Lyrae	Vega	0·14	0·123	27	63	A0
α Aurigae	Capella	0·21	0·077	42	150	G0
α Bootis	Arcturus	0·24	0·098	33	83	K0
β Orionis	Rigel	0·34	0·005	650	23 000	B8
α Canis Minoris	Procyon	0·48	0·288	11·3	5·8	F5
α Eridani	Achernar	0·60	0·045	70	280	B5
β Centauri		0·86	0·017	190	1 400	B1
α Aquilae	Altair	0·89	0·198	16·5	8·3	A5
α Orionis	Betelgeuze	0·92 var	0·005	650	13 600 var	M2
α Crucis		1·05	0·015	220	1 200	B1
α Tauri	Aldebaran	1·06	0·062	53	91	K5
β Geminorum	Pollux	1·21	0·114	29	25	K0
α Virginis	Spica	1·21	0·027	120	440	B2
α Scorpii	Antares	1·22	0·013	250	1 900	M
α Piscis Austrini	Fomalhaut	1·29	0·139	23	16	A3
α Cygni	Deneb	1·33	0·006	540	6 000	A2
α Leonis	Regulus	1·34	0·049	67	130	B8
β Crucis		1·50	0·011	300	2 100	B1

senting (in its modern version, introduced only by 1850) a logarithmic scale of intensity with an arbitrarily chosen zero point, defined so that the intensity of light of two stars differing by 5 magnitudes in brightness is in the ratio of 100. Accordingly, a difference of one stellar magnitude corresponds to an intensity ratio of $\sqrt[5]{100}=2\cdot512$. Moreover, our scale has been set up in such a way that the fainter the object, the greater its magnitude. Its zero point has been arbitrarily fixed to correspond to the apparent brightness of the stars like α Lyrae (Vega) or α Aurigae (Capella)—both well known stars of the northern sky. On this scale, Sirius—the brightest star of the entire sky—has been assigned a (visual) magnitude of $-1\cdot6$. Only planets and other bodies of the solar system can exceed Sirius in apparent brightness; Venus can attain $-4\cdot6$, while the brightness of the full Moon becomes $-13\cdot6$; and of the Sun, $-26\cdot8$. If we proceed to the other end of the scale, the faintest stars visible with the naked eye are approximately of the sixth magnitude (i.e., about 250 times fainter than Vega); the faintest stars visible through the largest telescopes are close to the 17–18th magnitude; and the faintest objects that can be photographed by our telescopes after long exposures approach the 23rd magnitude.

Consistent with our definition, two stars differing by 10 magnitudes differ in brightness by a factor of $100^2=10,000$; and a difference of 20 magnitudes corresponds to an intensity ratio of 100 million. The daytime Sun appears, therefore, to be about half a million times as bright in the sky as the full Moon, and a few hundred million times brighter than the planet Venus at maximum brightness. On the other hand, the latter can appear to be some 20,000 times as bright as the faintest stars visible to the naked eye.

It should be added that the term 'stellar magnitude' hails from pre-telescopic times, when astronomers thought that a brighter star was indeed larger in size than its less resplendent sisters—whereas what gave them that impression were the 'seeing discs' of the stars affected by atmospheric scintillation. It was not till after the discovery of the telescope that our astronomical ancestors found all stars in the sky to be essentially light points whose apparent brightness had nothing to do with size. However, for historical reasons, the term 'magnitude' stuck, and has survived as an anachronism up to the present.

Our Stellar Neighbourhood and Its Population

Whichever scale of units we express the apparent stellar brightness in, the result need not tell us much about the star itself; the latter may appear to us brilliant in the sky because it is intrinsically bright, or merely because it happens to be nearer than others. In order to obtain more meaningful comparisons, it is obviously necessary to normalize the brightness by reducing the measured magnitudes to what they would appear at some standard distance. Astronomers have chosen this distance to be ten parsecs (i.e., equal to the distance of a star whose parallax is 0.″1). If m denotes the apparent stellar magnitude of a star of parallax π, and M the *absolute* magnitude which the same star would exhibit at a standard distance of 10 parsecs, it can be shown that the inverse-square attenuation of brightness with distance leads to a relation of the form $M = m + 5 + 5 \log \pi$, provided that starlight suffers no loss on its journey through interstellar space by absorption. For example, if our Sun whose apparent magnitude on our scale is $-26 \cdot 8$ at a distance of one astronomical unit were removed to the standard distance of 10 parsecs or 2,062,650 astr. units, the attenuation of its light with inverse square of the distance would diminish its brightness $(2,062,650)^2$ times, and render its absolute visual magnitude to be $+4 \cdot 7$. At a distance of ten parsecs our Sun would still be visible to the naked eye at night, though it would be by no means conspicuous among its neighbours in the sky.

If all stars were of the same absolute (intrinsic) brightness, a knowledge of the latter should enable us to compute their trigonometric parallax (i.e., distance), from the measured apparent brightness with the aid of the foregoing equation. In actual fact, this is far from being the case—as can be gathered by an inspection of the data compiled in Tables II-1 and II-2, containing a list of the stars which we have identified at a distance no greater than 10 light years from the Sun, and similar data for the stars of the first magnitude, the ones that make the 'headlines' in the sky with their conspicuous apparent brightness.

Table II-1 contains a census of 12 individual stars from which the light needs to travel through space no more than ten years to reach us. Had we extended this limit to 5 parsecs (16·3 light years), the number of known individual stars encountered in a sphere of this increased radius around the Sun would have gone up to 50—a total of 37 stellar systems (some of which are double or triple) excluding the Sun. A similar sphere of 20 parsec radius would already include more than 900 single stars and systems consisting of almost 1,100 stellar components (probably more, since not all such stars may as yet have been discovered); and well over 3,000 individual stars should be encountered within a distance not more than 30 parsecs from our terrestrial abode.

But let us return to a sample of the nearest stars within five parsecs from us. If we look over their vital statistics, we shall note that—with two exceptions—none are very conspicuous in the sky; and they have been recognized as our close neighbours by their relatively large 'proper motions' (see p. 74 of Chapter III) rather than apparent brightness in the sky. In point of fact, only eight out of the total of 50 are visible to the naked eye in spite of their proximity; and some require fairly large telescopes for their detection. Only three stars in our sample turn out to be more luminous than our Sun. The brightest of them is Sirius A or α Canis Maioris, which is 8·7 light years away from us, and possesses an intrinsic luminosity of 23 times that of the Sun. Next comes Altair (the brightest star of the constellation of the Eagle—α Aquilae as the astronomers call it) at 16·5 light years, with a luminosity of slightly over 8·3 suns. The third is Procyon A (α Canis Minoris), about 5·8 times as bright as the Sun (these luminosities all refer to the visible light of these stars; somewhat different results would be obtained in total light emitted by such bodies). The brightest component of the triple system of the southern star α Centauri—our closest celestial neighbour—just about equals the Sun in luminosity. The intrinsically faintest star in the sample is Wolf 359 (so-called after its number in a particular stellar catalogue), which is less than 0·00002 times as luminous as the Sun. Although it happens to be the third nearest star to us in space—only 7·7 light years away—its apparent magnitude is +13·5; which means that a fairly large telescope is required to enable us to learn of its existence.

Table II–2 gives the vital statistics of the brightest stars in the sky—the 'first magnitude' objects. Although these stars do not differ much from each other in apparent brightness, they turn out to be located at widely different distances, and possess a wide range of intrinsic luminosities. All first magnitude stars are, in fact, intrinsically brighter than the Sun. The most luminous object among them is Rigel—one of the bright blue stars in the winter constellation of Orion (β Orionis). This star, which is some 650 light years from us, is about 23,000 times as luminous as the Sun. The next most luminous object of our sample is the reddish star Beteigeuze (α Orionis), with a variable luminosity which averages out at about 13,000 times that of the Sun. Next in line are the white stars Deneb of the northern constellation of the Swan (α Cygni), with a luminosity of 6,000 suns at a distance of 540 light years; and Canopus of the southern constellation called the Keel (α Carinae), 5,200 times as bright as the Sun, only 180 light years away from us. Such stars shine like beacons through vast expanses of space and would remain visible to the naked eye at ten times their distance from us.

But in our immediate neighbourhood it is a very different story. Of the fifty stars within five parsecs of us, only three exceed our Sun in brightness, while 46 are fainter—and of those 38 possess a luminosity smaller than one-hundredth of the Sun. The brightest star of the group—Sirius—contributes more light to our stellar vicinity than all the other stars of our sample combined. Moreover, the density of stars in space around us proves to be extremely low. The volume of a sphere of five parsecs (16·3 light years) radius includes some 18 thousand cubic light years; and is populated by only 50 individual stars separated from each other, on the average, by several light years. When we compare this distance with the dimensions of these stars themselves (the diameter of the Sun being only 4·7 light seconds) we realize that the sky around us is mainly empty space.

The tremendous emptiness of this space is illustrated by the following analogy, which is true to scale. If a sphere of the radius of 5 parsecs were reduced to one equal in size to our own Earth, the stars within this volume would be represented by some fifty odd balls—of the size of tennis balls, golf balls, or marbles—spread at random through the available space. Our own Sun would, on this scale, be not more than 6 cm in size (smaller than a tennis ball); and our Earth, a pinhead half a millimetre across, would revolve around it at a distance of 6·2 metres. Moreover, the nimble-footed photons of light—the fastest travellers in the Universe—can cross the expanse of our solar system (by traversing the orbit of Pluto) in less than 11 hours; but it would take them more than four years' journey across interstellar no-man's-land to reach the nearest celestial oasis of α Centauri; and a similar time again to the next. By hopping from one star to the next the individual photons would, of course, have to travel in a zig-zag manner; and a journey along straight lines might not bring them within hailing distance of another stellar oasis for thousands of millions of years of flight time (cf. Chapter XIII–1). Such is the insignificance of our home in space.

II–2: The Story of Starlight

The vital statistics of the stars listed in Tables II–1 and II–2 contain more information than we have made use of so far. We have been concerned up to now with the *quantity* of light sent out by the stars, of which we receive a small fraction diluted by distance. But what is the *quality* of this light—or, in more precise terms, its spectral composition—and what can it disclose to us about the nature of its source? That the sunlight illuminating our days, or the starlight our nights, consists of a mixture of different colours has been known since the days of Isaac Newton—and indeed before; for Nature decomposed sunlight into rainbow colours with the aid of atmospheric water droplets long before Newton (or anyone else) passed its beam through a prism to obtain what we call a 'continuous spectrum'. It is true that we had to await the advent of the quantum theory of light in the early years of this century to gain an understanding of its composition in terms of the physical properties—mainly the temperature—of the emitting source. Since that time we know, however, that the distribution of intensity in the continuous spectrum possesses a maximum at a certain wavelength λ characteristic of the temperature T of the emitting source (such that $\lambda T = 0 \cdot 365$ cm deg). Therefore, if we determine the value of λ in the spectrum of any celestial light source, Wien's displacement law can readily furnish its effective temperature T.

To give an example of the same process applied to more familiar surroundings, a white-hot body, or one raised to blue heat, is hotter than the same body when it was only red-hot; and what is true on the Earth continues to be so in the realm of the stars. In the case of our Sun, its continuous spectrum appears to be brightest at (approximately) $\lambda = 0 \cdot 6$ microns—a fact which shows that its effective temperature should be close to 5,800 degrees on the absolute (Kelvin) scale. For stars which are substantially cooler, or hotter, than the Sun the value of λ will drift out of the spectral domain to which our atmosphere remains transparent (*cf.* Chapter V–2) into the infrared or ultraviolet; so that only the slope of the distribution of brightness in their spectra can be ascertained by astronomical observations made from the surface of the Earth. Even this slope can, however—in the light of Planck's law— furnish a clue (albeit somewhat less dependable) to what astronomers call the 'colour temperature' of the respective source. Thus white-blue stars like Vega or Rigel are hotter (11,000°–12,000°) than the yellow Sun, and much hotter than the red stars like Antares or Beteigeuze whose effective temperatures are only about 3,500°.

The light of the stars holds more information in store for the observer who can decompose it into spectra of sufficient dispersion; for the colour bands of their continuous spectra are then found to be interrupted by a great many discrete *lines*—mostly dark, but occasionally bright ones—some very sharp, and others again of considerable width. These spectral lines have proved to be distinctive 'fingerprints' of different kinds of atoms capable of emitting, or absorbing, light passing through semi-transparent media; and if we match their measured positions in the spectrum of a star with those of a known sample in the terrestrial laboratory, such spectral analysis should permit us to ascertain, not only the chemical composition of the celestial body concerned, but also the physical conditions (temperature, pressure, surface gravity) at which the emission or absorption takes place.

An interpretation of the line spectra of celestial bodies constitutes a subject of some complexity; for atoms responsible for their formations are themselves quite complicated structures, built up from more elementary particles, whose number increases with the 'atomic weight' of the respective element. Hydrogen—the lightest of all elements and the most abundant constituent of most celestial bodies—simply consists of one electron revolving around a single proton. But uranium—one of the heaviest elements occurring in Nature in small but measurable amounts—possesses a nucleus consisting of 92 protons and 146 neutrons, around which 92 electrons revolve in several discrete shells; and this whole structure weighs 238 times more than a single hydrogen atom. Between hydrogen and uranium there are 90 other distinct elements arranged in what the chemists call the 'periodic table' of their properties—

elements which differ from each other by the number and arrangement of the 'electronic cloaks' shielding their nuclei (and in more than 250 varieties if we count their different 'isotopes' or atoms whose nuclei of different mass are shielded by identical cloaks of electrons).

The absorption or emission of light by different atoms is essentially (though not completely) controlled by the style of their electron envelopes; and occurs whenever their constituent electrons change places in the hierarchy. Such changes can be induced by a variety of processes—for example, by mutual collisions with neighbouring atoms or with other more elementary particles; or again by absorption or emission of light waves intercepted on the way; and other types of transition of the electrons from one place into another within the atomic structure can occur spontaneously (subject only to certain general rules). In other cases—when the external provocation has been greater than the structure of an atom can stand—electrons can actually be lost from its protective cloak; and until it can be recaptured the 'ion' mutilated in this way will acquire a positive charge (due to the fact that the sum of the negative charges of the remaining electrons can no longer neutralize the positive charge of the nucleus).

The variety of the line spectra which different atoms may produce under these circumstances is too bewildering for simple description. Whenever you discover in the spectrum of a star the lines of an element which you recognize, it is always bound to be some member of the 'club of the periodic table'; but it need not always be present in the same guise. When you meet such a member and recognize his identity, the first question which the astronomical spectroscopist will ask is the polite 'how do you do?' —to which the atom may reply (through its coded spectral message) 'pretty well', if it finds itself only in an excited state and otherwise in full possession of its electronic garb; or with a distressed 'so-so' message if we meet a temporarily discomfited atom whose electronic cloak has been tattered and torn in the scrimmage. An atom which has lost an electron is not unlike a man who has shaved off his beard; sometimes even old friends cannot recognize him at a glance!

The general nature of a stellar spectrum can thus not only disclose to us the chemical composition of the semi-transparent outer fringes of the stars ('stellar atmospheres') where such spectra originate, but can also describe pretty well the physical conditions of the environment—such as the prevalent pressure and temperature. For no element will 'show its hand' in the spectrum with equal readiness under arbitrary conditions, and most of them are quite sensitive to the climate at which they choose to do so; if these are not quite right they may decide not to make a premature appearance.

Their individual tastes for coming out in full bloom are very different by virtue of their atomic structure. For example, hydrogen remains largely in hiding until the ambient temperature exceeds 4,000–5,000 degrees; and its absorption lines do not fully develop till the temperature rises to between 10,000–11,000 deg, at which most of its atoms can become excited. With further increase of temperature, the strength of the hydrogen absorption lines begins, however, to fade again on account of the fact that an increasing fraction of atoms of this element becomes ionized, and thus loses the capability of absorbing or emitting light of discrete frequencies. With helium—the second most abundant element in the Universe—this even more so: its absorption lines will not show up in stellar atmospheres unless the temperature exceeds 10,000 degrees, and their 'most favourable climate' is much warmer. On the other hand, the grouping of atoms into molecules can occur—or survive—only in stellar atmospheres whose climate is cool. Molecules in the Universe behave cosmically like arctic snow crystals, and their natural habitat is (as we shall see in Chapter III-1) interstellar space; only a few species of them will survive at temperatures higher than 4,000 degrees.

A quantitative analysis of stellar spectra has shown that, by and large, most stars are monotonously alike when it comes to chemical composition—as alike as healthy human beings are in this respect. When some of the latter differ perceptibly from the common herd —by being deficient in calcium, iron, or vitamins—they are considered to be ailing, or otherwise falling into decrepitude. With the stars it is no different; for (as we shall explain in subsequent chapters) not all of them are of the same age or provenance; and, moreover, some of them suffer from specific afflictions manifest in their chemistry which we shall diagnose later.

However, when we survey the spectra of most stars around us in the sky, we find that a relatively small number of types occur repeatedly among them; and these have been described by early pioneers of the subject as 'spectral classes' of the stellar population at large. Shorn to their simplest features, they can be arranged in a scheme of the form

$$\begin{array}{c} \text{R—N} \\ | \\ \text{O—B—A—F—G—K—M} \\ | \\ \text{S} \end{array} ,$$

(with decimal sub-classes) representing essentially a sequence of objects of diminishing temperature. At the extreme left, stars of spectral type O show relatively few lines of ionized elements in their spectra, and emit most of their light in the ultraviolet, which is inaccessible to us on the ground; their effective temperatures range between 30,000 and 50,000 degrees (see Table II–3). On the other hand, spectral types listed at the extreme right of the foregoing scheme correspond to stars whose effective temperatures barely exceed 2,500–3,000 degrees and exhibit many absorption

TABLE II–3

Effective Temperature Scale of the Stars

Spectral Class	Effective Temperature
O4	40,000°K
O6	29,000
O8	22,000
B0	20,000
B3	17,000
B5	15,000
B8	12,000
A0	10,700
A5	8,700
F0	7,600
F5	6,600
G0	5,900
G5	5,200
K0	4,900
K5	4,400
M0	3,800
M5	3,000

bands of molecular origin. Most of their light is emitted in near infrared—at wavelengths too long to negotiate the passage through the terrestrial atmosphere; and the differences between individual branches of the scheme reflect real differences in chemistry of the atmospheres of the respective stars.

The spectral classification scheme on p. 58 has the stars arranged in the order of diminishing stellar temperature, and the sequence of its letters is purely heuristic.* Originally, other letters of the alphabet—since dropped—were used to describe spectra which proved to be exceptional rather than typical; and more recently, other characteristics were added to the surviving letters to represent, for instance the absolute luminosity of the object. However, the (one-dimensional) spectral types of the dozen nearest stars to us in space—as well as of the first-magnitude stars of our sky—are listed in the ultimate columns of Tables II–1 and II–2.

We have already mentioned that the volume of a sphere around us with the radius of 5 parsecs (16·3 light years) contains 50 individual stars; and a plot of their (visual) luminosity against the spectral class of each object is given in Figure 2.

Moreover, if we assign to each star an effective temperature appropriate for its spectral type (in accordance with a scale given in Table II–3), the radius R_* of a star ($*$) can be evaluated in solar units ($_\odot$) from a known luminosity L_* and temperature T_* with the aid of the formula $L_* = R_*^2 (T_*/T_\odot)^4$, based on Stefan's law for blackbody radiation (with $T_\odot = 5,800°$). The relative size of the nearby stars so computed is indicated in Figure 2 by the size of the individual circles. Although only three of these stars—Sirius, Altair and Procyon—outshine our Sun in brightness, five more (α Cen B, ε Eri, o_2 Eri, ε Ind and 70 Oph) outrank it in size.

The most striking fact disclosed by Figure 2 is, however, a remarkable relation emerging between the luminosities and the temperature (colour) of most stars. With the sole exception of five lonely points in the lower left-hand corner of our diagram (these are the famous 'white dwarfs' on which more will be said in Chapter III–2), the luminosities of all stars appear to be correlated closely with their colour. The fainter a star, the redder its colour;

---

*In the past a mnemotechnic ditty, 'Oh, Be A Fine Girl, Kiss Me Right Now, Sweet' helped many a student to memorize the odd sequence of letters in our classification. The spectral classes R and S do not differ from stars of class M by temperature, but chemical composition.

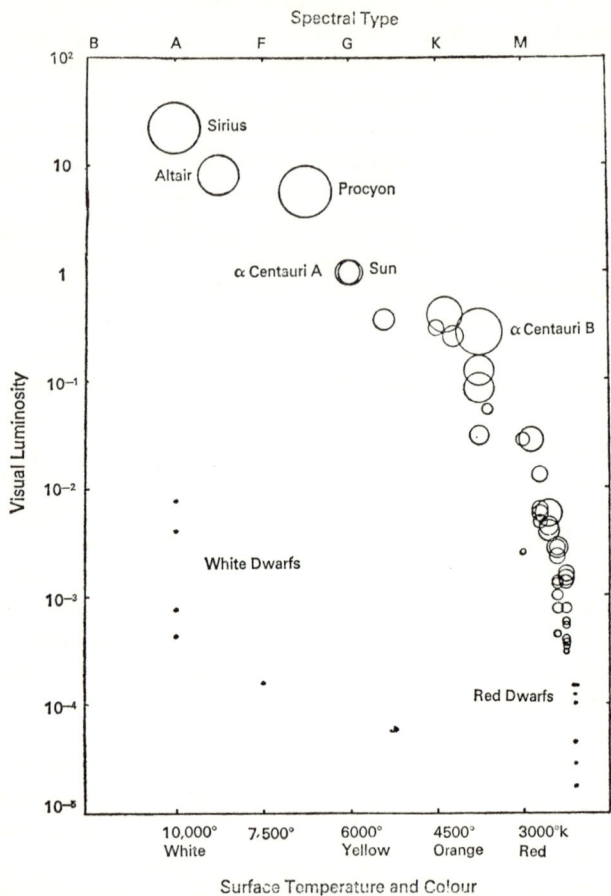

Figure 2 Hertzsprung-Russell diagram for nearby stars. Spectrum-luminosity relation and comparative diameters for stars within sixteen light-years. The spectrum depends on the surface temperature, which in turn determines the star's colour (After van de Kamp, 1954).

so that an arrangement of our sample of nearby stars in order of decreasing luminosity proves also to be a sequence of decreasing size and diminishing temperature. The astronomers refer to this array of stars on the luminosity-colour diagram as the 'Main Sequence', whose evolutionary significance for the life of the stars will be discussed in Chapter III–2.

Our Stellar Neighbourhood and Its Population

The overwhelming majority of the stars in our neighbourhood are smaller, cooler, and less luminous than our Sun. Such stars, nicknamed 'red dwarfs', constitute the backbone of the stellar population; but lacking the glamour of the 'headline' stars of Table II–2, they are found only by those who seek them; and prefer to live in obscurity as the best insurance for long life—a tactic which, as we shall see, applies to stars as it does to men.

II–3: Heavenly Twins

There is an important gap in the vital statistics of the stars in our neighbourhood, as given in the preceding section of this chapter. The measurements of distance and apparent brightness can furnish the luminosity of the stars; and their spectra indicate their temperatures which—combined with the luminosity—give a clue to stellar size. However, we still have to induce the stars to step on the scales to ascertain their mass.

The only way to determine the mass of any celestial body is to observe the effects of its attraction on another mass in its neighbourhood. A single star in space is a reticent object, unlikely to reveal to a distant observer much more information than we have inferred so far. If, however, another star happens to be in its vicinity, the two will be bound to revolve around the common centre of gravity of the system in an orbit whose size and period will at once disclose to us, not only the total mass of the system, but also the manner in which their mutual attraction falls off with their increasing separation. If, in addition, the motion of each star about the common centre of mass can be measured separately, the total mass of the system can be split up into the masses of its individual constituents.

In more specific terms, if $m_{1,2}$ denote the masses of the components of a binary system expressed in terms of the mass of the Sun being taken as unit, and P stands for their orbital period expressed in years of our terrestrial time, while a denotes the mean distance separating them in space (and expressed in terms of the Sun–Earth distance taken as the unit) then—according to a law discovered by Johannes Kepler as far back as 1618—these quantities should be related to the formula $m_1 + m_2 = a^3/P^2$, known as Kepler's 'law of periodic times'. Half a century later, Isaac Newton proved that if two bodies attract each other with a force falling off with the inverse square of their separation, Kepler's law represents a necessary consequence of their motion being an elliptical path around the centre of mass of the system which rests at the common focus of such ellipses.

Kepler's work in the early part of the seventeenth century demonstrated that the planets of our solar system indeed revolved around the Sun in this manner; and Newton proved that such laws are necessary consequences of the inverse-square law of universal gravitation. Did, however, the validity of this law extend beyond the confines of our solar system? This was not proven for almost a century following Newton's time—until William Herschel established in 1803 the existence of the first physical double stars in the sky and established the principal characteristics of their orbits.

That these orbits proved to be elliptical did not confirm as yet the validity of Newton's law to the exclusion of other possibilities. For example, if the components of double stars happened to attract each other with a force falling off with the inverse first power of their mutual separation—instead of with its square—their orbits would still be elliptical; but their centre of mass would coincide with the centre—rather than the focus—of the respective ellipses. Herschel—bless him—early discovered some binary pairs with markedly eccentric orbits, in which the displacements between the centre and the focus of the ellipse were considerable. In each case, the centre of mass proved to be in the focus of the respective conic—a fact which proved that Newtonian gravitation governed by the inverse-square law was indeed a universal force, operating everywhere in the Universe. Double stars provided astronomy at an early stage of its development with wings to cross vast expanses of space, and establish the validity of the same laws of nature far beyond the realm of the solar system.

But let us return to Kepler's law of periodic times, relating the orbital period of a double star and the size of its orbit with the total mass of the system. The period P in years can be determined directly by watching the system long enough, and so can the apparent size a'' of its orbit in seconds of arc. If, in addition, the annular parallax of the system has also been measured from periodic displacements of the whole system in the sky in the course of a year, the quantity a occurring on the right-hand side of Kepler's law will be given by the ratio of a''/π''. Hence, an observa-

Our Stellar Neighbourhood and Its Population 63

tional determination of P, a'' and π'' for any pair of stars can furnish directly the sum of their masses.

This is also all that we can hope to obtain from measurements of the apparent motion of one star around the other. In actual fact, of course, the two stars describe absolute elliptical orbits in the sky around their common centre of gravity characterized by apparent semi-major axes $a''_{1,2}$—such that $a'' = a''_1 + a''_2$, where $a''_1/a''_2 = m_2/m_1$. If, therefore, we can establish the individual values a''_1 and a''_2 in angular units from direct observations, a combination of Kepler's law with the above formula should enable us to determine the individual masses $m_{1,2}$ of the two stars.

Armed with this knowledge, let us turn now to the sky and attempt to pry out some more of its secrets. Of the quantities $a''_{1,2}$, P, and π'' required for a determination of the masses of the components of double stars, the most difficult one to obtain significantly from the measurements is usually the parallax π'', the value of which diminishes with distance. Therefore, the method we have in mind can only be practised with any hope of success among nearby stars. This limitation does not, however, reduce by much the potential gain that we can expect to make by this method; for double stars turn out to be quite abundant in our immediate cosmic vicinity.

If we take a census of all stars within five parsecs of the Sun, less than one-half are found to live as isolated individuals, and more than a half are known to constitute binary (or multiple) systems. A list of such *visual binaries* discovered so far within 10 parsecs from us is given in the accompanying Table II–4. Their identification in column (1) is given in abbreviated form (usually, the running number in the appropriate catalogue) to which astronomers often resort to identify faint stars which do not form an obvious part of a constellation. Only about half of the stars listed in Table II–4 could be seen without the aid of a telescope; and powerful optical means are required to resolve them into doubles. Their actual separations range from 10 to 100 astronomical units; and their orbital periods from a few dozen years to several centuries. The penultimate column of Table II–4 gives the total absolute magnitudes* of the constituent components; and

---

*Total absolute magnitude is a measure of the light emitted by the star in all wavelengths of its spectrum—not necessarily those to which our eyes are sensitive, or which can pass through the atmosphere. For very hot (or very cool) stars this total magnitude may exceed the visual magnitude by a considerable margin.

TABLE II-4

Visual Double Stars within 10 Parsecs from the Sun

Name	Parallax	Period (in years)	Spectra	Total Absolute Magnitude	Masses (in solar units)
α Centauri	0″.760	80.09	G1–K5	4.4–5.7	1.02–0.89
α Canis Maioris	0.375	49.94	A0–w.d.	0.8–10	2.24–1.07
α Canis Minoris	0.288	40.65	F5–w.d.	2.6–13	1.74–0.63
Krüger 60	0.249	44.46	M4–M6	9.1–10	0.25–0.15
o₂ Eridani	0.200	247.9	w.d.–M5	10.3–9.5	0.46–0.21
70 Ophiuchi	0.199	87.85	K1–K5	5.5–6.6	0.89–0.65
η Cassiopeiae	0.182	480	G0–K5	4.7–7.5	0.76–0.48
Furuhjelm No. 46	0.147	13.12	M3–	8.5–	0.36–0.29
ξ Bootis	0.145	149.9	G8–K5	5.4–6.8	0.91–0.79
Melbourne 4	0.142	42.09	K5–	6.0–	0.71–0.39
ξ Ursae Maioris	0.126	59.86	G0–G0	4.8–5.2	1.15–1.15
ζ Herculis	0.103	34.38	G0–K0	2.9–5.5	1.20–0.81

Our Stellar Neighbourhood and Its Population

the last column contains their masses (in solar units). Of the 24 stars listed in our tabulation, 17 are less massive and less luminous than our Sun.

In addition to the objects listed in Table II-4, there are at least eight additional stars within 10 parsecs which we know to be double because their positions do not stay put in the sky, but wiggle periodically in the course of their motion around the centre of mass of a system in which their companion is too faint to be actually seen or photographed. Sirius (α CMa) or Procyon (α CMi) are conspicuous examples of the stars which were found in the nineteenth century to possess such 'invisible' companions; and decades had to elapse before continuing advances in astronomical optics enabled us eventually to get a first glimpse of them. These discoveries did not, moreover, exhaust the possibility of the existence of further pairs of this nature. Among the so far unresolved 'astrometric' binaries known today, ξ UMa A represents a very close pair with an orbital period of only 1·83 years; and its unseen companion possesses a mass of only about one-third of that of the Sun. Or we come across such interesting objects as the Barnard's Star (see Table II-I), or 61 Cygni A attended by companions whose mass appears to be only a few thousandths of that of the Sun—i.e., of planetary rather than stellar order of magnitude.

On the other hand, we also know that double stars exist whose components are separated by thousands or tens of thousands of astronomical units. Because their orbital periods then run into millions of years, observations carried out in the course of a few centuries cannot detect early indications of their orbital motion. However the existence of a gravitational bond between their components is attested by the fact that they travel through space together—even though their orbital motion is very slow in comparison with their motion through space. We call them 'pairs of common proper motion'; and several such pairs are known to exist in our cosmic vicinity.

Visual binaries—ranging from unresolved astrometric doubles to wide pairs of stars with common proper motion—do not, moreover, exhaust the variety of double stars that may exist in the sky; for binaries with separation generally less than one astronomical unit would completely escape detection by the method which we have considered so far. In order to close this gap we must turn to other methods of celestial double-star hunting; and these will take us back to cast a second look at their spectra.

In the preceding section of this chapter we outlined some of the gains to be made from an analysis of stellar spectra. There are, however, still more facts that can be pried out of these informative stellar 'rainbows'. Light—like everything else—travels through space at a finite speed; and for light in vacuum this proves to be 299,860 km/sec. We also know that anything that moves towards you appears to be moving faster when you are going to meet it than when you stand still—let alone move away. Likewise, if a star in the sky should be moving towards us, the velocity of the light it sends out would appear to be increased by the relative velocity of the star itself. As a result, the apparent wavelengths of the light in its spectrum would all seem to have diminished; and, in particular, all discrete lines in the spectrum should be displaced towards the blue from their normal positions. Similarly, when a star is receding from us, all its spectral lines should be displaced towards the red.

The principle at the basis of these expectations is the *Doppler Effect*—called so after the Bohemian physicist Christian Doppler (1803–1854)—who first proposed it in 1842 to explain colour differences encountered between components of visual double stars known by that time. The real reason for these differences is—we know now—quite different from that envisaged by Doppler; it is due to different rates of stellar evolution for objects of unequal masses (see Chapter III–2), of which Doppler in his day had as yet no inkling. In spite of the fact that the Doppler effect was first invoked to explain phenomena to which it did not apply, Doppler's name has remained permanently associated with a principle which has become one of the cornerstones of astrophysical science, and to which Doppler himself had at least called attention.

In the domain of terrestrial acoustics, you experience the consequences of the Doppler principle while driving a car on the motorway whenever a reckless driver of another vehicle passes you in the opposite direction, making his way through the traffic with a thumb on his horn. The horn sounded by a moving vehicle will possess a higher pitch (corresponding to a shorter wavelength) while the vehicle is approaching at high speed, and will drop suddenly to a lower tone after the car has passed you and is receding to a distance. The acoustic consequences of the Doppler

Our Stellar Neighbourhood and Its Population 67

effect during such encounters are easily noticeable because the speed of sound emitted by the noisy vehicle—some 340 m/sec at 15°C—is only 7·6 times as great as the relative speed of (say) 100 miles per hour at which noisy horns often pass each other on our motorways. The speed of light in empty space is almost a million times higher; and although stars travel through space much faster than cars do on our motorways, as a rule they do not travel a million times as fast and, in consequence, the Doppler effect in their spectra is likely to be much smaller.

In general, the shift in wavelength due to the varying distance of the star from us should bear the same ratio to the wavelength as does the star's relative velocity v to the speed c of light. Since the ratio v/c is generally small for the stars, the Doppler shift should amount to a very small fraction of the wavelength—so small that we had to await 26 years for its detection (by William Huggins) in the spectrum of a star after Doppler qualitatively predicted its existence. Since that time Doppler shifts of this nature have been observed in the spectra of many thousands of stars.* Hot blue stars of spectral types O or B have been found to move rather sluggishly around us—like people in hot weather—with radial velocities of the order of 10–20 km/sec, while the cooler yellow and red stars in our neighbourhood appear to rush to and fro much faster. It should be stressed, however, that by the nature of the underlying effect measurable Doppler shifts can disclose only the *radial* component of the motion of a star—that of recession of approach; for if a star were moving perpendicularly to this radial direction—so that its distance from us would remain the same—no shift of the spectral lines would become apparent.

The Doppler principle which enables us to measure the radial velocities of the stars can also help us to study their possible binary nature. In 1889 it was discovered at Harvard Observatory that a star called Mizar—situated in the middle of the handle of the Big Dipper—sometimes showed single absorption lines in its spectrum, but at other times these appeared to be double; and this doubling was found to recur regularly in a period of 20·54 days. This phenomenon can only mean that Mizar actually consists of

---

*The Doppler shifts measured by the terrestrial observer include the effects arising from the annual motion of the Earth around the Sun, as well as from the diurnal rotation of our planet about its axis. Both must be taken into account when reducing the observations to obtain radial velocity with respect to the Sun.

two components revolving around their common centre of mass; but these are so close together that even through a telescope they appeared as a single point of light. Part of the time, the two stars in their orbits would be moving in opposite directions across our line of sight; and their two spectra would then be exactly superimposed. At other times—when the two component stars approach their maximum apparent separation—one of them would be approaching us just as the other would be receding, and their spectral lines would be displaced in opposite directions; thus unmistakably indicating the binary nature of the object.

Since 1889, stars disclosing periodic shifts of their spectral lines —so-called *spectroscopic binaries*—have been discovered in the sky by the thousand. Some show the lines of both components in the combined spectrum; others only one set of lines of periodically oscillating wavelength. For the two components of such a binary need not be of the same brightness, and sometimes one is very much fainter than the other. If, however, the latter is too faint to impress any lines of its own in the combined spectrum, the binary nature of the star can still be detected from the periodic changes in position of the lines of the visible brighter star.

What can the observed Doppler shifts of spectral lines tell us about the nature of the constituent objects? A combination of the orbital velocity, given directly by the observations, with the period of the spectral line shifts discloses the size of orbit, in absolute units, regardless of the distance of the system (provided only that the object is not rendered too faint by distance for its light to be decomposed into a spectrum with a dispersion sufficient to measure the Doppler shifts). Moreover, the probability of discovery of spectroscopic binaries (unlike that of visual double stars) actually increases with the increasing proximity of their constituent components; for the closer they are, the more rapidly they revolve; and the greater the corresponding Doppler shifts of their spectral lines.

Furthermore, a combination of the period and size of the orbit can offer a clue to the absolute masses of the constituent components of such a system—with one important proviso, however. Since the measured Doppler shifts of the spectral lines permit us to determine only the *radial* velocity of any star, the orbit constructed on their basis will represent only a *projection* of the actual orbit on a plane perpendicular to the line of sight. In other words, a knowledge of the radial-velocity changes of the components of a spectroscopic binary cannot furnish the absolute semi-major axes $a_{1,2}$ of the orbits of their components as such, but only their 'projected' values $a_{1,2} \sin i$; where the angle i denotes the inclination of the orbital plane to the celestial sphere. Similarly, the only direct information it can furnish on the masses $m_{1,2}$ of the constituent components are the values of the products $m_{1,2} \sin^3 i$. In order to free these data from the effects of projection to obtain the absolute masses themselves together with the dimensions of their orbits, it is necessary to ascertain the extent of the orbital inclination i by independent means.

This cannot, unfortunately, be accomplished as long as spectroscopic observations alone are at our disposal. However, under certain circumstances, the missing clue can be supplied by observations of the light variability of close binary systems—which is bound to occur whenever the inclination of their orbital planes to the line of sight of the terrestrial observer happens to be such that, twice during each orbital cycle, one component steps out in front of its mate to eclipse (partly or wholly) its apparent disc. This will, in general, happen the more readily the closer the components are in such a system (i.e., the larger their radii expressed in terms of their orbital separation), and the less the orbital plane deviates from the line of sight of the terrestrial observer.

When we come across such a pair in the sky, our spectroscopic binary becomes truly an *eclipsing variable,* which exhibits periodic light changes in the course of each eclipse. Between minima, the light of such a system remains generally constant (or will vary slightly on account of the mutual tidal distortion of both components, or because of the phase effects as each star illuminates the other). Within eclipses, however, the star will pass through light minima of characteristic form; and an analysis of the light curves exhibited during such minima can furnish many important clues as to the nature of the system in question.

The characteristic light changes of eclipsing variables are like telegraphic messages which such systems signal to us with clockwork regularity across the intervening gaps of space to attract attention to their nature; and provided that we can decipher correctly their particular Morse code, a very large amount of information can be obtained concerning various properties of their constituent stars. The harvest which we can reap from these observations includes the fractional radii of the two components, their fractional luminosities and—above all—the missing clue of the inclination of their orbital planes to the celestial sphere. If these data can be combined with the elements of their 'spectroscopic' orbits, we find ourselves in a position to deduce from all aspects of the combined evidence the absolute dimensions of the components of such eclipsing binary systems as well as their absolute masses.

Eclipsing binary systems—i.e., close binaries which by an accident of the orientation of their orbital planes with respect to our own position in space, happen to become eclipsing variables—occupy a position of particular eminence in modern astrophysics for several reasons. First, because of a prodigious abundance of such objects found almost everywhere in the sky. A census of the stars located within 20–30 parsecs from our Sun disclosed that at least seven (and, probably, several more) out of some 3,000 objects located within this distance are eclipsing variables; and if stars more massive than the Sun were considered, this proportion would be distinctly higher. If, however, a ratio of only this order were to prevail over the whole galactic system with its 10^{12} stars (cf. Chapter XI), the total number of eclipsing stars in our Galaxy would be enormous. Several thousand such stars have actually been discovered, and light curves established for several hundred of these; but the total number of such stars is quite beyond the hope of discovery.

Secondly, the significance of eclipsing variables is underlined by the fact that they represent the only class of double stars that can be discovered in more distant parts of the Universe. In the neighbourhood of the Sun—up to a distance of no more than about 50 parsecs—binary stars can be recognized by their orbital motion (or, for very wide pairs, by common proper motion of their components). Spectroscopic binaries can be identified with the aid of powerful modern reflectors up to a distance of one or two thousand parsecs; but beyond this limit double stars can be discovered if, and only if, they happen to be eclipsing variables.

Spectroscopic binaries which are also eclipsing variables have long been our principal source of information concerning the masses, densities, and absolute dimensions of the individual stars. A certain amount of data on stellar masses can, to be sure, be deduced from observations of visual binaries which are near enough

TABLE II-5
Some Eclipsing Systems which consist of Main-Sequence Stars

Star	Orbital Period (in days)	Spectra of the component	Total Absolute Magnitudes	Masses (in solar units)	Radii (in solar units)	Distance (in parsecs)
V 805 Aql	2·408	A2–A6	0·7– 1·6	1·85–1·50	2·16–1·84	240
σ Aql	1·950	B8–B9	−1·9– −0·9	6·80–5·40	4·2– 3·3	140
WW Aur	2·525	A7–F0	1·7– 2·0	1·92–1·90	1·92–1·90	77
AR Aur	4·135	B9–A0	0·3– 0·6	2·55–2·30	1·82–1·82	100
β Aur	3·960	A0–A0	−0·1– −0·2	2·33–2·25	2·48–2·27	27
Y Cyg	2·996	O9·5–O9·5	−6·0– −6·0	17·4–17·2	5·9– 5·9	1370
V 477 Cyg	2·347	A3–F6	1·7– 3·7	2·4– 1·6	1·5– 1·2	160
YY Gem	0·814	M1–M1	7·7– 7·7	0·64–0·64	0·62–0·62	14
RX Her	1·779	A0–A1	0·3– 0·7	2·1– 1·9	2·1– 1·8	220
TX Her	2·060	A5–F1	1·7– 2·5	2·1– 1·8	1·65–1·6	210
UV Leo	0·600	G0–G1	4·0– 4·1	1·36–1·25	1·21–1·20	71
U Oph	1·677	B5–B6	−2·4– −1·9	5·30–4·65	3·4– 3·1	310
V 451 Oph	2·197	A0–A2	0·0– 0·8	2·3– 1·9	2·4– 1·9	340
AG Per	2·029	B5–B7	−2·3– −1·7	5·1– 4·5	2·98–2·74	300
ζ Pho	1·670	B7–A1	−1·2– −1·0	3·0– 2·1	2·8– 1·6	70

to disclose their orbital motion. The number of such systems is, however, limited by their proximity to us; and the existing supply (*cf.* Table II–4) is not copious. Eclipsing binaries offer, on the other hand, an almost inexhaustible supply of data, only a minute fraction of which has so far been tapped; and a small sample is presented in the accompanying Table II–5. Moreover—unlike visual binaries—eclipsing variables can furnish absolute dimensions of their constituent components without a recourse to any estimate of their temperatures; and if their distance is known, their radius and luminosity can, in fact, be used to determine the effective temperature of the constituent stars. In this way, their 'colour' or 'ionization' temperatures (*cf.* Chapter II–2) are susceptible of independent verification.

The astrophysical data which can be deduced from the observation of eclipsing binary systems transcend, however, mere information concerning the masses and dimensions of their constituent components or the geometry of their orbits; for even their internal constitution can be deduced from outside. One link with it is a gravitational field which emanates from matter in the interior which the opaque layers concealing it cannot appreciably modify; and radiant energy originating in the deep interior, influenced by the structure of the intervening layers, will determine the distribution of brightness over the visible surface of the star. As long as this star is single, we have no way of gauging its external gravitational field at a distance, or of learning anything about the distribution of brightness on its surface. Place, however, another star in its proximity to form a binary; and the properties of the combined gravitational field of both components can at once manifest themselves in their motion (in particular, in the revolution of the apsidal line of their orbits); and the variation of light invoked by axial rotation of components distorted by tides raised by each star on the other—as well as during their mutual eclipses—will permit us to ascertain the distribution of surface brightness over the apparent discs of the constituent stars. These well deserve the name of 'heavenly twins'; for no other type of stars can tell us so much in so few words.

We are tempted to conclude that the stars in the sky behave like human beings. A solitary man—like a single star in the sky—is apt to be fairly reticent; you can describe his external manifestations up to a point, but cannot easily find out what makes him tick.

Place him, however, in company with another human being; and the intercourse thus initiated may disclose to a shrewd observer much more fully what is inside his mind. And—as with the stars —the extent of the intercourse will grow with increasing proximity of the individuals. You can afford to disregard your neighbour much better at a distance than if chance brings the two of you into close contact; and the closer you come, the more difficult will it be for you to ignore each other. With stars it is the same story; except that the laws governing the physical interaction of the components of close binary systems are much simpler and better understood than those of human psychology. As a result, the 'stellar psychologists' concerned with the study of manifold phenomena arising from tidal interaction, mutual irradiation, etc., of our heavenly twins, have been able to compile an extensive casebook of most exciting stories.

Lack of space prevents us from delving into the details of this casebook, but one fact cannot be passed without mention, the knowledge of which we owe exclusively to our heavenly twins: *the luminosity of a star appears to be closely correlated with its mass,* the greater the mass, the higher its luminosity. Figure 4 illustrates this empirical relationship between mass and luminosity for Main Sequence stars in our neighbourhood; though a discussion of its meaning has to be postponed until Chapter III–2.

CHAPTER III

Origin and Evolution of the Stars

THE STARS seem to look down upon us from their fantastic distances like incarnations of cosmic immutability. Yet this picture cannot be literally true; for if all stars—like our Sun—derive their radiant energy from gradually burning their nuclear fuel, they cannot go on doing so for ever, as the supply of fuel—no matter how large—is finite.

Moreover, Doppler shifts of the individual lines in stellar spectra disclose that stars are moving towards us, or away from us, in the radial direction. But if so, they may be moving also in a direction transverse to the line of sight—and thus, far from being 'fixed', may be gradually changing their position in the sky as well. Indeed, 'proper motions' of the stars, arising from this cause, were noted in isolated cases centuries ago. For example, Sirius and Arcturus—two of the brightest stars adorning our sky (see Table II–2)—have changed their apparent positions by $1\frac{1}{2}$–2 times the diameter of the Sun or the Moon between the time of Christ and our own day; and in our immediate cosmic neighbourhood, though not visible to the naked eye, stars are known (like Barnard's star, listed in Table II–1) that shift their place in the sky by distances equal to the apparent angular diameter of the Sun every 180 years.

The stars adorning the firmament of the heavens are then neither fixed in position, nor immutable in their light; the sky at night is really seething with action which we see arrested like a momentary glimpse—akin to a short-exposure still of a movie—because the time-scale of our own life is so pathetically short in comparison with the majestic rhythm of cosmic evolution. In particular, if stars do age as a result of a gradual depletion of their available nuclear fuel, they must also have been born at some time, and much later their light may become extinct.

Where do stars come from and how are they born? Once born, how do they live their lives? What experiences and adventures can they undergo in time and space in their youth; and what trials and tribulations are in store for them when the time comes for them to meet their end? Astronomy has already gone a long way to provide answers to at least some of these questions. In the first part of this chapter (Section III–1) we shall confine our attention to what one could describe as the pre-natal epoch of the stars —their conception in the local condensations of diffuse matter filling the space in between the stars; and in order to make our story intelligible, we must first detail some of the properties of this interstellar substrate. The second part of our narrative (Section III–2) will then take up the story of an ordinary star's life from the cradle to the grave. It will not be the life story of every star; for among them—as among human beings—exceptional beings arise which now and then may attract widespread attention while in the full bloom of their youth, or again by pathetic efforts to recapture it by extraordinary stunts late in their life.

We cannot leave out these showmen from our narrative because of their tendency to exhibitionism. Like men, all stars are created equal in everything except their mass and the quality of their substance; and these latter two parameters will largely control the manner in which each star can spend its patrimony acquired from the pre-stellar substrate. From birth, each star has been endowed with an inalienable right to burn hydrogen and other nuclear fuels as it can, at a rate appropriate to its circumstances.

But whatever these are, and whatever adventures the star may undergo, its whole life will be (as for most human beings) an almost uninterrupted sequence of giving away—its light, mass, and other forms of energy—until most of the available nuclear fuel is spent; and the stars which started their life with such a rich endowment of energy sources will end up as heaps of ashes before the gates of the stellar graveyard—inhabited by pale ghosts of stars that once upon a time were the glory of the sky, and whose light still travels through space on a journey without end long after its source has become extinct.

III–1: Interstellar Substrate

Soon after the discovery of the telescope, the early observers of the sky noticed that not all luminous sources in the sky possessed a starlike appearance. Some—not many—seemed to be distinctly fuzzy, looking like feebly shining clouds, which earned them the epithet of 'nebulae'. The first such object was discovered in 1612 by Simon Marius in the constellation of Andromeda; and in 1619 Cysat at Ingolstadt discovered one below the belt of the Orion. Thus at least two such objects became known to astronomers within ten years of the discovery of the telescope; and both were destined to serve as prototypes of two distinct classes of such object. We shall have more to say about Andromeda-type nebulae in the third part of this book; our present attention will be confined mainly to the nebulae akin to the feebly luminous cloud in Orion, which can serve as a representative example (*cf.* Plate 2).

The zeal of early telescopic observers soon detected many such nebulous objects in the sky; and by the end of the eighteenth century more than 2,000 of them were catalogued by William Herschel. A good many eventually proved to be dense star clusters, which were resolved into individual stars by telescopes of increasing size and optical power. However, others obstinately remained unresolved; and when the light of the Orion nebula was decomposed into its spectrum by Willliam Huggins in 1864, it was found to consist of a limited number of bright emission lines of the lightest elements (mainly hydrogen, nitrogen, oxygen and neon), with little or no indication of a continuous spectrum. This demonstrates that the luminous material must consist of tenuous gas at very low pressure, and not of solid particles.

Further investigation of this nebular matter disclosed an interesting fact: namely, that gaseous nebulae—like the one below Orion's belt (*cf.* Plate 2)—appear always to be associated with one or more hot stars of early spectral types which are imbedded in them, or stationed in their neighbourhood. This association between hot stars and gaseous nebulae is not accidental, but represents a real symbiosis; for the nebular gas is excited to shine by the radiation fed into it by the star—mainly at wavelengths too short to be visible to our eyes. This radiation is absorbed by nebular matter and re-emitted at longer wavelengths as light which we can see or photograph. Moreover, when we decompose this light into a spectrum, we find the latter to consist of a relatively small number of discrete emission lines, the measured wavelengths of which disclose the identity of the atoms or ions that gave rise to them. These prove to be mainly hydrogen and helium, with a sprinkling of nitrogen, oxygen, and neon; other elements are present only in amounts which a laboratory chemist would describe as impurities. The radiant energy of starlight which excites this emission can be compared to electrical current passing through a fluorescent tube used for artificial illumination. Extinguish this starlight, and you will quench the light of the nebula surrounding it almost as fast as you extinguish the fluorescent tube in your room by the flick of a switch.

Not all nebulae found in the sky are, however, of this type. In other cases—for instance, the nebulae surrounding the principal stars of the Pleiades (see Plate 3)—the stars associated with these nebulae are too cool to induce hydrogen to emit its characteristic line spectrum. Moreover, when the light of these nebulae is decomposed into a spectrum, it turns out to be a close replica of those of the stars which are imbedded in the nebular formation. Such nebulae are not clouds of fluorescent gas, but rather cosmic clouds of dust which reflect the light of the illuminating stars; hence, they deserve the name 'reflection nebulae'.

If the dimensions of the reflecting particles are large (or small) in comparison with the wavelength of light intercepted by them, the colour of the respective reflection nebula may differ but little from that of illuminating starlight. However, the scattering of light on solid particles may result also in its polarization—a phenomenon which can help us to reconstruct the shape as well as the nature of the particles responsible for the process. These particles prove to be elongated grains consisting mainly of carbon (graphite), silicates, and iron; with some admixtures of 'dirty ice' (consisting of ice flakes, frozen methane and ammonia). Ordinary ice (H_2O) does exist in interstellar space, though in not too large a quantity.

Far away from any bright star, cosmic dust clouds would remain dark and blend with the sky background imperceptibly to the human eye. When, however, they happen to interpose themselves between us and more distant stars in the background, their outlines may appear as 'holes in the sky' (Plate 4) obscuring the light of background stars. They are not completely opaque, to be sure, and stars located behind them shine through feebly; but their light is much redder, and also very noticeably polarized. Reddening and polarization in space go hand in hand; and from their combined effects we can fairly well deduce the density of solid particles in such 'dark nebulae', which sometimes assume quite dramatic forms (*cf.* Plate 5).

That clouds of dust exist around us in space has been known for a long time. The magnificent photographs of the Milky Way, taken by Barnard and other pioneers of astrophysics in the early years of this century, disclosed a profusion of dark lanes traversing the star background which indicates the presence of dust clouds between us and the more distant stars (see Plate 6); and in other, less conspicuous cases, more tenuous dust layers can disclose their presence by making the stars seen behind them redder than is appropriate for their spectra.

But even away from any obvious bright or dark nebula the space between the stars is not completely empty. Far from it; for it contains a remarkable assortment of ingredients which among them add up to a total mass comparable with that of the luminous stars. The discovery of this interstellar substrate goes back to the beginning of the present century. In 1904, the German astronomer Hartmann was studying by spectroscopic means the orbit of the components of the well-known spectroscopic binary δ Orionis— one of the three stars which constitute Orion's belt. As we explained in the preceding chapter, the orbital motion in such pairs manifests itself by periodic Doppler shifts of spectral lines of the two components, due to their varying velocity in the line of sight. All lines in the spectra of each component should exhibit such shifts (proportional to the wavelength) in unison. Hartmann's surprise was therefore great when he discovered that certain lines of ionized calcium failed to partake in the periodic shifts of all other spectral lines, and remained obstinately stationary—as though the orbital motion of the components of δ Orionis around their common centre of gravity did not concern them at all.

Since 1904, many other spectroscopic binaries were found to exhibit similar 'stationary' lines in their spectra; and it soon became apparent that such lines do not originate in the atmospheres of the respective stars, but along the line of sight separating us from them in a gaseous medium filling the entire interstellar space. Stationary lines of calcium and sodium were the first to be discovered because conditions prevailing in interstellar space are particularly conducive to their appearance; but other such lines were detected later which are caused by absorption of the neutral atoms of potassium and iron, or ionized atoms of titanium; or again (see Plate 7) by the molecular absorption of various compounds of carbon, nitrogen and hydrogen.* Quite recently, several of the more diffuse lines of so far unknown origin were even tentatively identified as being due to polyatomic organic compounds known as porphyrines.

How could molecules so complicated ever come into being in interstellar space? Or—an even more difficult feat—how could some of them combine to form solid crystals or grains of even sub-microscopic size? We do not know, and worse; for if theory alone were our guide, dust clouds would be about the last thing we should expect to exist in interstellar space. For even individual atoms in so tenuous a gas as we find there possess mean free paths which are of the order of hundreds of millions of kilometres; and the average time between their individual collisions should run into years and decades. A single sub-microscopic dust grain may contain hundreds of millions of individual atoms. When and how did they get assembled in one piece? Nevertheless, observations do not lie; and if they disclose that complicated molecules or dust particles are present in space, Nature must know how to produce them in the available time.

The spectral lines of interstellar origin are often distinguished from normal stellar lines by their narrow width (due to the low density and temperature of the medium in which they are formed). When spectra of distant bright stars are photographed with sufficient dispersion, their interstellar lines are often split up into several distinct components by Doppler shifts—a fact which indicates that the absorbing material along the line of sight is condensed into discrete *clouds,* endowed with different relative motions with respect to each other; each cloud being responsible for the production of a separate 'stationary' component of interstellar lines in the spectra. If we were to place a bright star sufficiently close to such a cloud, it would be converted to a nebula, such as we described earlier in this chapter. Only in the absence of the stars can such clouds preserve their anonymity.

In the proximity of bright stars, interstellar gas may be present in the ionized state and be heated by the star to approximately its own surface temperature. Beyond a certain distance from such stars the gas will, however, recombine and eventually settle down to enjoy some rest from the frivolous excitation offered by playful

*Such as CH, CH^+ and CN, or even HCN and HC_3N.

high-energy photons, which abound in stellar neighbourhoods before their stream gets weakened by absorption or diluted by dispersal into space. The physicists describe this blissful state of repose of an atom or a molecule as their 'ground-state', and most particles of matter filling the space between the stars can be expected to be in this state.

However, even when caught 'off-duty', some of this material may disclose its presence to us by a gentle 'breathing', due to spontaneous transitions of the electrons in the fine (or 'hyperfine') structure of their ground state. No atoms or molecules anywhere in the Universe sleep so deeply that their 'brain waves' are completely at rest; and this includes the simplest and commonest element of atomic hydrogen. Out of the sleep in its ground state, waves are continuously emitted by spontaneous transitions between different levels of its hyperfine structure; and since the energy difference between these levels is very small, the resulting waves propagate through space with a relatively low frequency of only 1420 Mc/sec—corresponding to a wavelength of $21 \cdot 1$ cm, well within the VHF domain of the radio spectrum.

It was a triumph of simple observational techniques when Ewen and Purcell at Harvard discovered in 1951 an emission line at this frequency in the radio spectrum of the night sky; and since that time the radio lines of several other interstellar molecules have been detected in a similar manner. Thus the OH-hydroxyl was found in 1963 to emit (as well as absorb) lines at wavelengths of 5, $6 \cdot 3$ and 18 cms. Water and ammonia emit at $1 \cdot 3$ cm; carbon monoxide at $2 \cdot 6$ mm; and even such relatively complicated molecules as those of formaldehyde, formic acid, or methyl alcohol were found in 1969–1970 to leave distinct imprints in the radio-spectrum of interstellar substrate, in the form of discrete emission lines in the cm-range.

Their discovery—in particular, that of the first atomic hydrogen line at 21 cms—opened up an entirely new and powerful way of exploring the structure and motion of interstellar matter surrounding us in space—its amount from the intensity of the emission, its radial motion from the Doppler shifts (to which the radio lines are subject in the same way as lines in the 'optical' part of the spectrum), and even its temperature from the broadening of the radio line profiles due to thermal agitation of the emitting particles. The radiation of a bright star can heat up the surrounding

Origin and Evolution of the Stars

gas to temperatures of several thousand degrees; but far away from such stars the temperature of interstellar hydrogen in its state of repose drops down to 80–100 degrees Kelvin (or about the temperature of our liquid air).

The density of interstellar gas—mainly atomic hydrogen—varies greatly, however, from place to place. In the optical part of the spectrum (which we can see or photograph) the line spectrum of interstellar hydrogen leaves no distinguishable trace; but in the radio spectrum its imprint is unmistakeable; and its density can be inferred from the intensity of its 21-cm ratio emission line. The outcome of such studies has disclosed that, between individual gas clouds, there are no more than a few hydrogen atoms to be found per ccm—and (since each hydrogen atom weighs only $1 \cdot 66 \times 10^{-24}$g) the density of so tenuous a substrate is scarcely more than 10^{-23}g/cm^3. Within gas clouds the density may be increased a hundredfold, and ten thousandfold or more in relatively dense complexes which we call 'gaseous nebulae'—like the one in Orion (Plate 2).

In denser parts of the Orion nebula the density of its gas may exceed 10^{-18} g/cm^3; still a pretty hard vacuum as far as our terrestrial notions are concerned, but a million times denser than the average density of interstellar substrate. A million atoms per ccm does not seem to be much to speak about (our own air at sea level contains 10^{15} times as many in the same volume); but if we were to fill with such gas a sphere of the radius of one parsec ($3 \cdot 09 \times 10^{18}$cm), the total mass inside it would be more than 30,000 times as large as that of our Sun. Not many parts of the Orion nebula are, to be sure, as dense as 10^{-18} g/cm^3; but its dimensions are several parsecs across and its total mass is certainly equivalent to that of tens of thousands of individual stars.

So large and massive a gas cloud cannot remain in a quiescent state for a moment. Applications of spectrographs to different parts of the nebula have indicated differential Doppler shifts due to turbulent motions with velocities exceeding 100 km/sec—belying the deceptive impression of calm given by Plate 2. The latter shows only a momentary glimpse of what is actually a seething cauldron of turbulent gas at high temperature—a veritable cosmic storm is raging there, which we are privileged to watch at a safe distance of some 500 parsecs. It is too far away to do us any harm (and, moreover, is receding from us at a mean velocity of some

18 km/sec); but a storm of this violence cannot last for a very long time—a few million years, perhaps, but no more.

But when it is over, what will be left in its wake, and what will happen to the turbulent gas of the nebula now in the active phase of its contortions? The answer is rather dramatic: for we know now that such contortions are the birth pangs of the stars—and will result in the formation of thousands of new stars which will add new glory to our skies. Some of them have been born already (like the stars in the Orion's belt), and others are being born virtually in front of our eyes; we can identify stars closely associated with the Orion nebula which must be less than one million years old.

Objects like the Orion nebula represent Nature's grand hatcheries of new stars, thriving on the breeding-ground of interstellar substrate whose composition—far from constituting a homogeneous medium—is largely bunched up in clouds. The reason for this clumpiness is no doubt turbulence in the medium from which our entire stellar system originated; but the steps which can lead to the collapse of individual clouds into stars we can reconstruct in greater detail. In order to lay down the groundwork for such a reconstruction we must, however, return once more to the dust in space which proves to play a crucial role in the process.

We mentioned earlier in this chapter that while interstellar gas consists predominantly of atomic hydrogen, interstellar dust is formed mainly by compounds consisting of heavier elements—such as carbon, nitrogen, oxygen, silicon and iron. The total mass of an interstellar dust cloud (like those shown, for instance, on Plate 6) can be inferred from the reddening or polarization of the light of background stars which shine through them; and is typically of the order of 10 solar masses. But the chemical elements, composing the dust grains which dim or polarize starlight, constitute only about 1% of the total cosmic matter—the remaining 99% being hydrogen (with possibly some helium). Therefore, a typical cloud whose mass contains 10 $\odot$ of dust, should possess also some 1,000 solar masses of hydrogen—an amount comparable with that in a typical interstellar gas cloud, observable in the 21-cm line of its radio spectrum.

If we can observe this line in the radio spectra of gaseous nebulae, it should be equally easy to observe the same amount of hydrogen also in the dust clouds. But when we turn our radio telescopes to them, their detectors of radiation at 1420 Mc/sec remain conspicuously silent—no atomic hydrogen appears to be present there at all. How to account for this anomaly? The only explanation seems to be the possibility that hydrogen in such clouds has been converted to another form which no longer emits any radiation at 21 cms—such as would be the case if atomic hydrogen gets converted to molecular hydrogen, which may even form solid hydrogen 'ice' encrusting the dust grains. In the open spaces between the stars this is impossible; molecular hydrogen in gaseous form cannot exist there because the general starlight—feeble as it may seem—would dissociate it more rapidly than it could form. Hydrogen which has frozen onto the dust cannot exist in open space either; for starlight warms up dust grains enough to preclude the formation of any 'hoar frost' of interstellar hydrogen on their surfaces.

But inside a dust cloud it may be a very different story. Starlight —the principal agent which keeps hydrogen in its atomic form— cannot penetrate far into a dark nebula because it is obscured by its dust; therefore, inside such clouds the prevailing temperature may drop far below 80°–100°K at which atomic hydrogen is maintained in open interstellar space. The actual value of this temperature was not established until quite recently from the measurements of the thermal profiles of the emission lines of the OH-molecules, found to be present in the radio spectra of certain dark clouds at wavelengths close to 18 cms. These lines proved to be so narrow as to rule out a temperature at their origin in excess of some 5°K. These are the lowest temperatures found to exist anywhere in Nature so far; and under these conditions, hydrogen would indeed be converted into solid ice encrusting other grains and adding to their mass.

The interiors of dark nebulae—a conspicuous example of which can be seen on Plate 5—are Nature's 'deep freezers' in space. They represent clouds laden with flakes of hydrogen snow, presaging snowstorms on a cosmic scale; and such snowstorms are the immediate precursors of star formation. What may set off the labour pains of such a process is again ubiquitous starlight—this time the pressure which light is bound to exert on any particle absorbing it.

The light of the stars carries not only energy, but also momentum; and a transfer of momentum is tantamount to pressure exerted on any surface which absorbs it. A single grain of dust in space may experience gentle radiation pressure exerted upon it from all directions; and if the field of radiation to which it is exposed is isotropic, the impulses received from light coming in all directions will cancel.

But this will no longer be the case in a dust cloud. On its periphery, particles are exposed to pressure by undiluted radiation of the nearby stars; but radiation from the opposite direction is found to be weakened by its passage through the cloud. As a result, peripheral particles find themselves exposed to a gentle but persistent inward pressure acting to move them towards the centre of the cloud. This pressure should tend secularly to diminish the size of the cloud, and increase its condensation; for the gas that may be intermingled with dust will be dragged along to follow the same general course.

Compression of the dust clouds by radiation of nearby stars need not represent the only way in which Nature can produce local condensations of interstellar material of increasing density. A turbulent flow of gas alone is bound to give rise to local condensations forming at random even in the absence of any dust; but no such ripples would escape eventual dissolution if dust were not present there in quantity. The reason is the fact that increasing condensation of gas entails an increase in its internal pressure and temperature, which will inhibit the growth of the condensation and bring about its dispersal before gravitational attraction can ensure the future nascent condensation as an independent dynamical unit.

In order that this should be possible it is necessary to remove excess heat from the interior of a growing condensation before the pressure due to rising temperature can arrest contraction; and this can be accomplished only by radiation while the cloud remains semi-transparent. In such a process solid particles still present in the cloud play a crucial role. Atoms or molecules of any gas are, in general, very inefficient cooling agents; for they can radiate away excess energy only in a discrete set of spectral lines or bands—the fewer in number, the lower the temperature. On the other hand, solid dust grains can radiate in a continuum of wavelengths—they can let excess energy get out through a much wider gate. The thermal properties of the dust are, therefore, crucial for determining how much heat generated during compression of the collapsing object—we can call it a 'proto-star'—is radiated away into space, and how much remains inside the configuration to increase its temperature.

This balance is of great importance for all the subsequent history of our collapsing object. As long as its internal pressure and temperature remain low, the incipient proto-star will have its immediate future controlled by self-gravity, and its material will start collapsing by free fall; the faster the fall, the denser it becomes. Also, at this stage, the collapsing cloud can fragment into smaller units—eventually giving rise to, not one, but several stars at approximately the same time; or even to a whole star cluster.* But as soon as radiation by dust can no longer keep up with the rate at which internal heat is produced by contraction, the temperature and pressure will rise and the first victim of the warming-up climate will be the dust itself.

All such dust will eventually revert into gas; but by the time this safety valve has been closed, self-gravity will already be in firm control; and initial collapse will be slowed down to an orderly course of contraction which will continue until the star can arrest it by unlocking the vast sources of nuclear energy contained in its material. These will enable the new-born object to attain a pressure in its interior which will be sufficient to counteract gravity and prevent further contraction of the whole configuration, but in so doing allow enough of this energy to leak out to tell the outside world that a star is shining.

This act represents only the first stage in a longer continuous process, which commenced with the development of an instability in the pre-existing interstellar substrate, several million years before the new-born star switched on the reserves of its nuclear power to adorn our sky in its own right. How long can it enjoy this privilege, what kind of trials and tribulations of stellar life are in store for it before nuclear sources run out and compel the ageing star to seek rest among the ghostly spirits of the stellar graveyard? In the next section we shall attempt to outline the life-story of a star from cradle to grave.

---

*We should also expect that only a part of the mass of the collapsing configuration will condense into individual stars; because once new stars are formed the remaining gas may be heated, ionized, and blown away.

III–2: The Life and Death of a Star

In the previous section of this chapter we gave, in outline, a pre-natal history of the stars in the womb of interstellar substrate, to the time when the self-gravity of a budding configuration takes control of its subsequent evolutionary course. This self-attraction will at first cause the configuration to shrink in size by free fall of its material towards its centre of mass—a collapse which will continue until it is slowed down and eventually arrested by gas pressure building up in the interior. The heat generated by compression will be distributed throughout the interior largely by convection currents which—at the advanced stages of this process—engulf the whole star.

By this time the star has already begun to shine with its own light—light derived from heat produced by contraction at the expense of its diminishing gravitational energy. At this time the surface shines feebly, but is very large. As a result, the luminosity of the star as a whole will keep decreasing with diminishing size, while its effective temperature rises slowly from red to white heat. At the same time, the impatient stellar infant emits more than light into space; it starts throwing off its surface material in angry puffs, in the form of an energetic stream of corpuscular radiation —known as 'stellar wind'—about one to ten million times more intensively than our Sun, and the other stars like it, are doing at the present time. This wind helps to clear up the debris left around in space from the formative pangs of the birth process, and may affect larger bodies—such as new-born planets, which are less easy to push away—in several ways which may leave visible traces in the structure of their surface material for posterity to decipher (see Chapter VII–3).

The gravitational contraction of new-born stars continues until the internal temperatures created by compression exceed some ten million degrees. When this happens, the first chapter in the history of a star—its early childhood—comes to an end; for by that time the physical conditions prevailing in the deep interior become sufficient to ignite the nuclear fuel which the new-born star acquired from the parent interstellar substrate.

What kind of fuel will it be that ignites most readily under these conditions? From the point of view of atomic nuclei, gas at

Origin and Evolution of the Stars

ten million degrees is merely lukewarm; at this temperature, plasma particles possess barely enough energy to reduce by well-aimed shots the defence barriers of only the lightest elements. Such elements are also the only ones likely to be present in stellar material in sufficient quantity to offer ready targets to ubiquitous cross-fire by plasma particles which have, by chance encounters, acquired sufficient velocity. Of these, light elements like lithium, beryllium or boron have already been largely destroyed (by conversion into helium) during the last stage of the preceding contraction, and (because of their relatively high perishability) are not present in Nature in quantities that could make significant contributions to stellar energy production later on. The only element which can do so effectively at this stage is the lightest and most abundant of them all: hydrogen.

The role which hydrogen and its conversion into helium can play at this stage of stellar evolution, and some details of the actual processes by which this can be accomplished, have already been outlined in Chapter I–2, in connection with our Sun. There we stressed the fact that neither the ignition, nor subsequent burning of hydrogen into helium can occur explosively. Far from it; for such a process will commence operating at so slow a rate that the nuclear fuel only smoulders rather than burns. And we may well be grateful to Nature for having arranged matters in this way; for a star in the initial phases of its evolution is filled to the brim with nuclear fuel, representing a gigantic hydrogen bomb whose premature detonation could bring the entire story of this chapter to an abrupt and premature end.

Once a star can switch on its central thermonuclear reactor to produce helium from hydrogen, the energy produced in this way can maintain internal pressure entirely adequate to completely arrest gravitational contraction; and the star can look forward to a long period of quiescent life of steady energy output during which its external characteristics—such as radius and luminosity—will alter little in the course of long intervals of time. Moreover, the energy output of the central thermonuclear reactor depends essentially on the temperature at which the reactor is run; and this temperature depends, in turn, on the extent of compression to which the configuration was squeezed by self-gravity of its mass. Therefore, the brightness of the stars living off the same kind of nuclear fuel should depend essentially on their mass—the brightness increasing with mass the more rapidly, the greater the temperature-dependence of the process.

Moreover—for a given type of fuel—the stellar luminosity should also be correlated with the radius and surface temperature of the star. Therefore, if we plot the luminosity of such stars against the

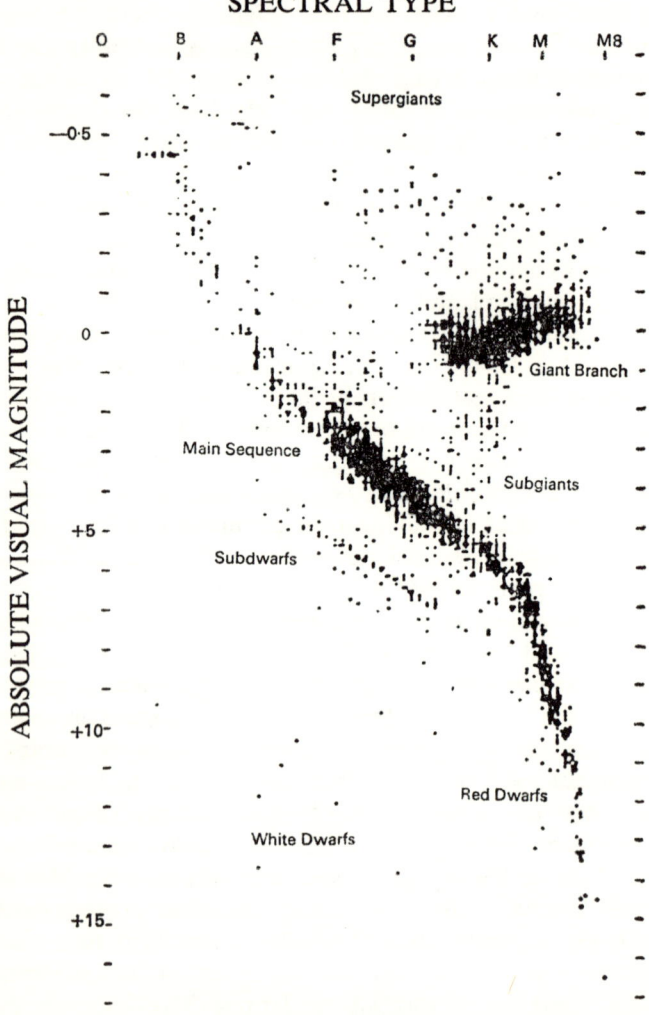

Figure 3 The Hertzsprung-Russell diagram for stellar population in our galactic neighbourhood. The significance of individual groups of stars is marked in accordance with the terms used in the text.

temperature of their surfaces (or spectra), we should obtain a diagram shown in Figure 3—usually referred to as a Hertzsprung-Russell (or, for brevity, HR) diagram,* on which such stars will cluster around a central band running diagonally downward from left to right.

Most stars picked up at random in any part of the sky will be located there by their characteristics, disclosing that they belong to the hydrogen-burning group. Figure 2 in Chapter II represents, in effect, such a diagram for the sample of stars found in the immediate neighbourhood of the Sun. Since hydrogen is the most abundant element of the stars as well as the easiest one to kindle, and its supply is likely to last for a very long time, a large majority of stars in the sky are seen now to be passing through this stage. The density of population of their locus in the HR-diagram has earned it the title of the *Main Sequence,* representing—in fact— the principal thoroughfare or meeting place of mature stars of the same generation, with a common past, common economic interests, and a common future.

The Main Sequence in the HR-diagram represents a locus populated by stars which derive their light from the combustion of the most effective and longest-lasting fuel available to them for the purpose; and that this happens to be hydrogen is an important reflection on the general state of our Universe as a whole, on which we shall have more to say in Chapter XIII of this book. Hydrogen-burning stars of the Main Sequence can look forward to a long astronomical future and an orderly life, for almost everything is precisely laid out for them in advance, and any youthful pranks are ruled out by inexorable laws of Nature.

In particular, all Main Sequence stars shine with very steady light—an attribute which they will lose as soon as they leave the Main Sequence, and will not recover again till the very end of their life. The reason is that the process of hydrogen-burning is regulated closely by built-in 'feedbacks' that can manipulate the controls of stellar thermonuclear reactors to ensure steadiness of output within a very narrow margin of uncertainty. For example, should nuclear fuel fail to maintain the required luminosity, gravi-

---

*To commemorate jointly the Danish astronomer Ejnar Hertzsprung (1873–1967) and the American astronomer Henry Norris Russell (1877–1957) who first constructed it in the early years of this century, and realized its significance as constituting a reflection of the evolutionary trends among the stars.

tational contraction of central regions will increase its output by raising the temperature. Similarly, any over-production would automatically entail expansion accompanied by cooling of the central regions. Thus, gravitational and thermal energy are ever ready to act as buffers against deviations from the luminosity appropriate for the mass, or as thermostats to control the rate of nuclear burning. So effectively do they accomplish this task that the output of hydrogen-burning reactors in the interiors of Main Sequence stars seldom deviates from the norm by as much as one part in a thousand.

The maintenance of this steady rate of energy production is also facilitated by the fact that (on account of the high opacity of stellar material) stars can maintain large reserves of radiation dammed in their interiors which can only slowly leak outwards. The amount of radiation bottled up by opacity inside a star is, in fact, so large that its gradual leakage could keep a star shining for millions of years after its production plant in the interior has gone out of commission. Should this happen to our Sun today, we would not know about it at all; and life on the Earth could go on, in fact, for several million years before our distant descendants living at that time would begin to suffer the consequences of a power cut.

Can all stars, however, attain the nuclear-burning stage on the Main Sequence? In order to do so, the initial contraction would have had to raise their central temperatures to levels in excess of 10 million degrees; and this will always happen as long as compression of stellar gas entails an increase of temperature. Beyond a certain degree of compression this can, however, cease to be true; for the gas may then become 'degenerate' in the sense that increasing pressure and density no longer affect the internal temperature. Appropriate calculations show that continuing contraction can render stellar gas degenerate before a temperature of 10 million degrees is attained in configurations whose mass is less than approximately eight per cent of that of the Sun. The evolutionary course of such starlets is then governed throughout by contraction; they can at no time unlock their nuclear energy sources; and such light as they emit is defrayed from gravitational energy lost by contraction.

Stars more massive than $0 \cdot 1 \odot$ can, however, always initiate the process of burning hydrogen into helium, which constitutes the

Origin and Evolution of the Stars 91

most important source of energy that can be converted to light. Stars with masses between 0·1–1·2 ☉ will do so by the helium synthesis described in section 2 of Chapter I in connection with the Sun, which falls into this range. Stars more massive than approximately 1·2 ☉ can accomplish the same feat more effectively by an alternative process which involves carbon and nitrogen as catalysts at intermediary stages. The outcome (and energy yield per unit mass) is the same, but at temperatures higher than 15 million degrees—attained in the interiors of stars more massive than the Sun—the 'carbon-nitrogen' cycle can consume hydrogen more rapidly than that based on the 'proton-proton' reaction described on p. 37; and stars operating their central thermonuclear reactors at higher temperatures can become considerably brighter. It is probable that a slight upturn in the slope of the Main Sequence apparent on Figure 2 just above the position

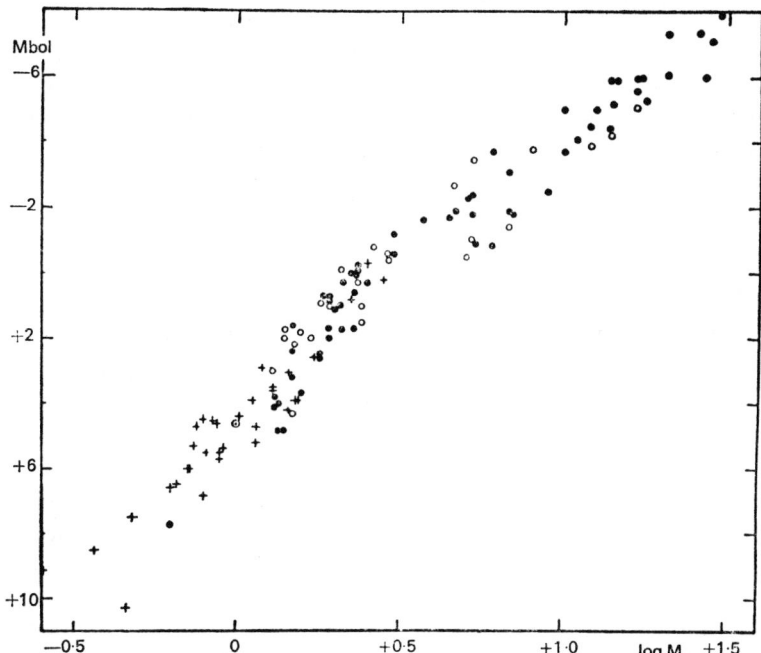

Figure 4 Mass-luminosity relation for Main Sequence stars. Objects marked on this diagram represent individual components of different types of binary systems (after Kopal, 1959). The symbol ☉ represents the position of our Sun.

occupied by our Sun, or in the mass-luminosity relation shown on Figure 4 for stars more massive than the Sun, is due to a changeover from proton-proton cycle to carbon-nitrogen cycle as the prevalent process of energy production by hydrogen combustion.

The greater brightness of a massive star requires a higher rate of energy production, and can be maintained only at the cost of a more rapid depletion of available nuclear reserves. How long can stars found at different parts of the Main Sequence go on maintaining their place in the face of diminishing hydrogen supply? Let us start with our Sun. The ages of the oldest samples of solid matter (meteorites, lunar rocks) found in the solar system reveal that our Sun arrived at the Main Sequence some 4·6–4·7 billion years ago to commence its cosmic career as a hydrogen-burning star. An analysis of its present chemical composition has disclosed, moreover, that its initial hydrogen supply has so far been diminished by less than one-quarter; therefore, the astronomical future of the Sun is still much longer than its past. For stars less massive than the Sun this is even more true. For example, dwarf stars like the components of the binary Krüger 60 (*cf.* Table II–4) could continue their modest existence as hydrogen-burning configurations for dozens of billions of years without undergoing much noticeable outward change; but for massive stars it is a very different story.

An empirical relation between mass and luminosity—as given by Figure 4—establishes that a star ten times as massive as the Sun should emit approximately 10,000 times as much total radiation; and stars 30 times as massive should be about a hundred thousand times as bright. Although such stars possess larger initial supplies of hydrogen, they spend it at so much more rapid a rate (i.e., they are running their central reactors at higher temperatures) that their life expectancies on the Main Sequence must be much shorter than that of the Sun. Stars of masses close to 10 $\odot$ will run through most of their available hydrogen in less than ten million years; and those of masses close to 30 $\odot$ will do so in a few hundred thousand years of our time.

While a star continues to burn hydrogen, its position in the HR-diagram will alter very little (as witnessed by a relatively small dispersion of the stars along the Main Sequence). When our Sun reached this stage, its initial luminosity was probably about 40% smaller than at the present time; but its size could have been essentially the same as today. It sounds paradoxical, but a typical Main Sequence star, as it evolves and consumes more and more of its hydrogen, gains somewhat in brightness and may become hotter (because of increasing transparency of its interior) in the course of time, though not inordinately so.

However, in the course of its long sojourn on the Main Sequence, the chemical composition of the star is bound to undergo a secular irreversible change. When the new-born star arrived there after a short period of contraction, material currents of its convective equilibrium ensured that its mass was well mixed and chemically homogeneous. Progressive depletion of hydrogen in the deep interior and its transmutation into helium must, however, cause the material to depart gradually from homogeneity—at least in stars of masses not much in excess of that of the Sun, which are in radiative equilibrium throughout their interiors. In a radiative core —with no convection—the abundance of hydrogen is bound to diminish inwards in the course of time; while more massive stars which burn hydrogen by the carbon-nitrogen cycle develop, as a result, convective cores in which all elements are well mixed, and in which all hydrogen will eventually be converted into helium. The shell surrounding this core may still contain hydrogen, but too cool to burn into helium; and with a temporary expiration of nuclear energy sources the star is bound to revert to gravitational contraction in an effort to establish a new balance.

In the course of this search, the contracting core (containing about one-tenth of the star's total mass) becomes rapidly more condensed, and its temperature rises to such an extent that hydrogen can resume burning in a shell surrounding the core. Such shell-burning stars exhibit other notable characteristics. Since the gravitational energy of a contracting core diminishes while the gravitational energy of the configuration as a whole must be conserved, it follows that its surplus in the core must be expended in the envelope— or, in other words, the star is bound to *expand*. Its size will rapidly increase, but its luminosity will not change a great deal; and, as a result, its surface temperature will diminish. The evolutionary track of such a star in the HR-diagram will lead it to evolve away from the Main Sequence—in the domain to its right —along evolutionary tracks leading to stellar configurations of increasing size on which astronomers have bestowed the epithets of 'sub-giants' or 'giants'. Some stars especially endowed with mass can eventually evolve into 'super-giants'—the largest and brightest stellar objects we know in the sky—shining like beacons and visible from afar in space with candle-power that may exceed 100,000 times that of our Sun.

This prodigious rise in celestial candle-power at the post-Main Sequence stage of stellar evolution is not caused by any new or more effective sources of nuclear energy being tapped, but rather to the increased ease with which radiation can escape from stellar interiors. As a star begins to evolve away from the Main Sequence to its right in the HR-diagram, its diminishing surface temperature stimulates a development of convective zones in sub-surface layers reaching deep in the interior. A convective zone facilitates outward energy transfer much more effectively than was the case in the radiative equilibrium of Main Sequence stars. And more: for deep sub-surface convection can revive a 'solar wind' of corpuscular radiation—important in the days of pre-Main Sequence contraction, and largely dormant during the hydrogen-burning past—and intensify it into an hurricane which can carry away a substantial fraction of the entire star's mass. During the evolutionary stage which maintains the stars on the Main Sequence, the light radiated away will diminish the total mass of such stars by less than one per cent; and apart from a secular decrease of this order their masses should remain constant. In their post-Main Sequence days the stars are, however, known to divest themselves—gradually as well as by isolated events—of a large part of the mass they still possessed on the Main Sequence; and to approach the portals of the stellar graveyard in a much more subdued and humble state.

The commencement of such a process can be followed along the evolutionary tracks which lead the incipient sub-giants on the giant branch to the right of the Main Sequence on Figure 3. The first phase of this process comes to an abrupt halt at the turning point of this track, when the temperature in the star's core—now consisting largely of helium—exceeds 100 million degrees. When this occurs, helium begins to burn to produce carbon and oxygen. The yield of radiant energy produced by this process is no longer comparable to that gained previously by hydrogen burning (only about 10 per cent of the latter per unit mass); nor will it last long—especially for stars of small masses where incipient degeneracy may give rise to a 'helium flash' that preempts this energy supply in a relatively short time. Whatever the time-scale of the process may be, however, the consumption of helium (synthesized previously from hydrogen on the Main Sequence) delivers much less energy than that which sustained the stars in the prime of their life; but while it lasts, it will enable the stars to enjoy a brief 'Indian summer' before the eventual approach of decrepitude.

The limitations of our present knowledge do not permit us to follow subsequent stages of stellar evolution otherwise than in general outline. At the exhaustion of each successive element of the periodic table by nuclear burning, short-lived gravitational contraction is bound to recur and—as long as compression can raise the temperature to ever increasing levels—heat up the central regions to the ignition temperature of the next fuel. As a result, more and more of the lighter elements are going to perish in the nuclear holocaust. Thus at temperatures between 600–700 million degrees carbon itself should largely vanish and be transformed into neon and magnesium; while temperatures in excess of 1,000 million degrees are necessary for a synthesis of the elements between silicon and iron.

Can, however, such temperatures be actually attained by contraction in stellar interiors? This depends essentially on the lengths to which stellar gas can go to avoid degeneracy (for in a degenerate gas compression can no longer raise the temperature); and this, in turn, depends mainly on the total mass of the respective configuration. We have already mentioned that stars with masses smaller than 0·08 ⊙ can never hope to ignite even their hydrogen. In order to ignite helium at 100 million degrees, a mass of at least 1·5 ⊙ is needed; and elements heavier than neon can be produced by thermonuclear processes only in very massive stars.

But what happens when this is no longer possible, and the star is aproaching the end of its tether? One of the sure symptoms of creeping old age in the stars is their growing inability to maintain a balance between the production of energy and its expenditure—or, in simpler language, to shine with constant light. As long as a star continues burning hydrogen on the Main Sequence, the controls of its central thermonuclear reactor maintain its energy production at a very steady rate. But as soon as the star departs from the Main Sequence to become a 'giant', its thermonuclear controls are much more difficult to maintain in steady adjustment;

and, as a result, the light of the star becomes unsteady—only slightly at first, but later to an increasing extent.

This is particularly true along the evolutionary track continuing past the helium-burning point of the giant branch, at which the track doubles back once more towards the Main Sequence (see Figure 3). While, at preceding stages, the light variability was small and irregular, past the helium burn-out stage it assumes more definite patterns. The most remarkable group of such stars are the 'cepheid variables—so-called after their prototype star of δ Cephei, discovered to be variable in 1784—which exhibit moderate light variation with clock-like regularity, in periods ranging from several hours to a few weeks. The most remarkable property of these stars is the close correlation between the absolute brightness of such objects and periods of their light variation—the 'period-luminosity' relation of cepheid variables—which discloses that the more luminous the star, the longer the period of its variability. This relation represents a most important tool for our exploration of the depth of the Universe—and the extent of the help which such stars have given us in this connection can scarcely be over-estimated.

The cause of such light variations is not fluctuation in the actual energy output of the star, but rather periodic oscillations set up in their surface layers which act as a 'light rheostat' controlling the outflow of radiant energy from the interior. In other words, the real causes of the light variability of the cepheids are not deep-seated, but quite superficial; and the surface pulsations which control the periodic 'gating' of energy outflow entail motions of very little mass.

The same is true of even more spectacular 'long-period variables' —akin to Mira Ceti—representing a group of very large but very cool stars (with surface temperatures around 3,000 degrees), whose visible light can fluctuate in much larger amplitudes (corresponding to a range between one and ten thousand in the observed amount of light) in longer periods that range from several months to a few years. Such large fluctuations in visible light are mainly due to the fact that the light emission of stars so cool is apt to drift periodically in and out of the spectral region to which our eyes are sensitive, or our terrestrial atmosphere transparent. The total light of such stars varies very much less than its visible range would seem to indicate—no more, in general, the cepheid variables—and their

Origin and Evolution of the Stars

variability constitutes (like that of the cepheids) a large superficial phenomenon.

But once the regions of light variability in the HR-diagram have been reached and traversed by stars with masses large enough to enable them to climb to the dizzy heights of luminosity on their evolutionary tracks (see again Figure 3), and with very little nuclear fuel or total mass left to enable them to maintain their former splendour, gravitational contraction takes over once more to send such stars in a tailspin in the direction of diminishing mass, size and luminosity. They pass along tracks which cross the Main Sequence to intermingle below it with stars whose initial mass did not enable them to undertake too long an excursion to the domain of giant stars. Such stars—called ignominiously 'sub-dwarfs'—continue to shine at the expense of their diminishing potential energy with a brightness comparable with that of the 'red dwarfs' at the lower part of the Main Sequence, but differing from them by higher surface temperatures and small dimensions. Such sub-dwarfs are typically one-tenth as large as the Sun, but several thousand degrees warmer on the surface.

The smallness of the size is a general indication of the extent to which gravitational contraction has by this time reduced the formerly proud stars. But the stars do not submit to their fate meekly, or at least some of them do not; and from time to time they recover at least a part of their former glory by 'relaxation oscillations', which are exhibited by certain variable stars that normally rest in a state of minimum constant brightness, interrupted now and then by spasmodic attempts to increase it. The longer the average time-interval between such outbursts, the greater the rise in light exhibited on such occasions. Most conspicuous recurrent objects of this type are called the 'Novae'—a class of new stars which suddenly appeared to our ancestors in the sky, seemingly from nowhere, only to peter out of sight of the unaided eye weeks or months later. Several of these 'guest stars'—as the Chinese used to call them—have appeared in the sky within our lifetime; and scores more were recorded by observers of the past.

Modern observing techniques have disclosed that in no such case was the star actually 'new', but rather that a previously faint star flared up—sometimes for a matter of hours or days—to become temporarily 1,000 to 10,000 times brighter than before; only to lose, in a short time, all its splendour and settle down to its former inconspicuous state. Protracted observation of many 'new' stars of the past has disclosed that their outbursts are recurrent in time, at intervals ranging from centuries to millenia. The underlying causes of this are probably gravitational; and—as we found for the cepheids or long-period variables—the real roots of the symptoms of their behaviour are only skin-deep. In the course of an outburst, a Nova may throw off into space one or more shells of its surface material accelerated to velocities in excess of that of escape from the gravitational field of the object. But the total amount of mass lost by each outburst appears to constitute but a minute fraction of the star's mass; and the star can repeat this strenuous exercise many times before beginning to suffer the consequences of such imprudent behaviour at so late a stage of its life.

Does every star at some evolutionary stage of its career have to perform such stunts to attract the attention of the star-gazers? We have reason to doubt it; for virtually all Novae (as well as 'explosive' variables of U Geminorum or SS Cygni type) have proved to be components of tiny 'heavenly twins'. Such binaries are very small—most of them could be packed inside our Sun with room to spare—and their orbital periods are measured in hours rather than days. Nevertheless, it appears that binary nature has something to do with the explosive tendency of its components; though a more exact diagnosis of the recurrent affliction of 'nova-itis', and its connection with the binary nature of the system in which it breaks out, still remains to be made.

However, while the sequence and course of chronic illnesses due to various deficiencies accompanying stellar old age cannot as yet be described in all its details, the final outcome is not in doubt. A continuing gravitational contraction—whose inexorable embrace the enfeebled stars are ill-prepared to withstand—will eventually compress their material to a state at which internal temperature can no longer contribute to pressure, and the star will become 'degenerate' in this sense throughout most of its interior. The dimensions of such stars will have shrunk typically from $0 \cdot 1\ \odot$ to $0 \cdot 01\ \odot$—i.e., become of planetary rather than stellar order of magnitude—and while their masses may still be comparable with that of the Sun, the mean densities may become ten to a hundred thousand times as large. Imagine—if you can—material so dense that several tons of it could be squeezed into a matchbox.

The stars formed of such material are known to us as 'white

dwarfs'—dwarfs because of their extremely small size, and white because their surfaces are still maintained at temperatures close to 10,000 degrees by conductive cooling of their interiors. Such stars continue to contract, but at so slow a rate that their frugal energy output can be met from their diminishing supply of potential energy for billions of years. The line spectra of some such stars still disclose the presence of hydrogen (possibly acquired by accretion from ambient interstellar substrate) in a sparse atmosphere floating on a degenerate core of heavy elements; but its interior has long ceased to act as a nuclear reactor.

Moreover, it is not only the mass of such configurations which gets compressed at white-dwarf stage to a state of high density, but also their magnetic field. The rotation of ordinary stars (consisting as they do of highly conducting plasma) gives rise to only weak general magnetic fields. That of our Sun does not seem to exceed one gauss in strength; though some Main-Sequence stars are known (such as the 'metallic' A-stars) whose magnetic fields not only run into several hundred to a few thousand gauss, but exhibit periodic changes of polarity which have earned them the epithet of 'magnetic variables'.

Now if a Main Sequence or giant star were to contract to white-dwarf stage without loss of its angular momentum, their periods of axial rotations would shrink from days to minutes of our terrestrial time; and their equatorial velocities would become so high that the spectral lines of such stars should be 'washed out' by Doppler broadening—unless we happen to view such a star from a direction parallel with that of its axis of rotation or nearly so; for in such a case axial rotation would generate no velocity component in radial direction and, therefore, no Doppler shifts.

No Zeeman splitting has been detected so far in the spectra of white dwarfs which show lines on their continuous background. However, quite recently (1970) the total light of some of these dwarfs was found to be polarized so strongly as to suggest the presence of magnetic fields of ten to a hundred million gauss. Such stars would, therefore, represent not only configurations of highly compressed mass, but also magnets of tremendous strength; and woe to any material susceptible to magnetic attraction which strays into such a field—it will never get away again.

At the white-dwarf state, most stars will have reached their final resting place in the HR-diagram; and will thereafter continue to wander through the fathomless depths of space like pale shadowy ghosts of the past—reminiscing about the days long gone when they still possessed the nuclear (or at least gravitational) means of showing off as dazzling beauties of the sky; and contemplating the glories and vicissitudes of stellar life which starts from dust and ends in the general paralysis of a degenerate state. Although white dwarfs no longer possess the means to advertise their presence, many of them have been spotted in our neighbourhood; such as the secondary components of Sirius or Procyon in Table II–1 or in Figure 2. Others, especially those which wander alone in space, are more difficult to identify as such at a distance; but there seems no doubt that their shadows lurk everywhere around us as silent reminders of the past.

Is this the way in which all stars are destined to fade away? In order to do so, the only necessary prerequisite is for gravitational attraction to compress them to a degenerate state and thus preserve them from a worse fate. Fundamental laws of physics disclose, however, that this can only happen to stars whose mass does not exceed approximately 1·4 times that of the Sun. We have good reason to believe that, by the time this criterion is called upon to decide the star's future evolutionary course, an overwhelming majority of them will pass its muster; for whatever their original mass may have been, most of them will have managed to divest themselves of enough superfluous mass at the 'giant' stage of their evolution.

However, it can happen—albeit very rarely—that an overweight star arrives at the gates of the stellar graveyard. If so, it will knock at them in vain; for inflexible laws prevent it from joining the other white dwarfs. A star thus ostracized and denied the blissful repose which comes with degeneracy will be punished for its avarice in holding on to too much of its mass too long by a torture worthy of the ancient Tantalos: for unable to become degenerate, it has no other choice than to submit to an ever-tightening grip of its gravitational attraction—and become a 'pygmy' rather than a 'white dwarf'—until it attains the stupendous density of the order of a million tons per cubic centimetre. At this compression (at which the entire mass of our Sun could be confined to a sphere no more than 100 km in diameter—of asteroidal rather than planetary size) the nuclear structure of matter gives in, and the star itself—or what is left of it—becomes reduced to a neutron core.

Such an event entails very dramatic consequences. The collapse itself of so large a mass in a matter of seconds would give rise to so terrific an implosion that its consequences would rend the whole star asunder and disperse most of its matter into space. An observer watching the event from a safe distance would then witness a cosmic catastrophe to which astronomers refer as the explosion of a Supernova. The term itself is barely adequate to describe the stupendous scale and nature of the event involved in the process; for while the individual nova outbursts represent a star 'blowing its lid off', a Supernova explosion signifies the final and irrevocable suicide of the star as a whole, and the dispersal of most of its mass into surrounding space. Stars too massive to afford a quiet cosmic burial among the white dwarfs are destined to disposal by cremation in a flash of nuclear fire; and the message of each such event is transmitted on the wings of light to the far corners of the Universe.

An exploding supernova can outshine for a few days a whole galaxy of thousands of millions of stars—in startling contrast to the insignificance of its remnant, a neutron core of only dozens of kilometres across that will continue seething with unrest for hundreds of thousands of years. We have good reasons to surmise that such Supernova remnants are identical with the 'pulsars' discovered in recent years, on which more will be said in the next part of this chapter. For the present we propose, however, to abandon the Ariadne's thread of theoretical reasoning which led us through the labyrinths of stellar interiors to reconstruct the stories of their lives—from their conception in the womb of interstellar substrate and birth by gravitational attraction, to their lingering death in the graveyard of white dwarfs, or to the grand *auto-da-fé* of a Supernova explosion—and examine briefly the extent to which our story is actually being borne out by the observed properties of the stars around us.

III–3: Inquest by Observations

The first observational test which we can apply to our theoretical expectations concerns the observed distribution of stars in the empirical HR-diagram (see Figure 3). The test is positive—in so far as real stars are found to be in all regions of the diagram where they should be; they have the anticipated properties and are in approximately the estimated numbers. This static test is necessary, but clearly not sufficient; for it affords only a momentary glimpse of the current distribution of stellar population of different mass, age, and initial composition.

A much more discriminating test is provided by the observed properties of double stars—our 'heavenly twins' of Chapter II-3—for the following reason. Our previous theoretical outline of the life-story of a star has made it clear that its entire course from cradle to grave is predestined by three Norns—Mass, Chemical Composition, and Angular Momentum. The first two are really decisive. Stars of the same mass and initial composition will always go through life in the same manner; and their subsequent fortunes can differ only to the extent implied in the difference of these initial conditions.

If we pick out at random any two stars in space around us, they may be of quite different ages; and their initial mass and composition may likewise have been different. Consider, however, two components of a close binary system: their proximity ensures that both must have been formed virtually at the same time, and from material of almost identical composition. Moreover, their mutual gravitational bond will keep them together and make divorce impossible no matter how long they live; so that we can compare them at any time. The only difference in their subsequent careers could be caused by the unequal amount of mass with which they may have been endowed at the time of the origin of the pair.

Therefore, if our theoretical story of stellar evolution follows the correct line of reasoning, we should expect that the Main Sequence components of close binary systems of the same mass would also be identical (or similar) in all other external characteristics—such as size and temperature or spectrum. Conversely, however, the components should differ in temperature or size the more, the greater their difference in mass. This is exactly borne out by the observed facts—such as those summarized in Table 5 of Chapter II, of which we can consider β Aurigae as an example; and we conclude that, to this extent, our theoretical expectations are in full agreement with what we see in the sky.

When one (or both) components of a close binary evolve from the Main Sequence, the situation becomes less simple, because we anticipated that an evolving star may lose a part of its initial mass. Such an anticipation is indeed borne out by the fact that, in binary systems with sub-giant (or giant) components, the latter invariably proves to be the less massive of the two although it is considerably more evolved; and if so, excess mass was obviously lost somewhere in the process. Such systems have not been listed in Table II–5, but many are known—the well-known eclipsing variable star Algol (β Persei) represents perhaps the most conspicuous example.

The double stars referred to in Chapter II–3 include, however, other overwhelming instances of pairs in which one component must have lost the greater part of its initial mass before reaching its present advanced state of evolution. For consider the well-known visual pairs of Sirius or Procyon (*cf.* Table II–4) in which a Main Sequence star is attended by a white dwarf. The present mass of Sirius B is equal to 1·1 ⊙; as against 2·2 ⊙ for Sirius A. It is almost certain that two stars as close to each other as these originated at the same time, and from very much the same primordial matter. If, however, Sirius B has already attained the white-dwarf stage while its mate is still lingering on the Main Sequence, it must obviously have passed through a major part of its evolution at a very much more rapid pace.

But this would be consistent with the known high temperature-dependence of nuclear energy sources only if, initially and through most of its long past, the mass of the present Sirius B was actually larger than that of its mate—probably several times as large. If so, however, this once primary (and now secondary) component of the Sirius system must have passed through the stage of being a red giant while its original secondary (and since primary) component was—and still is—basking in the Main Sequence. Whether or not the major part of the mass of the present Sirius B was lost at its giant stage, or during its subsequent collapse which ended in the formation of a white dwarf, is not yet possible to calculate with any assurance; but that its evolutionary process was bound to entail a large mass loss is scarcely open to doubt.

Observations in recent years have, moreover, provided us with dramatic new evidence documenting the catastrophic evolution of ageing stars in neutron cores. We mentioned on p. 101 that the most drastic example of stellar variability is the explosion of a

Supernova—when for a short time (ranging from days to weeks) a single star in the throes of this cataclysm can radiate as much light as a whole galaxy. Such events attract a more than galaxy-wide audience; they can be seen at a greater distance of space than any other event in the Universe.

Because of their conspicuous nature, individual Supernovae have been detected in considerable numbers in external galaxies in the past 40 years—in particular, by that indefatigable veteran of the field, Fritz Zwicky—and from the statistics we surmise that, on the average, not more than a few Supernovae flare up in each galaxy per millenium. In our own Milky Way, three such events are on record in the past thousand years, two of which (Tycho's Supernova of 1572 and Kepler's object of 1604) flared up within 32 years of each other; but it is the event of the year 1054 A.D. to which we shall confine our attention.

In the absence of any Western sources, Chinese chronicles have preserved for us the fact that in the year 1054 A.D. a 'guest star' appeared in the constellation of Taurus, which for a time was bright enough to be noted in daylight; and it remained visible to the naked eye for almost two years. Several centuries later, astronomers found in approximately the same place a faint nebulous object—on which William Herschel bestowed the name of 'Crab Nebula'. Observers of recent decades have established spectroscopically that this nebula expands with a high velocity of close to 1100 km/sec; and a backward extrapolation of this motion discloses that the size of the present nebula (some 5 minutes of arc across) would by 1054 A.D. have dwindled to a point.

Moreover, the image of the nebula on photographic plates taken in the past 60–80 years has grown appreciably in size (by about $20''$ per annum); and a comparison of the observed radial and lateral velocity of expansion reveals that the object must be at a distance of more than 1,000 parsecs from us. Consequently, the absolute (visual) magnitude of the exploding supernova in 1054 must have been close to -16th magnitude. This was, however, a long time ago; for the light message which reached the Earth in the year 1054 had to travel through space for almost 3,300 years to its terrestrial destination. Therefore, the explosion of our Supernova actually took place about 2200 B.C.—some four thousand years ago, before the time of Abraham, before the Old Kingdom of Egypt was in decline or Sargon ruled in the Valley of the Euphrates

Origin and Evolution of the Stars

and Tigris; and millenia had to come and go before their descendants would eventually decipher the meaning of the stupendous cosmic event.

The Crab Nebula as we see it today (cf. Plate 8) derives some of its light from the emission of hydrogen—whether mainly stellar or interstellar we cannot as yet say—but the bulk of it is made up of the highly polarized light of relativistic electrons, accelerated to their energies by the explosion. Is there anything left of the original stellar object? The American astronomers Baade and Minkowski, who made fundamental contributions to the study of the Crab Nebula more than a quarter of a century ago, pointed out that near the centre of its optical image there exists a very faint stellar object (of approximately 16th apparent photographic magnitude) showing a spectrum completely devoid of lines. Baade and Minkowski conjectured that this may be the actual stellar remnant of our Supernova. For a long time the correctness of this identification hung in the balance. But it was dramatically vindicated in 1968 when several observers detected that it is a variable star of most peculiar characteristics: namely, that it emits a sequence of millisecond pulses in an extremely short period, one-thirtieth of a second—and is a variable star with characteristics which earned its class the name of 'pulsars'.

The central star of the Crab Nebula was not the first pulsar to be discovered—the first such stars in the domain of radio-frequencies were detected a year before—but it was the first pulsar exhibiting a regular sequence of pulses in exactly the same period not only in the radio end of its spectrum, but also in visible light, and even in the domain of X-rays. Subsequently, another remnant of an ancient supernova, in the southern constellation of Vela, was found to be associated with a pulsar with a somewhat longer period of 0·089 second; and about 50 other pulsars have now been detected by radio-astronomers.

The most significant feature emerging from the evidence to hand is that two pulsars with the shortest known periods are associated with the visible remnants of supernovae—the Crab pulsar ($P=0.033$ sec) with one of the most recent galactic events of this type, and the Vela pulsar ($P=0.089$ sec)—much fainter—with an older supernova remnant (as evidenced by a more advanced decay of the nebula around it). The rest of the known pulsars are not connected with any detectable nebulosity, and their periods are longer (typically, of about one second). However, the periods of all pulsars are secularly increasing at a rate which appears to be the greater the shorter the period separating successive pulses. For example, the Crab pulsar is lengthening its period by 13·3 microseconds per year; and the Vela pulsar, by 4·3 microseconds; while pulsar periods close to one second are increasing them at a reduced rate of a few tenths of a microsecond per annum.

These figures lead us to surmise that the period of the stellar remnant of the Crab Nebula shortly after the event of 1054 A.D. was not longer than 0·020 of a second, and will increase to one second in about 10^5 years. At a rate of one supernova per galaxy every 1,000 years, our Milky Way system should then have produced about 100 of them in 10^5 years; and with 50 pulsars already known (while others may yet be awaiting detection), it is reasonable to assume that such configurations represent the necessary evolutionary stage of all stars after Supernova explosions.

What kind of configurations are our pulsars? In one sense, their designation by this term is a misnomer; for such stars cannot pulsate in their periods in the same sense as the cepheids or long-period variables; nor can they again constitute sufficiently close pairs of heavenly twins. According to all probability, the pulsar periods are identical with the periods of axial rotation of the respective configurations; and their light surges are due to the 'searchlight effect' of a beam of radiation emitted by a small part of the surface and sweeping through space in a certain solid angle. Detailed mechanisms by which radiation in the entire span of the spectrum can leak out of such an object in a directional beam are still under discussion; but the following general features can be regarded as fairly well established.

First, stellar remnants rotating with periods between 0·03 to 1 second must be extremely small in size; for otherwise centrifugal force would tear the configuration to pieces. For example, should the mass of the Crab pulsar be comparable with that of the Sun, the radius of a configuration rotating with a period of 0·033 sec would have to be smaller than approximately 140 kms in order to prevent centrifugal force exceeding gravity on the equator; and its mean density should not be less than 10^{12} g/cm^3. It is evident that the internal structure of such configurations—likely to consist of a nuclear liquid contained in a solid shell—will be governed by laws of physics very different from those which governed stellar evolution in the past; and we shall not attempt to unravel them by inviting the reader to rush where angels fear to tread, and disregard the signs saying 'Men at Work, Pass at Your Own Risk'.

But we do not want to expose our readers to the risk of possible misinformation at this junction so far away from the beaten track. We propose to cast a retrospective glance at all that we have learned about the stars and their evolution in earlier parts of this chapter. We wish to stress that the stars in the sky, of which our Sun is but one, represent standard products of Nature in their mass-range, and constitute a basic class of celestial objects which Nature used as building bricks for the construction of larger edifices in the Universe—to the architecture of which we shall turn in the last part of this book. The formation of the stars from the diffuse matter in interstellar space, already outlined in Chapter III-1, is not a special process, but an inevitable link in the cosmic evolution of matter from which our Universe is constituted; an evolution which starts with condensation, and ends with a dispersal—by 'stellar wind' or more catastrophic events—of at least a part of the condensed matter into its formerly dispersed state.

Physically speaking, a 'star' can be defined as a condensation of matter prevalent in space at the respective stage of the Universe into self-gravitating units assuming the form of gas spheres, the mass of which ranges between 10^{32}–10^{35} grams. That mass of this magnitude must remain gaseous is a direct consequence of the temperatures raised by self-compression; and that a single star in space must be spherical is ensured by the requirement that it assumes a form of minimum potential energy; and this (in the absence of any external forces—such as are exerted, for instance, by the attraction of another star in its neighbourhood in double-star systems) is a sphere.

Moreover, the requirement that the masses of the stars remain very largely within the range of 10^{32}–10^{35} g is enforced by physical laws which are no less stringent. If the mass of a self-gravitating cosmic configuration were much less than 10^{32} grams, conditions in its interior would never become extreme enough to unlock energy sources sufficient to make it shine as a star. On the other hand, if its mass were larger than 10^{35} grams, such a flood of nuclear energy would be produced in its interior that the star could not remain together as one mass.

Within the 10^{32}–10^{35} g mass range, the stars can differ greatly in size, and even more so in luminosity (by a factor in excess of 10^9); but the relatively narrow mass range is imposed by the nuclear structure of matter of which the stars consist; and is an indication of the sensitivity with which the energy-producing nuclear processes react to the climate prevalent in stellar interiors.

Among the configurations within the permitted mass-range we have encountered in the sky the following three groups of stars which differ from each other in basic physical aspects:

Normal Stars—the most abundant species—consist of gas in which the pressure and density depend on the temperature. Such stars derive the energy which makes them shine from nuclear transformations in their deep interiors, supplemented (at times of need) by gravitational energy that can be tapped on contraction. Most stars in the sky—all those visible at night to the naked eye—belong to this class.

For a large part of them, the actual energy source is the burning of hydrogen into helium, because hydrogen happens to be the most abundant (as well as efficient) nuclear fuel which lends itself for this purpose. In the HR-diagram (p. 88) such stars can be distinguished by occupying a strip which we call the 'Main Sequence'. Their sizes range mainly between $0 \cdot 5$ ☉ at the lower end of the Main Sequence (in the lower left-hand corner of the HR-diagram), to 5 ☉ or more near its upper end; and their mean densities exceed but little the range of $0 \cdot 05$–10 times that of the Sun. Their central temperatures range between 10–25 million degrees; and their central densities are about 100 times as large as their mean densities (somewhat less so for massive hot stars; and several times more for the red dwarfs).

Once such a 'normal' star begins to feel a hydrogen deficiency in its central parts and evolves away from the Main Sequence to become a 'sub-giant' or a 'giant', its radius may increase many times; and while the gravitational contraction of its core causes its central temperature to increase gradually up to 100 million degrees, the ratio of its central to mean density may increase from a hundred to a million or more. At the same time, the star is likely to undergo an extensive loss of mass; and its light—formerly steady —may become increasingly variable.

By the time the stars have reached the turning-point of the giant branch of their evolutionary track in the HR-diagram and double back towards the Main Sequence, they parade in their elevated positions in the HR-diagram under manifestly false pretences; for by then they have lost a large part of their initial mass, and maintain their extravagent luminosities increasingly at the expense of internal heat which can no longer be replaced. The variability of light—conspicuous at times—represents the visible symptoms of their distress, and heralds the stage at which the star will cease to be 'normal' (in the sense that ideal gas laws are valid throughout the interior) and falls prey to 'hardening of the arteries' of its structure with the onset of what physicists call the 'degeneracy'.

Degenerate Stars—the second distinct group of stellar objects—are configurations in which a continuing gravitational contraction has reduced their matter to a state in which the internal pressure and density no longer depend on the temperature. While stars of small masses (less than about $0 \cdot 08$ ☉) can reach such a state directly by continuing gravitational contraction, most of them can do so only after hydrogen has been depleted in their interiors. Even under these conditions the rules of admission to the community of degenerate stars require that each postulant must first divest itself of any mass in excess of (approximately) $1 \cdot 4$ ☉. Provided these conditions can be met, every 'normal' star will eventually evolve into a degenerate star. The onset of degeneracy is gradual rather than cataclysmic; and spasmodic distress signals in the form of ordinary Nova explosions can only prolong the ordeal, but will not alter the final outcome.

When the transition to a fully degenerate state has been completed, our stars have bcome objects of planetary size—of radii ranging between $0 \cdot 01$–$0 \cdot 001$ ☉, and mean densities 10^5–10^8 g/cm³. However, in spite of such extreme conditions, degenerate stars continue to shine very feebly (at the expense of very slow gravitational contraction); and although very many have no doubt ended up in a sink of this state, their low luminosity does not make them very conspicuous in the sky, and their existence can be detected only in close cosmic proximity. The faint companions to Sirius or Procyon are typical examples of this group of stars, whose appearance has earned them the name of *white dwarfs*.

The third distinct group of celestial objects, which differ drastically in their external appearance as well as their physical structure from normal stars or white dwarfs, are the *Neutron Stars*, of which at least some manifest themselves in the sky as 'pulsars'. Such stars are the probable result of the gravitational collapse of an ageing stellar configuration whose mass, well in excess of 1·4 ☉, does not enable it to become degenerate. The typical densities of stars of this group are between 10^{12}–10^{14} g/cm³; and their typical dimensions are asteroidal rather than planetary (10–100 km). Gravitational compression of matter to such fantastic densities requires very strong gravitational fields to bring about implosions lasting only seconds; and the transition of a former star to a neutron core constitutes a truly cataclysmic process, whose external manifestations—visible across vast gaps of space—are the explosions of Supernovae.

The existence of all three distinct groups of stellar configurations—normal stars, degenerate stars, and neutron stars—have already been attested by astronomical observations which have acquainted us with their fundamental properties and differences. The observational documentation of the stars' life during the 'normal' stage of their evolution is extensive; and the vital statistics of white dwarfs and of the processes which make them tick are likewise adequate. The existence of neutron stars has been borne out by observational evidence which is less than four years old; but in spite of its recent origin, its interpretation seems to leave little room for doubt.

Do the neutron cores formed by Supernova explosions represent the ultimate stage of stellar evolution? Not necessarily so; for some contemporary theoreticians believe it is possible that such cores may contract further—until they eventually vanish from sight! For according to the general theory of relativity, a sufficiently dense body can warp space-time around it in such a way that no light can leave it with finite frequency. As a result, bodies can exist which cannot be seen by an outside observer, although they can still communicate with the outside world through their gravitational field. Such 'stars'—if they exist—cannot, therefore, leave any trace on our photographic plates, or be noticed by a photocell; yet their presence in double-star systems could be detected from the orbital motion which their mass may force the visible component of the pair to describe around their common centre of gravity.

No such 'invisible' component of any known heavenly twin (Chapter II-3) has so far been identified with a gravitational 'black hole' in the sky; and no wonder. For if such 'black holes' are evolutionary descendants of neutron stars, they should be even scarcer in space than the 'pulsars'; and no more than about 50 of the latter have so far been found in our entire galaxy. However, even in the absence of any observations, the theory of relativity discloses that the critical radius for this ultimate withdrawal of an astronomical body in its own gravitational nutshell is given by $2 \cdot 96 \, (M/M_\odot)$ km, where M denotes the mass of the respective configuration. For a configuration of 1·5 times the mass of the Sun (which can no longer become degenerate), this critical radius turns out to be slightly less than $4\frac{1}{2}$ kms.

Should, therefore, our Sun ever contract to such a size without loss of mass, our Earth and other planets would still continue revolving around it, but without being able to see it at all. Such configurations are described as 'black holes'; and to fall into such a hole may be the ultimate fate of very massive stars. No specific instance of such a hole has been found so far, but they may exist; and with the discovery of the first gravitational coffin of this kind the observational documentation of all essential stages of stellar evolution from the cradle to the grave will become complete.

PART TWO

The Solar Family and our Terrestrial Cradle

IN THE preceding part of this book we got acquainted with the community of stars in our neighbourhood, of which our Sun is one. We learned that—like human beings—the stars around us prefer to live in pairs; and the principal distinguishing mark of such pairs is the 'mass-ratio' of their components. A large majority of double stars discovered so far possess mass-ratios in the neighbourhood of unity; for pairs in which each component 'pulls the same oar' as far as attraction is concerned and makes a comparable contribution to the total light of the system, are easiest to spot and identify at a distance.

With diminishing mass, the contribution of the less massive component of the pair begins to peter out in such a way that its light disappears out of sight long before the effects of its attraction become negligible. The gravitational effects of any star are proportional to the magnitude of its mass and diminish with it linearly; while (for a large majority of stars) its light diminishes as a third or fourth power of this mass. In a typical binary consisting of two Main Sequence stars whose masses may happen to be in the ratio of three-to-one, the more massive (brighter) component will be made by its mate to move around the common centre of gravity in an orbit one-third in size of the separation of the two stars. However, the light of the less massive star should then contribute only one or two per cent to the light of the respective binary system; and as such it will be lost completely in the glare of its more brilliant companion, beyond any possibility of observational detection.

Therefore, less massive companions in binary systems whose components differ greatly in mass can generally be detected—if at all—only by the effects of gravitational attraction which the small mass will exert on the motion of its more substantial mate. A careful search for the existence of such 'astrometric binaries' in our stellar neighbourhood led to the discovery of systems with 'invisible' companions possessing not more than one or two per cent of the entire mass of the system—the famous 'Barnard's star' being perhaps the best-known example of such a system.

Since the detailed mechanism of the origin of the binary stars in general is as yet unknown, we cannot estimate the probable proportion of binaries with such large mass-ratios solely on theoretical grounds. However, if we could place the immediate surroundings of some of our stellar neighbours under a more detailed scrutiny than is possible with our telescopes (at least as long as we have to carry out our observations through the terrestrial atmosphere), we should no doubt find other stars possessing companions whose mass amounts to less than one per cent of that of the principal component. Although we do not know—nor can we reliably estimate—how many such systems there are in the Universe around us, we know one quite well, because we happen to be a part of it: namely, our *solar system* with its family of *planets* which we can observe at close range from a ringside seat at the circus; for our Earth—the cosmic cradle of our own race—happens to be one of them.

The existence, in our immediate cosmic neighbourhood, of starlike objects in the sky which do not conduct themselves like others and do not remain fixed in position on the firmament of the heavens has been known to human beings on this Earth since the dawn of civilization. Five of the stars adorning the night sky have been found not to stay put, but to wander among the rest in a quite complicated manner. Different names have been attached to them by different nations; but they are best known to us under the Latin names of Mercury, Venus, Mars, Jupiter and Saturn; the first two being visible alternately in the morning or evening sky, while the last three can shine throughout the night.

These five 'wandering stars' or planets were joined—though only relatively late in the history of our science—by our Earth, which was recognized as another wanderer around the Sun in the early part of the seventeenth century; and the years 1781, 1846 and 1930 brought telescopic discoveries of an additional three planets —Uranus, Neptune and Pluto, no longer visible to the naked eye— which complete the principal members of the solar system as we know it today.

This system contains, to be sure, many more denizens than its nine planets. Several of the latter are encircled with families of *satellites* of their own; and one—Saturn—is girdled by a ring of an untold number of smaller particles. Moreover, the Sun itself is surrounded by a loose ring of 'minor planets' or asteroids, filling up a part of the space gap between Mars and Jupiter. Last but not least, a large part of the interplanetary space (down to its innermost precincts) is traversed by solitary eccentric travellers of peculiar structure and composition—generally known as *comets*—whose rapid disintegration on cosmic time-scales leaves behind them swarms of meteors or 'shooting stars' if their cosmic journey happens to be terminated by the Earth, whose atmosphere brings them to a brief but fiery end.

We propose to describe the principal properties of our fellow-inhabitants of the solar system divided into kindred groups. The *major planets*—Jupiter, Saturn, Uranus and Neptune—represent the major contributors by mass to our system. By their composition—if not structure—they resemble our Sun more than the next group of planetary bodies—generally referred to as *terrestrial planets*—comprising our Earth, Venus, Mars and Mercury with Pluto. Lastly, the asteroids are often lumped together as *minor planets*, and have much in common with small planetary satellites and meteorites.

Because of a similarity in mass, composition and internal structure, all the major planets will be dealt with in the same section. Of the terrestrial planets, Mars and Venus—our brother and sister in space—can be described in greater detail than is so far possible for Mercury or Pluto; while the Earth—our cosmic cradle which nursed our ancestors and ourselves to our present degree of development—will call for privileged treatment; and so will its faithful companion and our nearest celestial neighbour, the Moon.

CHAPTER IV

Major Planets of the Solar System

THE MAJOR part of the mass of our solar system, other than that constituting its central star, is stored in four planetary bodies—Jupiter, Saturn, Uranus and Neptune—which revolve around the Sun in that order and at a mean distance ranging from 778 million kms for Jupiter to 4,498 million kms for Neptune, in orbits of very small eccentricity and situated almost in the same plane. When these distances are expressed in terms of the Sun-Earth separation taken as our 'astronomical unit', Jupiter is found (cf. Table IV–1) to revolve 5·2 times as far from the Sun as our Earth; and Neptune, almost 30·1 times as far. The light from the Sun, which needs a little over eight minutes to reach our Earth, traverses these distances in 43 and 250 minutes respectively.

The orbital periods of the major planets range from 11·86 to 164·8 of our terrestrial years. But orbital motion is not the only source of momentum which these planets possess; for they also all rotate about an axis which, for all of them but Uranus, is moderately inclined to their orbital planes. The velocity of their axial rotation is high: the duration of a day on all four ranges from about one-half to two-thirds of the terrestrial one; for Jupiter, it amounts to only a little less than 10 hours of our time. All four major planets are attended by families of numerous satellites (from 2 for Neptune to 12 for Jupiter) revolving around their central planet in equatorial orbits differing widely in size. In addition, Saturn has been endowed by Nature with a tenuous ring in its equatorial plane (cf. Plate 10), whose mass represents (probably) the remnants of a former satellite that ventured to approach its central planet at too close a range and was torn to pieces by its attraction.

The masses of the major planets range from 0·000955 ☉ or 318 terrestrial masses (⊕) for Jupiter, to only 14·6 ⊕ for Uranus. Their difference in size is likewise considerable; for while the equatorial diameter of Jupiter amounts to 142,700 kms—i.e., more than eleven times as large in size as that of the Earth—Neptune's globe is only 44,600 kms across. When, however, we divide the mass by the volume, the mean densities prove to be very much alike, ranging between 0·7 g/cm³ for Saturn to 2·2 g/cm³ for Neptune (*cf.* column 4 of Table IV–2).

This mean density of the major planets constitutes one clue to their composition and internal structure. The other is their polar flattening due to axial rotation—i.e., the extent to which the

TABLE IV–1

Kinematic Properties of Major Planets

	Jupiter	Saturn	Uranus	Neptune
Mean distance from the Sun (in A.U.)	5·204	9·548	19·20	30·08
Light transit time (in minutes)	43·27	79·34	159·5	250·1
Orbital Period (in years)	11·86	29·46	84·02	164·79
Orbital eccentricity	0·048	0·056	0·047	0·009
Orbital Inclination to the Invariable Plane	0°.0	1°.2	−0°.5	0°.5
Period of axial rotation (equatorial)	$9^h 50·5^m$	$10^h 14^m$	$10^h 45^m$	$15·8^h$
Inclination of equator to orbital plane	3°.1	26°.7	98°.0	29°.0

planetary globe as a whole yields to the prevalent centrifugal force. On account of their relatively rapid axial rotation, all the major planets are appreciably flattened at the poles; and the amount of this flattening leads (by a fairly straightforward chain of reasoning) to the conclusion that a ratio of the central density to the mean density of the respective planet is roughly as given in the penultimate row of Table IV–2. These values indicate only a moderate degree of central condensation—larger than for our

Earth (where the ratio ρ_c/ρ_m is only about three), but much smaller than in the Sun or the stars.

According to the requirements of hydrostatic equilibrium, the pressure at the centre of Jupiter (of mass $1\cdot 90 \times 10^{30}$g) should attain $1\cdot 1 \times 10^{14}$ dynes/cm²; and for Saturn somewhat less. These pressures should be sufficient to compress the constituent material of these planets to central densities of 4–5 g/cm³ for Jupiter and Saturn—as inferred from the observed mean densities and

TABLE IV–2

Physical Properties of Major Planets

	Jupiter	Saturn	Uranus	Neptune
Mass (Earth = 1)	318	95·2	14·6	17·2
Diameter (equatorial) in km	142 700 (11·20⊕)	120 800 (9·48⊕)	47 300 (3·71⊕)	44 600 (3·97⊕)
Mean Density (in g/cm³)	1·34	0·71	1·56	2·22
Ratio of ρ_c/ρ_m	3·1	6	1·8	2·1
T (surface; at noontime) in °K	135	105	65	50

extent of polar flattening of these planets. The mean densities indicate, moreover, that the bulk of their mass must consist—as in the stars—of the two lightest elements, hydrogen and helium; for no other mixture could render the globes of the major planets so light. Indeed, more detailed computations of hydrostatic balance indicate that the mass of Jupiter must consist of about 66% of hydrogen (i.e., somewhat smaller a proportion than we find at present in the Sun) by weight; and of Saturn, 60% (a smaller proportion in spite of its lower mean density; for its smaller mass will subject it to less compression). The main part of the balance of the mass in Jupiter and Saturn is almost certainly helium; though in Uranus and Neptune quantities of carbon, nitrogen and oxygen must be present, for their smaller masses would not compress a hydrogen-helium mixture to the observed mean densities of these planets by self-attraction.

What are the temperatures likely to be attained in the interiors of the major planets? In order to account for their densities, it is necessary that the bulk of hydrogen must be present in their interiors in *solid* state; and this requirement by itself imposes an upper limit on temperatures at which this can be true. Under pressures prevailing in the Jovian or Saturnian interiors, hydrogen can remain solid up to temperatures of about 7,000°K, but no higher; and this is probably the limit (about the same as we shall find inside our Earth) which their internal temperatures cannot exceed. Helium—in contrast to hydrogen—does not solidify at any pressure. If the relative abundance of helium inside Jupiter and Saturn were, however, greater than we estimated, gaseous helium would be very much more compressed than solid hydrogen, and the central condensations of these planets would be higher than is consistent with their observed flattening at the poles.

On the other hand, hydrogen is known to solidify at low temperatures or high pressures (and, at pressures of 10^{13}–10^{14} dynes/cm^2, a few thousand degrees is still a 'low' temperature) into a substance which behaves like a metal. The presence of a metallic core inside Jupiter is indeed attested independently by a powerful magnetic field emanating from its interior, of the strength of several hundred gauss (a thousand times stronger than that of our Earth)—as disclosed by the radiation emitted by the planet in the domain of radio-frequencies. Whether or not Saturn (or Uranus and Neptune) possess similar fields has not yet been made clear by direct observations, but remains a distinct possibility.

A further confirmation that the major planets are globes of partly frozen, partly liquefied gases is the fact that—unlike the Earth—they do not rotate as rigid bodies, but—like the Sun—their angular velocity of axial rotation varies somewhat with the latitude. Thus while in the equatorial regions of Jupiter the sidereal day lasts 9 hours, 50 minutes and 30 seconds, at 'moderate' latitudes its duration has increased to 9 hours, 55 minutes and 41 seconds. On Saturn, the equatorial length of the day is equal to 10 hours and 14 minutes, while at ±40° latitude it has increased to 10 hours and 41 minutes. These results demonstrate that neither one of these planets rotates like a rigid globe, but behaves as a fluid capable of differential rotation.

Like the stars, planetary bodies of the mass and composition of the major planets will be surrounded by extensive semi-transparent layers which we call their 'atmospheres'. That this is so has been disclosed by observations almost since the time of the discovery of the telescope; and all the features we can see on the apparent discs (cf. Plates 9 and 10) of these planets are essentially due to atmospheric phenomena. More recently, the spectra of all major planets have disclosed powerful absorption bands of methane—and that of Jupiter, of ammonia as well—which, together with molecular hydrogen and atomic helium, constitute the bulk of the mass of their semi-transparent outer layers. In fact, most of this mass is probably—as in the interior—just a mixture of molecular hydrogen and atomic helium; while compounds of hydrogen with carbon and nitrogen constitute the rest.

The temperatures prevalent in the semi-transparent layers of major planets are generally low. If the Sun were the only source of heat received by the planet, its diluted radiation could raise the daytime temperatures on Jupiter to about $105°$ K ($-160°C$); and that on Saturn, to $80°K$ ($-190°C$); but the absolute temperatures of Uranus and Neptune are only $55°$ and $43°$ K, respectively. Direct measurements of infrared thermal emission reaching us from these planets established the actual temperatures to be 10–30 degrees higher than these theoretical values. On Jupiter and Saturn, afternoon temperatures prove to be almost the same as in the morning (a fact due to the rapidity of their rotation, and to the efficiency with which temperature differences are eliminated by atmospheric circulation); while the night-time temperatures cannot be measured directly because—on account of their distance—the apparent discs of all outer planets are always seen at a virtually 'full' phase (the maximum phase-defect by which Jupiter can depart from it does not exceed $12°$, and for more distant planets such a defect becomes even smaller).

Although, therefore, all major planets are essentially 'cold' bodies, and show no evidence of any appreciable source of internal heat of their own,* and their masses are a thousand to ten thousand times smaller than that of our central star, their chemical composi-

---

*It is true that the measured effective temperatures of Jupiter and Saturn appear to exceed by 10–30 degrees those that could be accounted for by insolation alone. This difference can be easily explained by a very slow secular contraction as the only source of internal heat.

tion appears to be very much akin to the Sun. When, however, we turn to another group of planets—the so-called 'inner planets' revolving in closer proximity to our Sun—we encounter a group of bodies which differ from the major 'outer' planets in chemical composition even more profoundly than they do in mass or size. Just as the group of the major planets is dominated by Jupiter, the primacy among the inner planets by mass and size belongs to the Earth—our cosmic home and the cradle of our life.

CHAPTER V

Our Earth—Its Origin, Structure and Evolution

IN THE preceding chapter of this part of our book we got acquainted with the principal planetary members of our solar family, as well as with its lesser constituents roaming endlessly in space around us. Two members of this system have not yet been touched upon in our narrative; we propose now to single them out for special attention. They are, of course, our mother Earth and its faithful satellite, the Moon. If we do this at a somewhat belated stage of our narrative, it is in recognition of the fact that—by its physical characteristics—our Earth cannot claim any particular distinction among the members of our planetary family, let alone in the Universe at large. However, in one respect it is unique, at least within the confines of our solar system: for it is the only planet in this system which gave rise to *life*, and ultimately became a cradle for such civilization as we possess today. The Earth has also become the first celestial body to provide a springboard for gradual penetration of the greater depths of the Universe around us; and in what follows we may outline a few first steps which led in this direction.

For a long time in the past—centuries and millenia—the Earth was to our ancestors a flat disc supporting the vault of the sky overhead and covering up an imaginary underworld. In the earliest literary monuments of the ancient Greeks—the spiritual ancestors of astronomical science—some 3,000 years before our time, the Earth was still a flat circular disc the dimensions of which were largely indefinite. According to Hesiod, an iron anvil would take nine days to fall from Heaven to Earth, and another nine days from Earth to Tartarus. The vault of heaven remained immovable for ever in one position; while the Sun, Moon and the stars moved around underneath it—rising from Oceanus in the East and plunging again into it in the West.

This was the mythology of the pastoral age; and the early Greek accounts did not differ essentially from those developed previously in Egypt or Mesopotamia. However, not long after the time of Hesiod (the first half of the eighth century B.C.) an idea emerged which—for the first time in the history of mankind—raised mythological speculations about the world around us to the rank of scientific thought: namely, the conjecture that the Earth was a sphere. This conception probably emerged from the Pythagorean school of philosophy which flourished in southern Italy in the fifth-sixth centuries B.C.; and tradition attributes it to Pythagoras or his pupil Parmenides. There is no indication that they would have borrowed it from any non-Greek source. It is, however, also more than probable that the Pythagorean reasons behind their hypothesis of a spherical Earth were essentially aesthetic, and their doctrine may have run as follows: the most perfect shape of a body is a sphere. The heavenly bodies are perfect; the Earth is a heavenly body and, therefore, spherical. Such speculations might possibly pass for philosophy at that time, but not for science as we understand this term today.

The first scientific argument proving the Earth to be spherical was advanced in the 4th century B.C. by the great encyclopedist Aristotle (384–323 B.C.), who (in his book *De Coelo*) stated that the Earth must be a sphere because the outline of its shadow cast on the Moon during lunar eclipses appears always to be circular. Whether this argument—entirely sufficient to a modern mind as a proof of the proposition—was original, or whether Aristotle merely reported an opinion already pre-existent, we do not, unfortunately, know; for very little scientific literature has reached us from pre-Aristotelian times. The fact remains that the spherical form of the Earth was deduced from astronomical observations not later than the middle of the third century before our era, by a geometrical argument the validity of which has not weakened during the ages. A knowledge that the Earth is a sphere has therefore been in the intellectual possession of mankind for at least 2,300 years.

Once we admit the Earth to be a sphere, the question is bound to arise: what is its *size*? It was obvious already to Aristotle and his contemporaries that the Mediterranean basin in which they lived constituted only a very small part of the Earth's surface. In the century following Aristotle's, Eratosthenes of Cyrene (276–194 B.C.)—a great geographer of the Hellenistic period who seems to have spent most of his life in Alexandria—succeeded in determining the dimensions of the Earth within a few per cent of its actual value by a triangulation of the arc of meridian between Syene (Aswan in Egypt) and Alexandria. Some uncertainty as to its accuracy arises from the fact that the unit of length (an Alexandrian stade) in which Eratosthenes expressed his result is not known to us exactly today; but according to all evidence we possess, the Eratosthenian value of 252,000 stades for the Earth's circumference corresponds to 37,500 km (23,300 miles)—a value which errs by only $6\frac{1}{2}$ per cent. Thus, in spite of the necessarily rather crude observational techniques of Eratosthenes and his contemporaries, these ancient geometers provided posterity with a very realistic approximation of the actual size of the Earth—and one which was not improved for the next two thousand years. For it was not till the latter part of the seventeenth century—when a more precise knowledge of the size of the terrestrial surface became essential for the political ends of leading world powers busily carving it up among themselves for exploitation—that we eventually arrived at the present value of the mean radius of the terrestrial globe as being equal to 6,371·04 kms.

The next datum concerning the vital statistics of our planet which should interest us in its *mass*. As the Earth's size, once established, proved to be the basis for a determination of cosmic distances of increasing magnitude, so the Earth proved also to be the first celestial body whose mass was determined by our ancestors. Neither the Greeks nor the scientists of any other ancient civilization had any idea of the actual magnitude of the terrestrial mass; nor did they express any concern about it. This ignorance lasted well through the Renaissance up to the times of the beginning of modern science in the early seventeenth century. Johannes Kepler and Galileo Galilei—the two founding fathers of the new astronomy—did not know any more about the mass of the Earth than did Aristotle two thousand years before.

The method by which this problem could be approached was born with Newton's theory of universal gravitation; for it was not till then that the mass of a body was correctly related with the force exerted by its attraction. Isaac Newton (1642–1727), who discovered the law of gravitation, did not, however, know the mass of the Earth any more than Kepler or Galileo; or, for that matter, Aristotle. It is true that the discovery of the inverse-square law of attraction enabled Newton to relate the magnitude of the terrestrial mass $m_\oplus$ with the acceleration g of a particle falling towards it by a simple equation of the form $g = Gm_\oplus/r_\oplus^2$, where $r_\oplus$ denotes the distance of the falling body from the Earth's centre (i.e., the local terrestrial radius), and G, the 'constant of gravitation'. The acceleration of an apple that fell from a tree in Newton's orchard at Woolsthorpe in 1665 or 1666, or indeed the acceleration of any mass-particle falling in the terrestrial gravity field, was already measurable then with fair accuracy; and the absolute value of the terrestrial radius $r_\oplus$ was likewise known (since 1671) with adequate precision. However, the foregoing relation between g, $m_\oplus$, and $r_\oplus$ involves also the constant G, the value of which was not yet known to Newton; nor indeed for some time after.

Newton himself only guessed at it by assuming that the mean density of the Earth was between 5 and 6 times that of water*—a remarkably lucky estimate considering the fact that nothing was known in Newton's time about the state of the Earth's interior, and that common rocks found on the Earth's surface possess densities of between 2·8—3·3 g/cm^3. For, once we assume a given density for the Earth, the known dimensions of its globe permit us to evaluate its total mass $m_\oplus$; and, consequently, G from known values of g and $r_\oplus$. This Newton did; and from a value of the gravitation constant so determined he went on to estimate the absolute masses of the Sun and of other planets. Strictly speaking, however, what Newton did was to estimate the mass *ratios* between the Earth and the Sun or other planets, which could be converted into absolute masses of the other bodies only if that of the Earth was estimated.

The first empirical determination of G independent of any estimate of the mean density of the Earth as a whole was attempted in the early part of the 18th century by Bouguer from the measured deflection of a plumb-line (i.e., a difference between the positions of a geographic and actual zenith) in the proximity of the mountain Chimborazo (altitude 6,254 m) in the Equatorial Andes, the total mass of which (consisting as it does of rocks of known density) could be estimated more directly than that of the Earth. In 1772, the same experiment was repeated with greater success by Maskelyne, who used for this purpose the mountain Shehallien in the Scottish Highlands because of its simple geometrical shape. In the 19th

---

*'*Verisimile est quod copia materiae totius in terra quasi quintuplo vel sextuplo major sit quam si tota ex aqua constaret*' (*Principia*, Libri III, Propositio 10).

century and later, the value of G was specified with much greater accuracy in the laboratory (by measurements of a mutual attraction of bodies of known mass with the aid of torsion balance, or other less direct methods); and today it is known to be equal to $6 \cdot 67 \times 10^{-8}$ cm^3/g sec^2. If we combine it with the observed gravitational acceleration of free fall $g = 9 \cdot 82$ m/sec^2 corresponding to a distance $r_\oplus = 6371$ km from the Earth's centre, the mass of the Earth necessary to produce the requisite acceleration turns out to be $5 \cdot 98 \times 10^{27}$g; and corresponds to a mean density of the terrestrial globe of $5 \cdot 52$ g/cm^3—well within the limits anticipated by Newton almost three hundred years ago.

V–1: The Anatomy of the Earth and its Composition

In the opening section of this chapter we enumerated the principal physical characteristics of our planet, and outlined the way in which they have been determined by different types of observations. Let us now turn to the interior of the terrestrial globe, which remains off limits to the experimenter, but whose structure supports the surface, and accommodates the total mass of our planet within its observed size.

How is this mass distributed within the Earth? The fact that the Earth's mean density proves to be almost twice as large as that of the rocks we find on the surface makes it evident that our Earth does not constitute a simple homogeneous rock; but that its denser material must be largely confined to the centre. That this is true was first indicated by the extent to which the diurnal rotation of our planet has managed to flatten its globe at the poles by centrifugal force. This phenomenon was discovered through the changes in the rate of march of a pendulum clock at different latitudes (due to a change in local gravitational acceleration), by Richer and his colleagues on an expedition to triangulate the distance to Mars in 1671–72 between Cayenne (in French Guiana) and Paris; Newton correctly interpreted this phenomenon as being due to the spheroidal shape of our planet. Now the extent to which a rotating globe yields to centrifugal force and becomes flattened at the poles depends on the internal structure of the spheroid; and a ratio of the centrifugal force arising from daily rotation to the observed flattening, which at the poles amounts to

Our Earth; Its Origin, Structure and Evolution

22 km, points to the fact that the central density of our globe is equal to three times its mean density—or approximately 17 g/cm³. Therefore, the extent to which the terrestrial globe yields to the centrifugal force invoked by its axial rotation discloses that, in the central parts of our planet, the density of the material should exceed that of iron, and approach that of gold (at zero pressure).

The polar flattening of the Earth—like that of any other planet—offers only one glimpse into the internal structure of its globe: namely, the ratio of its central to mean density. A more detailed examination of the Earth's interior is, however, possible by a study of shortlived and recurrent disturbances in the Earth's crust commonly called 'earthquakes'—those freakish tremors of the ground which are provided from time to time by sudden slides (or other kinds of adjustment) inside the Earth's crust, especially in those parts of it (such as the regions of recent mountain-building activity) which are tectonically unstable. The phenomena invoked by such tectonic disturbances can be used by geophysicists to explore the interior of the Earth down to its core.

The methods employed for this purpose bear, in fact, a basic similarity to those which the old-time family doctors used to study the state of their patients' lungs—by observing the acoustic effects of percussion on the chest. The geophysicists concerned with the state of the Earth's interior do the same thing in principle, but on a different scale. Since the mass of the Earth is so large, obviously no percussion by human hand would be of any avail (unless nuclear explosives are used for this purpose on a larger scale than has been done so far); but—fortunately for us in this connection—the Earth itself occasionally suffers from disturbances, in the form of earthquakes, which can play the role of natural percussions. All we need to do is to wait for them to occur and listen to their message.

Virtually all earthquakes originate in slips or other tectonic disturbances of the Earth's crust at a relatively shallow depth below the surface; for over 20 per cent of such events their foci (or 'epicentres') are located at a sub-surface depth of less than 100 km—a layer only skin deep in comparison with the dimensions of the Earth as a whole. Therefore, while the mechanical effects of such earthquakes in the proximity of the epicentre may sometimes be devastating and cause immense losses of life and property, inhabitants of other parts of the world learn about such events only through various news channels hours or days later—unless they employ special listening devices which can bring them a direct intelligence of seismic disturbances through the Earth's crust. The stethoscopes which the geophysical doctors use for this purpose are called 'seismometers'; and their sensitivity is such that virtually thousands of seismic events are recorded by them for every one that can be noticed by the man in the street.

What kind of murmurs are forthcoming from the bowels of the Earth, and what can they tell us? Let us consider first the types of messages which can be transmitted to stony layers of a planetary interior—regardless of their origin. The physicists call these 'elastic waves'; and they are basically of two kinds. Consider an elongated iron rod—such as a crowbar or a traverse. If we hit its long end with a hammer, the material of the rod will be compressed under the force of the impact, and this compression will be propagated along the rod in the form of a 'pressure' wave. The different parts of the rod will be displaced periodically by such a wave to and fro in the direction of propagation of the disturbance (i.e., along its length); and this is why we call such a wave 'longitudinal'. Ordinary sound waves represent another familiar example of such longitudinal wave motion in gas.

A different type of oscillation will result if we shake the end of the bar by hitting it with the hammer on the side. Such a stroke will not compress the material significantly (as the rod can respond to the impulse by bending), but rather displace some parts of the rod relative to others. Such 'shear' deformations will also propagate along the rod, but the motion of individual sections in this case will be perpendicular to the direction of the propagation; and these we speak of as 'transversal' waves. Unlike longitudinal (pressure-) waves, transversal waves cannot occur in gaseous (or, generally, fluid) media and are characteristic of the solids alone.

Should we now administer to our rod a sidewise blow with a hammer (i.e., from a direction inclined to the bar's axes of symmetry), both kinds of waves will be excited in its material at the same time, and propagate through it with an appropriate speed. In most types of solid matter—such as the terrestrial rocks —the 'pressure' (P) waves travel faster than the 'shear' (S) waves; but the absolute velocity of propagation for each depends on the elastic properties of each particular type of rock and on its density.

Now if—in place of a rod—we consider a solid sphere gently

tapped by a hammer, the physical effects produced by such an impulse will be qualitatively not unlike those produced by earthquakes in the globe of our planet: elastic waves of both kinds will radiate out of the point of impact (analogous to an 'epicentre' of a shallow earthquake) and set the sphere in vibration, an effect reminiscent of global earthquake effects. In the case of the Earth,

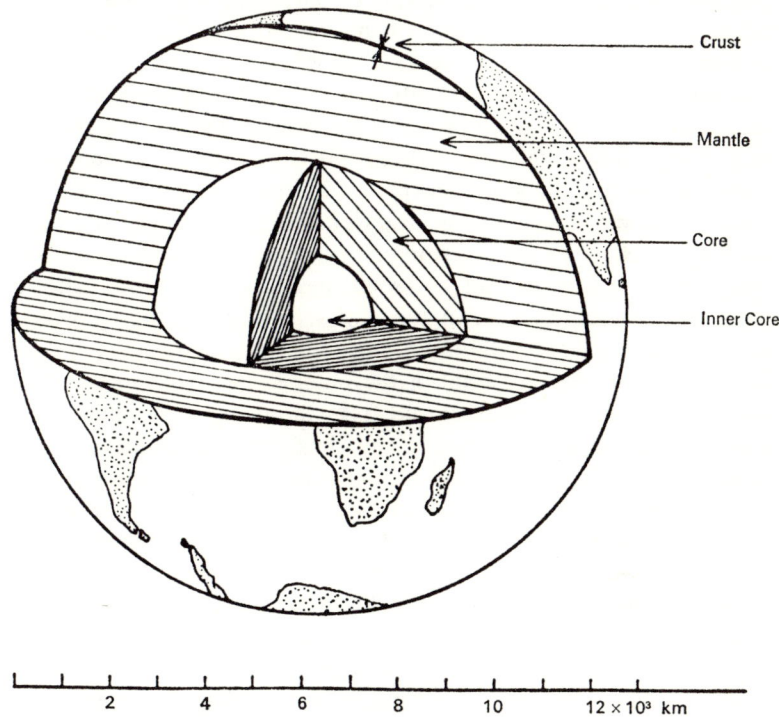

Figure 5 A schematic cross-section of the interior of the Earth, illustrating the principal parts of its anatomy.

the vibrations caused by earthquakes are monitored by geophysicists applying their stethoscopes to the terrestrial surface rocks in a great many places. From the form of the records as well as the time-lags with which such messages reach different parts of the world geophysicists have succeeded in the past fifty years, in reconstructing the physical structure of the Earth's interior almost as accurately as could be done by direct borings through our planet.

As a result of such studies, the internal structure of the Earth has been laid bare to us almost as completely as if we could X-ray it throughout its mass.

What has this internal structure of our planet proved to be in the light of seismographic records gradually accumulated since the beginning of this century? The principal result has been a realization that the Earth as a whole consists (cf. Figure 5) of two distinct parts: a *core,* whose radius of 3,470 km represents a little more (54%) than a half of that of the terrestrial globe, surrounded by a *mantle* making up the rest of our planet. The volume of the core represents, therefore, only about 16% of that of the Earth as a whole, 84% of which is occupied by the mantle; but by its structure and composition the core proves to be as distinct from the mantle as to form a veritable 'planet inside a planet'.

How did the geophysicists discover the existence of this core hidden so deeply in the interior of our planet? Its principal giveaway characteristic proved to be its inability to transmit elastic shear waves—one of the two types of seismic messages by which an intelligence of an earthquake can be carried to distant parts of the Earth. The solid material of the mantle was found to transmit both 'P' as well as 'S' waves; and from the delay with which such waves traverse a known distance the density of the different layers in the transmitting mantle can be deduced with fair accuracy.

When, however, the earthquake occurs in the opposite hemisphere of our planet, a curious phenomenon has long been noted by seismologists: that at a certain distance one part of the message —namely, the shear waves—suddenly disappears from the seismic record—as though this source has set below the 'horizon' of the receiving station. This horizon has been located to lie just about 2,900 km below the surface of our planet; and the core enclosed within it has been found to shield completely from shear waves any locality lying in its 'shadow'. But, as we have already mentioned, an inability to transmit shear waves is characteristic of any material in a fluid state. Hence, we conclude from the seismic evidence at our disposal that the simplest model of our Earth consistent with its observed elastic properties must comprise at least two distinct regimes: a fluid core surrounded by a solid mantle.

A more detailed study of the elastic properties of the Earth, as deduced from the seismic evidence now at our disposal, has disclosed a number of other features characteristic of the interior of our planet. Thus the outer *crust* of the Earth on which we walk and which supports the land masses of our continents extends to only about 33 kms below the mean surface of our planet. The mean density of the material constituting this crust ('lithosphere') is between $2 \cdot 6$–$2 \cdot 8$ g/cm^3 (corresponding to that of basaltic rocks), and increases thereafter by self-compression throughout the mantle up to about $5 \cdot 7$ g/cm^3 at its bottom where pressure has risen to over one million atmospheres. As far as the composition is concerned, the indications are that the outer part of the mantle (down to a sub-surface depth of about 400 kms) consists of rocks whose principal chemical constituents are oxygen, silicon, and aluminium; while in the deeper strata aluminium may be gradually replaced by magnesium.

At the interface between the mantle and the core—some 2,900 kms below the Earth's surface—the density of the material appears to jump suddenly from $5 \cdot 7$ to $9 \cdot 4$ g/cm^3 at a pressure of $1 \cdot 4 \times 10^{12}$ dynes/cm^2. So large a discontinuity strongly suggests that the solid mantle and fluid core differ not only in the physical state of their material, but also in their chemical composition. In point of fact, a density of $9 \cdot 4$ g/cm^3 or more can be naturally accounted for only if we assume that the composition of the core is essentially *metallic,* the principal constituents of which are iron and nickel; with some admixture of molten silicate rocks.* Although the core occupies only 16% of the Earth's volume, the relatively high density of its material makes it represent over 31% of the Earth's mass. Moreover, there are indications that, inside this core (whose mass behaves as a fluid) an 'inner core' exists—of the radius of some 1,250 km—in which the density of the constituent material has reached 17 g/cm^3 at the centre; and the pressure exceeds $3 \cdot 6$ million atmospheres. The material of this inner core may consist of pure metals, which the prevailing pressure has again compelled to solidify.

Altogether, the overall chemical composition of the differentiated

---

*Certain scientists have conjectured that the material of the core represents a high-density modification of compressed silicates similar to those constituting the mantle. According to this view, the material of the core and the mantle is essentially the same; only its density jumps up discontinuously when a certain threshold pressure is attained at the interface between the two regions. There exists, however, so far no independent proof that this actually occurs in Nature —inside the Earth or in the laboratory.

Earth (which averages the properties of the core and the mantle) appears to be as follows. The iron content of our planet (stored mainly in the core) should account for almost 39% of its mass; while oxygen—the second most abundant element by mass—contributes about 27%. Silicon accounts for 14%; magnesium, 11%; sulphur and nickel add about 2·7% each; and aluminium with calcium, about 1%. All other elements (sodium, etc.) are present in amounts adding less than the two remaining per cent of the total mass of our planet, of which 31·4% is stored in the core, 68·1% in the mantle, and 0·5% in the crust.

What is the temperature prevalent inside the Earth's mass from its surface to the core? At the surface on which we live our climate is essentially controlled by the Sun; and so is the ground temperature down to a depth of a few dozen metres. However, since the early days of mining it has been established that, at greater depths, the ground temperature not only ceases to respond to seasonal changes on the surface, but begins to increase steadily inwards—a phenomenon which suggests that the Earth possesses its own internal heat supply which gradually leaks out to the surface. This increase in temperature—amounting to 30°C per kilometre of depth (or 16°F every 1,000 feet)—is remarkably uniform in all parts of the world regardless of the 'boundary conditions' (be these tropical or arctic); and suggests a deep-seated location of the heat source.

Since, moreover, the average temperature of the Earth's surface is about 15°C, a simple extrapolation of the 'geothermic degree' of 30°C/km inwards discloses that the temperature of the rocks constituting the Earth's crust should rise to the boiling point of water at a sub-surface depth of only $2\frac{1}{2}$ kilometres. If water from the surface leaking through occasional cracks reaches this depth, it should begin to boil and be ejected by vapour pressure in the form of hot springs or geysers, familiar in many parts of the world. Should, moreover, the inward rise in temperature continue at the same rate beyond the explored regions through at least the outer part of the terrestrial mantle, the temperature of the melting point of rocks (about 1,500°C) would be reached at a sub-surface depth of only 50 kms—comparable with the depth of the 'combustion chambers' of the majority of the terrestrial volcanoes dotting like warts the loci of tectonic instabilities on the face of the

Earth. Volcanic eruptions represent occasional outbursts of deep-seated geysers in which molten lava plays the role of water.

The source of heat which keeps the volcanic chambers going may be partly mechanical (and due to frictional dissipation of motion into heat); but the origin of the general source of heat which keeps the interior of the Earth at a relatively elevated temperature is not in doubt. For in addition to such primordial heat of condensation as the Earth may have acquired at the time of its formation, its chemical composition contains traces of certain radioactive elements which produce heat by their spontaneous disintegration at a slow but very steady rate. The principal elements occurring widely in Nature, which are known to do so in a measurable amount, are uranium (U-235 and U-238), thorium (Th-228) and—among the lighter elements—the radioactive isotope of potassium (K-40), all of which play an important role in geophysics. Their role as secular indications of time will be discussed in the next section of this chapter; for the present we are interested only in the potential heat supply which they can provide to warm up the intestines of the Earth.

The percentage contents of these elements in common surface rocks available for precise chemical analysis is minute: granites or basalts from different parts of the world are found to contain approximately one part per ten million by weight of uranium, decaying spontaneously into lead at a rate which diminishes the amount of uranium to a half in $4 \cdot 5 \times 10^9$ years. Thorium (constituting about four parts per hundred million of the Earth's crust) is decaying into lead with a half-life of about $1 \cdot 4 \times 10^{10}$ years; and in so doing these elements keep releasing a minute amount of heat. Such heat sources represent a very minute trickle which may seem scarcely to deserve even a mention. No matter how small this trickle may seem to be, however, it acts dependably for a very long time—billions of years, in fact—and the temperature to which it can eventually give rise depends on the balance between heat generation and loss: heat being produced throughout the entire volume of the body in question (provided that the radioactive material is uniformly interspersed), and lost by conduction (or radiation) through the surface.

If you pick up a piece of granite containing (say) one part per ten million of uranium by weight and hold it in your hand, you will not be able to detect any increase in temperature of the stone over that of its surroundings, because radiogenic heat produced by uranium decay is being very effectively drained off (by conduction) into the matter with which it may be in contact. However, a ratio of volume to surface grows with the size of the body in question; and if you could exchange your piece of granite for the Earth as a whole, it would be a very different story. The answer can be obtained by computations which do not leave much room for doubt, and whose outcome proves to be almost embarrassing: namely, it shows that if the mass of the Earth throughout its interior contained as much uranium or thorium as we find on the surface, the amount of radiogenic heat produced in a few billion years and bottled up inside our planet (because escape by conduction represents a very slow process) would have raised the internal temperature of our planet far beyond the melting point of its constituent material not only in the core, but also throughout the greater part of its mantle.

And yet the seismic observations of the shear waves propagating freely through the mantle demonstrate that this cannot be the case! Therefore, we are driven to the conclusion that the terrestrial surface crust has been *enriched* with radioactive material, far beyond the contents prevalent in the deep interior, by nuclear processes which accompanied the last formative stage of our planet; and (as we shall see later) the same appears to be true of our Moon as well. When one takes into account the effect of pressure on the melting point of terrestrial materials, it transpires that the temperature prevailing at the interface between the mantle and the core cannot exceed about $4,000°C$. Near the Earth's centre the temperature may attain $5,500°-6,000°C$—values not very different from the effective temperature of the solar surface—but the pressure is so high there (and increasing more rapidly than the temperature) that the metallic material of the 'inner core' may again behave as a solid. It is only the material of the core proper—comprised in a shell between the radii of 1,250 and 3,400 km from the Earth's centre—that behaves like a liquid; and thermal *convection currents* inside this shell (produced by superadiabatic temperature gradients) can give rise to a 'self-excited dynamo' in conducting material that is responsible for the maintenance of the Earth's *magnetic field*.

Lastly, one comment should be added concerning the temperatures prevalent in the Earth's interior: they must vary in the course of time. A warm Earth must be continuously redistributing its internal heat supply by conduction, and losing some of it by radiation into space. On the other hand, new heat is constantly being produced by spontaneous disintegration of radioactive elements in the interior. Should the principal source of heat warming up the bowels of our planet stem from radioactive disintegration of long-lived elements like uranium, thorium, or potassium—with half-lives of billions of years—it follows that the Earth is very probably still warming up at the present time—albeit at a very slow rate—and was internally cooler in the past.

If so, however, it is possible that the metallic core which extends now to 54% of the terrestrial radius did not exist in the primordial Earth, but that its iron and nickel pool was only gradually extracted by secularly rising temperature from rocks in which they occur in small amounts. The new-born Earth need not, therefore, have possessed the same degree of differentiation in internal structure as transpires from the seismic evidence today; nor need the present profile of our planet represent as yet any final stage of its evolution. In particular, the continuing production of heat by radioactive elements now in the Earth's interior, and the consequent rise in its temperature, may cause the metallic core of our planet to grow further for the next two or three billion years, and attain dimensions still several per cent larger than they are at the present time; but none of us is going to live long enough to have a chance to verify this by direct observation.

V–2: The Surface of the Earth and its Evolution

In the preceding section we briefly outlined a profile of the Earth's interior, and described the physical conditions prevailing in its different zones, on the basis of evidence supplied mainly by the readings of the seismological 'stethoscopes' of the geophysicists. In the present section we intend to emerge from the deep interior and turn our attention to the outermost shell of the Earth which we referred to as the 'crust' of our planet, extending not more than 30–40 kms in depth below the surface. The mass of this shell constitutes a very small part—about one ten-thousandth—of the mass of the Earth as a whole. Nevertheless, this crust represents the part of the terrestrial anatomy which we know best, and the outermost part of this crust, with its continents and oceans, represents the terrestrial home which has nurtured us and our ancestors from time immemorial.

Physically speaking, the crust of the Earth consists of rocks whose average density ranges from about $2 \cdot 8$ g/cm^3 in the continental land masses to $3 \cdot 3$ g/cm^3, characteristic of ocean beds and rock lying below. Chemically speaking, the principal constituents are oxygen (to about 47%), silicon (28%) and aluminium (8%), followed by iron, calcium, and other elements in diminishing amounts. These elements do not occur anywhere in the Earth in a pure state, but in solid compounds which are so complicated—and form such intricate molecular structures—as to have given rise to a whole science of mineralogy. Now mineralogy is, in general, of little interest to astronomers, because a solid state of matter is extremely rare in the Universe; the milieu in which stellar astronomers feel most at home is plasma. However, in our solar family Nature has presented us with certain—albeit small—samples of solid matter in the form of planets, comets, meteorites, or interplanetary dust which are of intense interest to students of the solar system.

So intense has this interest become of late, and so important the message enshrined in natural minerals of different cosmic origin, that astronomers concerned with the study of our immediate neighbourhood had to overcome their natural aversion to the complicated terminology with which mineralogists tried to protect their professional domain. In what follows we will try to protect our readers as far as possible from too many proper names, and simplify the situation by describing the rocks which form the bulk of the terrestrial continents as 'granitic', and the lower-lying and denser strata as 'basaltic'—simplifications which may also find their use on other bodies of the solar system (such as the Moon). While granites occur only in the outermost parts of the Earth's crust, basaltic composition extends considerably deeper; and volcanic eruptions disgorge basaltic lavas which originated in subterranean melting-pots 50–100 kms below the surface.

But let us now confine our attention to the continental surface of the Earth on which we walk or travel. Its granitic composition makes it considerably lighter than the basaltic substrate on which the terrestrial continents virtually 'float', on account of their smaller mean density, in accordance with the requirements of hydrostatic equilibrium or—as the geophysicists prefer to express it—the principle of isostasy. How is it possible for one stone to float on another merely because its mean density is smaller than that of its substrate? For does not seismic evidence disclose that the Earth's crust transmits both the 'pressure' as well as 'shear' waves excited by the earthquakes—a fact which shows that its layers behave like an elastic solid rather than a liquid in which things can float? Strange as this may seem, the rocks constituting the Earth's crust—and maybe even the mantle—may sometimes behave as if they were solid as well as liquid at the same time—depending on the length of time during which they are exposed to stress.

To give an example of such a behaviour under conditions which are familiar in daily life, suppose that we take a stick of ordinary sealing wax and hit it with a hammer. The stick will, of course, break into many pieces—as if it were a piece of glass. But if we put another stick of the same wax in a jar and forget about it for long enough, in a year or so we shall find that it has spread all over the bottom of the jar as if it were a liquid. In the same way, a metal coin placed on a seemingly solid surface of tar will sink through it if given enough time; while a piece of cork will move upward through 'solid' tar and eventually float upon it as if it were water. All solid materials which are not crystalline can react to external stimuli as if they were rigid or fluid—depending only on the fact that the stimuli to which they are subjected occur on a time-scale which is short or long in comparison with what physicists call the 'Maxwellian relaxation time' of the respective solid, which for the rocks found in the Earth's interior lasts only days (or, at most a week or so) of our terrestrial time. To an impulse administered to them by an earthquake which lasts only some minutes, the terrestrial crust and the mantle will respond by vibrating like elastic solid; but to a permanent centrifugal force produced by diurnal rotation, the Earth responds by becoming flattened at the poles to exactly the same extent as if its entire mass were fluid.

Other phenomena can be recalled to show that, in response to a long-lasting stress, the stony crust of the Earth behaves as if its layers were fluid. For example, during the last ice age the Scandinavian peninsula was covered up by a heavy ice-cap which melted away with the advent of the present warmer (interglacial?) climate. As a result of a gradual lifting of this load, the altitude of the Fenno-Scandian land-mass above the sea-level has been rising at a rate of about half a metre per century—and remnants of the fishing villages of a thousand years ago are now found to be quite far from the shores. Partly in compensation for this uplift, other regions of the neighbouring land masses (such as the northern shores of the Baltic Sea, or the Low Countries) are secularly sinking—though, fortunately for their inhabitants, at not so alarming a rate. Other examples from different parts of the world could be quoted to prove the striving of the terrestrial land masses towards isostasy—a tendency differing only in scale from that which urges a piece of cork to push its way upwards through solid tar and eventually float upon it in accordance with the law of Archimedes.

But if the individual blocks of continental land masses can float upon their heavier substrate by virtue of their greater buoyancy, they should likewise be capable of making *lateral* motions if impelled by internal forces to do so. Different lines of geophysical evidence disclose that such 'continental drift' is indeed operative on the Earth on a time-scale which can profoundly alter the face of our planet several times in the course of its existence. It seems that not more than a thousand million years ago our Earth still possessed only one continuous continental area surrounded by ocean on all sides. Its diversification into the present five continents and many smaller islands may have occurred since that time, by a process which left behind enough clues to enable us to reconstruct at least the main features of its course.

These clues are indeed plentiful. Consider, for instance, the marked similarity between the west coast of Africa with its Gulf of Guinea and the east coast of Southern America. Although the two are now separated by the southern Atlantic some 2,000 kms in width, the surmise that they were once in contact is supported not only by a common orientation of the remanent magnetism of the rocks found along both coastal lines, but also by the fact that the fossils of many species of animal and plant life found there show close similarity up to the Cretaceous period of the Mesozoic age after which they begin to differentiate. This latter phenomenon suggests that the present Africa and South America were parts of the same continent as late as about 100 million years ago; and that their present separation occurred gradually since that time. Should, moreover, this separation have grown at a uniform rate,

Our Earth; Its Origin, Structure and Evolution 141

it would correspond to a relative drift with a velocity of about 3 centimetres per year, or 0·1 mm per day. When, therefore, you next cross the Atlantic from London to New York, remember that the distance between the two places on your arrival would have increased by about 30 microns while you were in the air, or by half a milimetre if you travelled by ship. Not a great change, perhaps, but also not one that would escape the attention of the geophysicists.

In the same way—by using the clues offered by paleontology and paleomagnetism—we can trace a gradual separation of Australia from south-east Asia which occurred at an earlier age; and other parts of the world disclose by and large the same story. For instance, the Antarctic rocks recently yielded the fossilized jawbone of an amphibian animal—long extinct—which flourished in tropical climates some 200 million years ago. Identical fossils have been found in Australia as well as in South Africa, thus proving that at some time in the dim past the three blocks of land masses were really one; and that the present Antarctica was not then covering the South Pole.

Before we consider the question concerning the forces that could have split the primordial continent asunder and sent its splinters drifting in different directions on the surface of our globe, let us inquire about the *age* which elapsed since the rocks constituting the continental land masses solidified. As has been well known since the beginning of this century, this age can be ascertained from the continuous ticking of tiny atomic clocks embedded in small amounts in most rocks occurring in Nature—in the form of certain radioactive elements which disintegrate spontaneously at a known rate.

One particular 'atomic clock' well suited for the measurement of long geologic time is radioactive potassium (K-40) which disintegrates (by the capture of an electron) into one kind of the inert gas argon (Ar-40). Laboratory measurements have disclosed the rate of this disintegration to be such that one-half of potassium-40 will decay into argon-40 in a time close to 1,270 million years —quite oblivious to the physical conditions (temperature, pressure) obtaining in its neighbourhood. The decay product—argon—is a gas which would escape freely from a liquid, but becomes imprisoned in the crystal lattice of a mineral the moment the latter solidifies. If—at a later date—we grind a sample of such a mineral to powder and capture gas escaping from it on heating, the ratio of the decay product (Ar-40) to its mother substance (K-40) still left in the sample will indicate—like a hand on the cosmic clock—the time that has elapsed since the sample solidified; and neither temperature, nor pressure to which terrestrial rocks can be exposed, can alter in the least the regularity of its march.

Other chains of radioactive disintegrations—such as those based on the uranium-lead or strontium-rubidium decays—can be used for the same purpose. But they all possess one feature in common: namely, they start marking time from the moment when the rock containing them has solidified; and their dials are automatically set back to zero whenever the respective mineral has been remelted—just as (on a different time-scale) the radioactive carbon-14 dating tells the archaeologists the age of any organic tissue, measured from the moment when the respective organism stopped its intake of ^{14}C from the atmosphere on cessation of breathing at the time of death.

When the radioactive potassium-argon, rubidium-strontium, or uranium-lead methods were used to determine the time which has elapsed since the solidification of the terrestrial rocks found in different parts of the world, a result of profound interest came to light: namely, that *the oldest rocks found anywhere on the surface of the Earth are no more than 3·5–3·6 aeons* (i.e., billion years) *of age, and at least one aeon younger than the oldest known meteorites;* and the majority of them are much younger. If we assume that the Earth as a whole is about 4·6 aeons old (and recent age determinations of lunar rocks, to be described in the next chapter, bear this out), it follows that the first billion years of the Earth's age represent a veritable 'dark aeon' of our planet, from which no direct information can be found in the geological record. Does it mean that the Earth as a whole could have been molten during that time? Very unlikely; for had it still been so 3·5 aeons ago, its present temperature would be very much higher than that indicated by geophysical measurements, and our globe could possess no elastic mantle of the present size; the cooling of a planetary globe of the size of the Earth is an extremely slow process.

Such being the case, the only reasonable explanation of the relatively low ages of the terrestrial rocks is to admit that *the rocks now forming the crust of our planet were not a part of its surface from the beginning of its existence, but emerged there from the interior at a later date.* We are driven to such a conclusion by the fact that large parts of the terrestrial surface—and not only of its continental areas, but also of the 'abyssal plains' of its ocean floors—appear to be remarkably young, with their tiny nuclear clocks re-set for the last time not more than a few hundred million years ago. The physical mechanisms which could account for this phenomenon are thermal convection currents driven by the 'heat engine' in the terrestrial mantle.

That elastic rocks in the solid mantle could be susceptible of motions associated generally with fluids is an audacious concept. Nevertheless, the rate of these postulated motions is so slow, and their time-scale so enormously long in comparison with the Maxwellian relaxation time of the Earth's crust, that slow convection in the mantle (stimulated by superadiabatic temperature gradients) remains a physical possibility. And its existence could enable us to kill two birds with one stone: namely, to provide a motive mechanism for the 'continental drift', as well as for a 'consumption' of surface rocks which are at times drawn deep enough into the mantle for re-setting of their 'nuclear clocks'. The time interval at which this seems to have recurred appears to be generally a few hundred million years. Only in rare parts of the terrestrial surface— along the 'nodes' of the convective motion—can rocks be found which are substantially older. Such regions are the archaic Canadian shield, or the Central and South African plateau, where rocks as old as $3\frac{1}{2}$ aeons of time have been discovered in the past few years; but solid relics of the days gone by so long ago cover no more than a few per cent of the terrestrial surface, the rest being of much younger provenance.

One side-thought may, perhaps, be added here to connect with these concepts another phenomenon well known to us from geography: the existence of continental mountain chains—such as the Alps, the Himalayas, or the Andes—stretching sometimes for thousands of kilometres in length. How old are these chains, and how did they come into being? We know that all mountains (other than purely volcanic cones)—not only those parts of them which loom above the surface, but also their subterranean 'roots' —consist of relatively light rocks characteristic of the continental crust. If the continental land masses—thousands of kilometres in size, but not much more than 20–30 kms deep—float on the denser mantle like pancakes carried adrift by the slow convection streams, what is more natural than that the thin continental pancake does not always move as a rigid block, but becomes warped in places where lateral pressure is unable to push the land in front everywhere at the same speed?

This may be the origin of 'folded' mountain chains so typical of the terrestrial landscape (and conspicuous by their absence on the Moon)—like the Pyrenees, Alps and Carpathians in Europe, the Caucasus, Pamir and the Himalayas in Asia, or the great chain of the Andes and the Rocky Mountains running from Patagonia to Alaska along the entire west coast of the American continent. The geologists studying the detailed anatomy of the face of the Earth tell us that all these mountains (with a host of their less conspicuous links) originated by folding in the relatively recent past—only some 20 to 30 million years ago—as a part of an orogenetic process which took place at the time of the transition between the Miocene and Pliocene periods of the Tertiary epoch. We do not know what caused Mother Earth to warp her face by this particular grimace at that time. We know, however, that a similar process had taken place at least twice before—as represented by the so-called Hercynian and Caledonian mountain building in the Permian and lower Devonian periods of the Paleozoic era some 250 and 400 million years ago. The mountains of those ages are very much less conspicuous, and less attractive to the mountaineer as climbing propositions, because erosion by water and air has almost levelled them off after such a long period of time. But the latest era of mountain formation—the Alpine movements —managed to lift rocks containing fossils of creatures living in the sea almost to the height of Mount Everest; an eloquent testimony to the tremendous forces engaged in the building up of the mountains.

So far we have been speaking of the surface of the Earth as if it were a solid land mass—which, of course, is not the case; for no less than two-thirds of it are ocean basins which are filled with *water*. The basins themselves represent shallow—albeit extensive —pockmarks on the face of the Earth, as their maximum depth below sea-level (11,000 metres) exceeds by only two kilometres the altitude of the highest mountains (8,884 metres) on land. Just as the latter are largely localized in chains (like the Himalayas

Our Earth; Its Origin, Structure and Evolution

with their eight-thousand-metre peaks), the greatest abyssal depths at sea are found in relatively narrow trenches (like the Marianna or Tonga trenches in the Pacific, or the Puerto Rico trench in the Atlantic). Ten kilometres represent less than one part in six hundred of the terrestrial radius, and less than one-half of the amount of polar flattening produced by the daily rotation of our planet. If pockmarks as shallow as the terrestrial ocean beds were marked to scale on a globe of one metre in diameter, both the Atlantic and the Pacific (not to speak of smaller oceans) would represent on it depressions barely one millimetre deep—indentations scarcely noticeable to the palm of a hand passed over the globe.

Examined in greater detail, however, the ocean floors are far from smooth. If we could siphon off all the water from the Atlantic, we would find on its floor the largest mountain chain on the Earth—the famous mid-Atlantic range running in the north-south direction with a deep central crack, the origin of which is probably connected with the phenomenon of continental drift. No mountain range on Earth even approaches the length and average height of this mid-Atlantic range. The highest mountains on the Earth are not to be found in the Himalayas, but actually rise from the floor of the Pacific. The famous Hawaiian volcanoes Mauna Kea and Mauna Loa in mid-Pacific attain altitudes of only 4,208 and 4,170 metres above sea-level; but they rise from an ocean floor 5,800 metres deep, so that their actual altitudes above the surrounding abyssal plain are close to 10,000 metres—more than 1,100 m higher than the altitude of Mount Everest above sea-level.

The ocean beds on the Earth are, of course, not empty, but filled with water constituting the terrestrial *hydrosphere*. The total mass of this water is only a little more than one ten-thousandth of the mass of the Earth as a whole. If it were distributed uniformly all over the globe, it would cover the Earth with an ocean about 1,800 metres in depth. Chemically, ocean water is far from pure; for each cubic kilometre (weighing one billion tons) contains, on the average, 19 million tons of dissolved chlorine, 10·6 million tons of sodium, 1·3 million tons of magnesium, and proportionally smaller amounts of other elements* which make it truly 'salt' water—chemically as well as by taste.

Where did all this water come from? We are fairly sure that the new-born Earth contained no water on its surface—that it was

*Among them we should also find about 300 kg of silver, and 4 kg of gold.

born 'dry'—and that its oceans were later exuded from the interior by thermal cracking of the hydrates. Let us try to explain what we mean. The molecule of water (H_2O) is a cosmically common and very stable product of Nature. We have found (by means of its radio-emission) that it exists in interstellar space in the form of tiny ice crystals; and we know of many minerals on the Earth—such as obsidians and many other kinds of volcanic glasses—which contain as much as 10 per cent of water molecules by weight imprisoned in their structure. The mineralogists call such specimens the 'hydrates'. At normal temperatures prevalent on the surface of the Earth such hydrates are, in general, stable and can retain their water for an indefinite length of time. A moderate heating (to temperatures between $500°-1,000°C$), is, however, sufficient to break the chemical bonds keeping the H_2O molecules within the fold of the molecular structure of hydrates, and expel them in the form of steam which can condense into liquid water. Temperatures of this order are likely to have been exceeded in most parts of the Earth's interior. If so, however, the hydrates that may have been contained there are already largely despoiled of their water supply. If water was originally present in the primordial material from which the Earth was formed in solid state to an extent of one part in 10,000 or more, the thermal cracking of the hydrates, and outward seepage as superheated steam, could have eventually produced as much water as we find in all the oceans of the Earth.

How old are the oceans? While nothing is known about the possible hydrosphere of our planet in the first 'dark aeon' of its existence, the oldest preserved rock strata—more than three billion years of age—already bear evidence of the existence of 'sediments' which required water for the formation of their deposits. Moreover, the original 'juvenile' water squeezed out by heat from the Earth's interior probably contained few salts dissolved in it before it emerged to the surface. Chemists estimate that, in order to acquire its present salinity, sea water must have been on the surface in a liquid state for not less than three billion years—an important fact for the emergence of life on this planet, which we shall discuss in a later chapter.

The continents and the hydrosphere thus form the topmost layer of the Earth's crust, constituting a skin whose depth barely extends to two parts in a thousand of the terrestrial radius. The present distribution of the continents and oceans on the terrestrial globe is familiar enough to us all from our geography lessons at school; but its detailed features are largely incidental, and a consequence of the present height of sea-level. The 'continental shelves'—the real coast-lines of the large land masses, along which the continental shores descend steeply to the ocean floors—do not parallel the outlines of dry land with any fidelity. For instance, if the present sea-level were to drop only 100 metres (which could happen if more water were trapped in the polar caps of our planet during a severe ice age), the European shores would run about 200 kms west of the British Isles (including Ireland); and the latter would become integrated as a part of the European continent—as indeed they geophysically are whether their inhabitants like it or not. On the other hand, should our sea-level rise by not more than some 150–200 metres (as it could if our present polar caps vanished during a warm spell of cosmic climate), the geography of our globe would likewise change almost beyond recognition. Almost half of Western Europe (including large parts of France, Germany and the Low Countries), and most of the eastern and southern United States too, would disappear below sea-level; and changes in many other parts of the world would be no less striking. Perhaps it was with such a possibility in mind that William Shakespeare, in his *Winter's Tale*, made the king of the central European land of Bohemia a sea-coast ruler!

The anatomy of our planet does not, however, end with this surface; for the latter is surrounded by a gaseous envelope known as our *atmosphere*. That a terrestrial planet of the mass of the Earth borders on interplanetary space by an atmosphere is not accidental, but a logical consequence of the same kind of processes which have endowed our planet with its hydrosphere. If the latter originated by a defluidization of the Earth caused by a gradual build-up of radiogenic heat in its interior, the atmosphere originated by its de-gassing—through the liberation of volatile compounds from the interior, whose molecular weight is sufficiently large to prevent their escape from the gravitational field of the Earth. A gradual formation of the hydrosphere and atmosphere represents, therefore, two different aspects of the same process. Moreover, an atmosphere capable of exerting adequate air pressure is necesary for the maintenance of any liquid on the surface. Planets can exist which possess atmospheres but no hydrospheres (Mars and Venus represent conspicuous examples of this kind in our solar system); but the converse is impossible on physical grounds.

The composition of our atmosphere is in agreement with our expectations based on the ability of our Earth to retain gases above its surface. Hydrogen or helium—the commonest elements in the Sun—are too light to be present in our air except in insignificant traces. The principal constituents of our atmosphere prove to be nitrogen (75·5% by weight) and oxygen (23·1%), followed by argon (1·3%), neon (0·0013%), and diminishing amounts of other inert gases (helium, krypton, xenon) present in quantities so minute that a chemist might describe them as 'impurities'. Variable amounts of water vapour (0·01–0·1%) and carbon dioxide (0·03%) add up to the rest of the natural composition of our atmosphere. Its contamination by human action (like that of the water) we propose at present to pass over in silence. This composition proves to be remarkably uniform throughout at least the first 100 kms of atmospheric altitude—testifying to the efficiency with which gases of very different molecular weight are intermixed by atmospheric air currents.

The total mass of the terrestrial atmosphere—close to $5·3 \times 10^{21}$g—constitutes about one-millionth of the mass of the Earth as a whole, and only 0·3% of that of our hydrosphere. Nevertheless, in one respect its presence looms more impressively: by its extent. The bulk of its mass is confined to its lowest layer which the meteorologists describe as our 'troposphere', and which extends to a mean altitude of 11–14 kms. It is this zone which is primarily responsible for external manifestations of our weather—with its rain or shine, its winds and occasional storms due to the vagaries of its meteorology; in brief, for most phenomena of Nature which make one day different from the next. The highest mountains on the Earth just approach the top of this layer; and big modern jet planes skirt it in flight.

When you fly in a jet and look out of the plane window away from the Sun, you will notice that the pale blue sky over the airport deepens considerably—this is because the 'sky blue' of our daylight is caused by the scattering of sunlight on air molecules, the density of which diminishes with altitude. Sky blue is indeed produced by an interaction of sunlight with particles which are very small in comparison with the wavelength of the visible light. Should these particles grow large—such as those constituting dust or smoke disgorged from our chimneys—light scattering of a different kind will arise which gives the sky an indifferent 'milky' appearance. At the top of the *troposphere,* the air is already so rarefied that the mean ambient pressure is only 26% of that prevailing at sea-level; and you may recall that flight captains of jet planes at cruising altitudes report outside temperatures around minus fifty degrees centigrade, while ground temperatures at the airport may have made you long to get into the air-conditioned cabin of your plane.

These are the conditions prevailing at the base of the terrestrial *stratosphere*—the layer which overlies the troposphere, and so called because the barometric drop in temperature throughout the troposphere comes to an end at about $-55\,°C$, the temperature prevalent higher up. Most of our weather has happened well below these altitudes which, until quite recently, could be penetrated only by large balloons, and where even now only the vapour-trailing supersonic jets are scribbling in the deep-blue sky, their shorthand of the future.

This stratosphere extends for many miles, to altitudes well above the ceiling of any plane or balloon; heights to which man has penetrated only by means of rocket propulsion. At altitudes commencing at about 60–80 kms (oscillating between day and night) we encounter another distinct layer of considerable practical interest to the inhabitants of the Earth. At those heights the ambient air pressure is only about 5×10^{-5} part of an atmosphere; and the air density, about 9×10^{-8} g/cm^3. Air so rarefied becomes, however, so easily ionized by energetic radiation of the Sun that the number of electrons encountered there may amount to as much as 10^6 per ccm. Such a layer, extending almost up to 300 kms in altitude (and possessing a fine structure of several consecutive layers) acts like a metallic mirror or mesh which can reflect downwards high-frequency radio waves—and scatter backwards any similar waves which reach our Earth from outer space.

The actual level of this *ionosphere,* as well as its transparency, oscillates between day and night; and its outer rim may attain altitudes not far from 300 kms above the surface of our planet. The temperatures prevalent at these levels go up and down, reaching values well in excess of those encountered on the surface. Their significance is, however, only to describe the mean velocity of agitation of individual gas particles at those levels—without regard for the fact that the number of such particles is dwindling so rapidly that they could give no physiological sensation of heat. To give an example: at an altitude of 200 kms the individual gas particles are moving to and fro at speeds which correspond to a kinetic temperature of about a thousand degrees centigrade. However, the mean free path of such particles between individual collisions is over 200 metres—much larger than the dimensions of a human body.

If, therefore, you were to stretch out an unprotected hand into such an environment, it would freeze immediately to a solid in spite of the fact that—as the aeronomists tell you—the ambient medium is 1,000°K hot. Its individual particles move fast enough to correspond to such temperatures; but very few of them would hit you to make you aware of their speed. A gas of the density between 10^{-11} and 10^{-14} g/cm³ obtaining in the ionosphere at altitudes ranging from 100–300 kms may be nothing much to speak about in spite of its fantastic temperature; and certainly its total mass does not exceed about a million tons. But the region filled by it is still capable of giving rise to the beautiful displays of 'polar aurorae'; and the air density in its lower layers is sufficient to light up the majority of the meteors or 'shooting stars' by atmospheric resistance.

Above this ionosphere, the remaining air becomes already so rarefied, and the mean free path of the individual particles so large, that we no longer deal with gas, but with an assembly of individual particles which describe ballistic trajectories of increasing length between individual collisions that become increasingly rare. This is the terrestrial *exosphere,* through which our planet borders on interplanetary space; and through which some of the more energetic particles—whose speed may temporarily exceed the escape velocity from the terrestrial gravitational field—may be lost to our planet.

Thus, in our brief survey of the structure of our planet, we have found the Earth to consist of a solid 'inner core' of nickel-iron, of a radius of some 1,250 kms, surrounded to 3,470 kms by a liquid shell of the 'core' consisting of much the same material (except, possibly, for an admixture of a certain amount of molten silicates), and overlaid by a 'mantle' of silicate rocks covered on the top by the 'crust'. It is this crust which supports our continents and oceans; and it is protected from above by a gaseous 'atmosphere' of several distinct layers gradually petering out into outer space.

This atmosphere contains relatively little mass. A column of gas of 1 cm² cross-section weighs only 1,034 grams, and exerts an average pressure of 10^6 dynes/cm² (one bar)—capable of balancing a column of mercury about 760 mm in height—which we call 'one atmosphere'. Nevertheless, gas at this pressure is sufficient to keep our oceans and other waters of the land from evaporation, and provides enough oxygen to sustain the metabolism of all living creatures which populate this Earth. And to one group of these creatures—namely, the star-gazers—some of its properties are of paramount interest; for the atmosphere filters (and otherwise modifies) all light reaching us from the celestial bodies, and thus restricts the amount of information which we on the surface of the Earth may hope to deduce from it. As the greater part of this book is based on such information, in what follows we shall detail some of the limitations which the atmosphere puts in our way.

It may seem surprising that our atmosphere—far from being transparent—is really opaque to most kinds of light reaching us from space. The radiation which can penetrate to the ground without much hindrance is, in fact, limited to two discrete and well-separated domains of the spectrum. The first is a relatively narrow 'optical window' between wavelengths of approximately 2,900 Å and some 10,000 Å—including the light visible to the human eye from violet to deep red. The fact that this 'visible light' falls in the domain of atmospheric transparency is no accident; for the sensitivity of the human eye (as well as the light receptors of most other animals) developed throughout the ages so as to take the best advantage of available sunlight, which reaches us largely through the same gap. The second 'window' through which our atmosphere becomes transparent opens up in the radio-domain of the electromagnetic spectrum, extending from wavelengths of approximately one millimetre up to several metres.

What sets these limits of atmospheric transparency? The violet edge of the 'optical window' around 2,900 Å is imposed abruptly by the absorption of the ozone molecules, extending broadly between 25–40 kms aloft. Ozone constitutes the principal source of absorption for ultraviolet light down to 2,000 Å wavelengths; while between 2,000 and 1,300 Å this role is taken over by the ordinary (diatomic) oxygen molecules which become ionized by energetic sunlight. These molecules absorb in extreme ultraviolet so effectively that the intensity of incoming light is reduced to a half at altitudes in excess of 200 kms, where the residual air density is only one billionth of that prevailing at sea-level.

On the other hand, towards the red end of the optical window, atmospheric transparency becomes increasingly impeded by absorption of the molecules of water vapour and carbon-dioxide, which blots out most of the spectrum between 1 and 1,000 micron wavelengths. This absorption does not set in as abruptly as does the ozone absorption below 2,900 Å; for in this domain there are at least two additional half-open windows (between 8–12 microns and around 25 microns) through which some infrared light from space can actually reach the ground. However, beyond some 30 μ's the atmospheric absorption becomes so impenetrable that even the Sun does not begin to emerge through it till at sub-millimetre wavelengths. Between 1 mm and a few metres—in the domain of the radio spectrum—atmospheric transparency becomes once more almost complete, until it is eventually quenched by the reflecting properties of the ionosphere. Charged particles of the ionized layers, which act as concave mirrors reflecting back to Earth shortwave radio signals of ground-based transmitters, will act as convex shells in reflecting back similar waves reaching us from space.

In the face of all this it is intriguing to speculate how much better we—that is, astronomers—would be if oxygen and its compounds were totally absent from our air. In such a case, the continuous atmospheric transparency would extend from wavelengths of about 1000 Å to some 10 metres or 10^{11} Å; only the extreme ends below and above these limits would continue to be blotted out by the absorption of ionized nitrogen—both atomic (N^+) and molecular (N_2^+), and by the scattering of free electrons liberated by this ionization. But all this is idle speculation; for without atmospheric oxygen (which may, indeed, be all of organic origin) no comprehending eye could contemplate the grand panorama of the Universe with the curtains fully drawn; all the precious light would be wasted on dead rocks.

To summarize: apart from the relatively narrow 'optical window' between 3,000 Å and 10,000 Å, and a much wider 'radio window' between 1 and 10,000 mm wavelengths, our atmosphere on the ground is almost totally opaque to light reaching us from the Universe. Moreover, in order to free ourselves from these limitations it is not sufficient merely to ascend above the main atmospheric air mass, but to attain altitudes at which the air density becomes less than 10^{-9} of that at sea-level. Below these levels the damage caused by absorption becomes extensive and irreparable. Moreover, the absorption itself does not constitute the only source of harm to the telescopic images of celestial objects observable on the ground; for even more serious damage can be caused by anomalous refraction as well as diffraction of light passing through tropospheric layers of increasing air density not very far above the ground.

In order to explain such phenomena, let us point out that no telescope which astronomers use for their work really commences with its objective or mirror used to collect light, but rather many kilometres above it—where the plane wave of light from space will undergo its initial distortion in layers of unequal temperature, and suffer anomalous refraction and diffraction in turbulent air long after it has been pruned by selective absorption very much higher up. For the atmospheric density and temperature do not only vary with height, but also laterally because of motions which constantly agitate the air (winds!) and cause ceaseless fluctuations in its local index of refraction. The visible outcome is the phenomenon of 'scintillation' of starlight, giving rise to shimmering discs in place of the point-like images of the stars which we could expect to see with our optics outside the atmosphere. 'Twinkle, twinkle, little star' may be an amusing ditty to a child; but one often capable of driving an astronomer to distraction.

But there is another (more beneficial) role played by the atmosphere—and hydrosphere: in controlling the *temperature* prevalent on the surface of the Earth. As is well known, all heat we receive on the surface comes from the Sun—the internal heat of the Earth makes itself felt at a depth commencing a few hundred metres below the surface, but its flux is too low to have any influence on our weather. The amount of heat received from the Sun is very close to 2 $cals/cm^2min$; and most of its energy is carried by 'white light' to which our atmosphere is almost completely transparent. What is the temperature at which our planet should be maintained by such a flux?

Since the (average) distance of the Earth from the Sun amounts to 149 million kilometres or 214 solar radii, each square centimetre of the terrestrial surface should receive about one $(214)^2$th or a 46,000th part of the heat passing through each square centimetre of the surface of the Sun. This (as we have already seen on p. 26 is about 1.39×10^6 ergs/cm²sec, sufficient to maintain the temperature of the Sun at its 5,800°K. As, moreover, this flux is (approximately) proportional to the fourth power of the absolute temperature, it follows that, at the sub-solar point in our tropics, our temperature should be $\sqrt{214}$ times (or about 15 times) less than that of the Sun, which is approximately 120°C—higher by 20° than the temperature of boiling water! Now everyone knows that—notwithstanding the tales of old navigators in ancient times —this is just not the case, even in the 'torrid zone' of the tropics. Noon temperatures of 40–45°C are sometimes recorded in desert climates; but scarcely more. The average global temperature of the Earth proves to be close to 15°C; and in many climates it does not vary very much between day and night, or from one season of the year to another.

The cause of this phenomenon is not hard to find. Like the Sun, the Earth (like any other body maintained at non-zero temperature) not only absorbs heat, but also emits it at a rate proportional to the fourth power of its absolute temperature, in accordance with what the physicists call 'Planck's Law'. And this law rules that not only all light absorbed must be fully re-emitted, but also that this must take place at wavelengths which become longer the lower the temperature of the emitter. While at the temperature of the Sun (5,800°K) this occurs mainly at wavelengths which correspond to visible light, at 380°K a Planckian radiator emits mainly in the infrared—with a maximum around wavelengths of 10 microns (i.e., 0·01 mm).

A light of this 'colour' is, of course, completely invisible to the human eye, and incapable of impressing a photographic plate; though it can be measured by other devices. But—and this is essential for our narrative—it will also experience a great difficulty in penetrating through our atmosphere out into space. As we have already said earlier in this section, this atmosphere is almost completely transparent to the bulk of 'white light' which we receive from the Sun. On the other hand, two of its minor constituents— namely, water vapour and carbon dioxide (constituting together no more than about 0·1% of the entire air mass)—render our atmosphere almost completely opaque to infrared light given off by the Earth. The bulk of heat emitted by its surface is effectively trapped by the absorption of CO_2 and H_2O molecules in our atmosphere which thus acts like a greenhouse.

And not only the atmosphere, but also the oceans of the hydrosphere of our planet contribute to a mitigation of the extremes of the temperatures encountered on the Earth. Some $70 \cdot 8\%$ of the surface of our planet is covered with water; and this water is a substance possessing many remarkable properties. Because of its very large heat capacity, the oceans can absorb a large amount of heat from the Sun without becoming too hot, and lose much of it without becoming too cold. Thus our hydrosphere can be compared with a savings bank for solar radiation, receiving deposits in seasons of insolation and paying them back in time of want.

And not only do our oceans receive deposits in seasons of insolation. Since water can move and circulate in the hydrosphere —not only through the brooks and rivers, but also through the agency of ocean currents—it can not only preserve heat received from the Sun during daytime, or in the tropics, but also transport it to other parts of the world which may be less generously blessed with sunshine. A closed-loop heat engine responsible for such a circulation takes many forms: water evaporating from tropical seas can be transported as clouds by winds over the continental regions, where a part of it may be extracted by precipitation and provide a source for the brooks and rivers which take it back to sea. Or, ocean currents driven by convection on a rotating globe— of which the warm Gulf Stream in the Atlantic, and the cold Humboldt current in the Pacific constitute the best known examples —can re-distribute much larger amounts of heat across the vast expanses of the oceans, from which they are picked up by atmospheric air currents and transported by them to regions which are inaccessible to water. The Atlantic trade winds skirting the surface, which propelled the caravels of Columbus on their maiden voyage to the New World; or the 'jet stream' which impedes the west-bound air traffic at stratospheric altitudes—all are part of the general air-water circulatory system, which has maintained our terrestrial abode as a home fit for the development and maintenance of life. Without these great stabilizers of temperature present everywhere around us, our terrestrial environment would be as bleak and forbidding a one as we shall find, in the next chapter, to exist on our Moon. It is the terrestrial air and water—inseparably connected with each other—that have enabled our Earth to become the sole cradle of life in the solar system; and how this happened we shall proceed to describe in the next chapter.

CHAPTER VI

Life on the Earth

IN THE preceding chapter we gave a brief outline of the principal physical properties of our mother planet, and of the inanimate processes which have been shaping its face from time immemorial. In doing so we have, however, deferred mentioning one particular facet of it which is intimately connected with our existence: that—in the fullness of time—the surface of the Earth became the cradle of *life*. It will be the aim of the present chapter to try to explain how and why this has happened on our planet alone; and to outline the past of this wonderful and unique development, in so far as it can be done by an astronomer.

When our Earth emerged from its first 'dark aeon' of which we know so little, its surface as well as (as far as we can say) the composition of its atmosphere was similar to what it is today (with the possible exception of its oxygen content). The rare strata of rocks preserved from the ages of $3-3\frac{1}{2}$ aeons before our time already exhibit, however, unmistakable effects of the action of air (winds) and water in their sedimentary structure—thus demonstrating that at that time water already existed on the Earth's surface in liquid form. And more: the microscopic structure of such rocks already exhibits tiny spots which modern paleontologists tentatively consider to be fossil remnants of organisms animated by life.

What is life, and what distinguishes it from inanimate matter? In its rudimentary form, living matter can probably be defined as the structure of certain types of complicated molecules (possibly of single giant molecules) which endows their system with two characteristics unique and fundamental to life: the possibility of *metabolism* (i.e., the energy exchange with its surrounding medium), and the capability of *self-reproduction*.

Not all types of molecules are, however, capable of these two symptoms—metabolism and self-reproduction—which we regard as essential to life. In order to be able to do so, they must attain the degree of complexity and sophistication which the rules of atomic physics make possible only for the compounds of one element which is common enough on the surface of the Earth: carbon. Unlike most other elements, the atoms of carbon can combine with those of oxygen and nitrogen—another pair of cosmically common elements—into molecules which may consist of thousands or even millions of individual atoms; and this very complexity can eventually enable them to perform the functions which we have described as characteristic of life. Such molecules can—as far as we know—be formed by naturally occurring inorganic processes (such as the interaction of elements in solutions; under the effects of electrical discharge; etc); but owing to the number of the 'building bricks' which must be brought together to form such 'organic' molecules of gigantic size, it is not possible to conceive of their origin elsewhere than in liquids whose main ingredient is *water*.

Therefore, life on Earth almost certainly originated in water; and could not have come into being unless water existed on the surface in liquid form. In addition, it needed light—provided by the Sun—to activate the production of oxygen—that life-sustaining gas of our atmosphere—from carbon dioxide as a by-product of the photosynthesis process carried on by green plants since the early days of the history of our planet; but light whose quanta are too energetic (such as the ultraviolet, or X-rays) would have again done more harm than good to the nascent organic molecules by photodissociation, and had to be removed from sunlight by atmospheric absorption.

These facts should help to explain why life did not originate (or, if it did, why it did not develop) on any other planet or other body in the solar system apart from the Earth. The existence of liquid water depends on the life-bearing planet being at the right distance from the Sun—within the 'temperate zone', where liquid water can exist on the exposed surface, the mean temperature of which must lie between freezing point and boiling point. Moreover, since these limits cannot be exceeded without the destruction of previously formed organic products, it follows that the planet in question must also rotate fairly rapidly about an axis which is normal to its orbital plane, or nearly so; for otherwise the day-to-night variation of temperature could easily exceed the permissible limits (as it does on the Moon).

Third, not only must liquid water exist on the surface of a

planet that can give birth to life; but this planet must also be surrounded by a gaseous atmosphere that fulfils several essential tasks. This atmosphere must exert a pressure sufficient for the maintenance of liquid water on the ground (otherwise it would quickly boil off and evaporate into space); its absorption must remove the unwanted wavelengths from the illuminating sunlight; and its composition must be such that it contains all the ingredients necessary for the formation of the organic molecules, but not those which could be harmful to them. Ingredients essential for such life as it eventually developed on the Earth are gaseous elements with atomic weights between 10 and 20—from nitrogen to neon. Of the two lighter gases—hydrogen and helium—the latter is largely irrelevant because of its chemically inert nature, while hydrogen only too readily forms compounds (with carbon or nitrogen) which can be lethal to life. On the other hand, gases heavier than neon are increasingly scarce in the Cosmos; and increasingly prone to form lethal compounds as well.

These considerations should increasingly single out our Earth as the only hopeful harbinger of life in the entire solar system. A planet on which life can be conceived must not only have its distance from the Sun, but also its mass, confined within fairly narrow limits. Too large a mass—like those possessed by the major planets of the solar system between Jupiter and Neptune—would enable the respective bodies to retain too much harmful hydrogen in their atmospheres; while planets or satellites of small mass, like that of the Moon—especially if they happen (like Mercury) to be too close to the Sun—can scarcely retain any atmosphere at all. Venus does possess an extensive atmosphere; but its surface is too hot to permit any life to originate or develop; while the conditions prevailing on Mars are so marginal as regards its vestigial atmosphere as well as climate, that living matter—if it ever formed there—would have remained arrested in the earliest stages of development.

In our solar system, therefore, the Earth alone offered a reasonable chance for the origin and development of what we call life. That this is so is well known to us; but this fact could also be inferred by an extra-terrestrial intelligence from observations at a distance, by such reasoning as we have developed so far. The *evolution* of life in the course of ages constitutes a fascinating story. For the living organisms—once formed—continued to evolve under the influence of the same processes which gave them birth. In the simplest form, *the evolution of living organisms can be defined as the extent of their failure to reproduce* from generation to generation *in exactly the same form*. If each offspring were to become an identical replica of its progenitors—as the latter were of their own parents—the first would have reproduced indefinitely in the same form ever after.

In actual fact, no physical system or organism—inanimate or living—can be reproduced in exactly the same form because the process resulting in reproduction can never be exact, due to deviations and faults which are inherent in any stochastic system consisting of many components or particles. Whether such deviations are caused by processes which are *systematic* (such as natural selection, struggle for life, etc) or *accidental* (such as mutations of the genes produced by radiation damage and other types of external interference) is a task for the biologists to decide; and they are as yet far from unanimous as to the relative importance of various contributing factors acting at different times. However, to an interested onlooker—such as the astronomer concerned mainly with the outcome—the evolution of species as recorded in the fossil record of the geological strata of the Earth is a truly remarkable story.

As perhaps could have been expected, the beginnings of the evolution of life on our planet were slow, and its records scanty—due to large-scale alteration (by pressure and heat metamorphosis) of rock strata deposited in the second and third aeon before our time. There is some evidence that when the evolution of life reached a mono-cellular stage, Nature may not yet have settled experimentally the question of the type of metabolism likely to be most successful under terrestrial conditions. It did not, in particular, single out those deriving their energy from oxidation—possibly because free oxygen may not yet have been as important a constituent of our atmosphere as it later became. At least bacteria are still living today which thrive on decomposition of methane or sulphur-dioxide rather than oxygen—to which oxygen is, in fact, lethal. It may be that such bacteria constitute the surviving remnants (in arrested evolutionary stage) of different types of life with which Nature experimented before it convinced itself that organisms whose metabolism is based on oxidation will be more

Plate 1 A star called the Sun – photograph of the Sun in the light of the hydrogen line Hα, showing distinctly the structure of the solar atmosphere in the neighbourhood of sunspots (by courtesy of Dr. John Hagen, Pennsylvania State University, U.S.A.).

Plate 2 (left) The great nebula in Orion (Messier 42 = NGC 1976), photographed in blue light with the 100-inch telescope of the observatory at Mount Wilson (reproduced by courtesy of the Hale Observatories, California Institute of Technology).

Plate 3 (above) Reflection nebulae surrounding the principal stars of the Pleiades cluster, photographed with the 48-inch Schmidt telescope of Mount Palomar Observatory (reproduced by courtesy of the Hale Observatories, California Institute of Technology).

Plate 4 A "Hole in the Sky" – a dark cloud of cosmic dust imposing itself on a star field of the southern Milky Way. A photograph taken with the 24-inch Bruce refractor of Harvard Observatory in South Africa and reproduced by courtesy of Dr. H. Shapley.

Plate 5 The "Horsehead" dark nebula just south of Zeta Orionis (below Orion's belt) as photographed in red light by the 200-inch Hale Telescope at Palomar Mountain (reproduced by courtesy of the Hale Observatories, California Institute of Technology).

Plate 6 Star clouds in the Milky Way – in the region of the galactic centre in Sagittarius, photographed in red light with the 48-inch Schmidt telescope at Palomar Mountain (reproduced by courtesy of the Hale Observatories, California Institute of Technology).

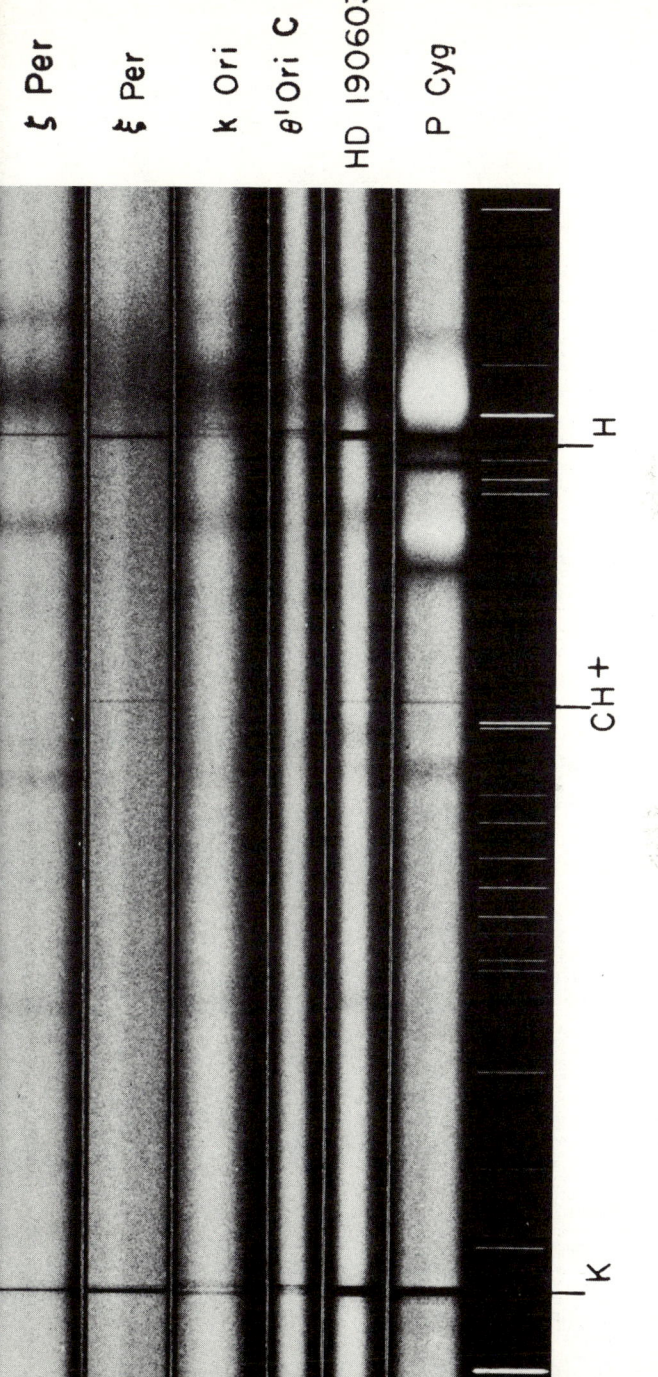

Plate 7 Spectra of distant stars showing positions of interstellar absorption lines with their fine structure, taken with the 100-inch telescope of Mount Wilson Observatory (reproduced by courtesy of the Hale Observatories, California Institute of Technology).

Plate 8 (left)   The Crab Nebula in the constellation of Taurus, remnant of a gigantic explosion of the Chinese Supernova of 1054 A.D., photographed in red light with the 200-inch Hale Telescope at Palomar Mountain (reproduced by courtesy of the Hale Observatories, California Institute of Technology).

Plate 9 (above)   A photograph of the planet Jupiter, in blue light, taken with the 200-inch Hale Telescope at Palomar Mountain. Apart from equatorial bands of ammonia clouds, the photograph shows the Great Red Spot and the Jovian Satellite Ganymede with its shadow. (Reproduced by courtesy of the Hale Observatories, California Institute of Technology.)

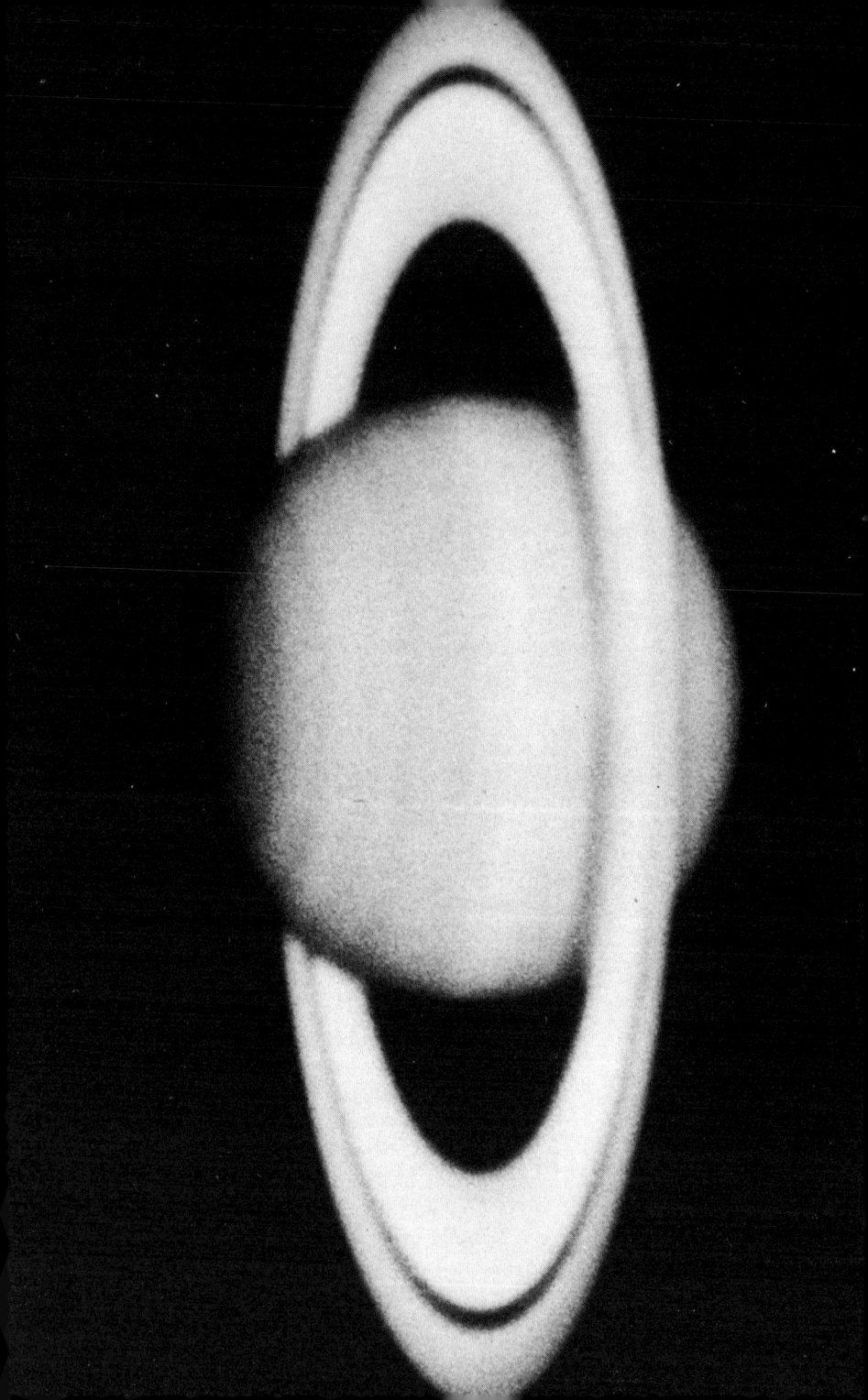

Plate 10 A photograph of the planet Saturn with its rings, taken with the 43-inch reflector at the Observatoire du Pic-du-Midi and reproduced by courtesy of the Director of the Observatory.

Plate 11 A photograph of the Earth taken from an Apollo spacecraft in July 1969. Most of Africa and portions of Europe and Asia can be seen in this spectacular photograph. The spacecraft was more than 270,000 kilometres from Earth. Reproduced by courtesy of NASA.

Plate 12   Man on the lunar surface. This photograph of eerie beauty was taken by U.S. Astronaut Neil Armstrong and shows Astronaut Aldrin standing in what he called the "magnificent desolation" of the lunar landscape. Reflected in his visor are Armstrong with his camera, the American Flag, the television camera and, at right, part of the Lunar Module. Reproduced by courtesy of NASA.

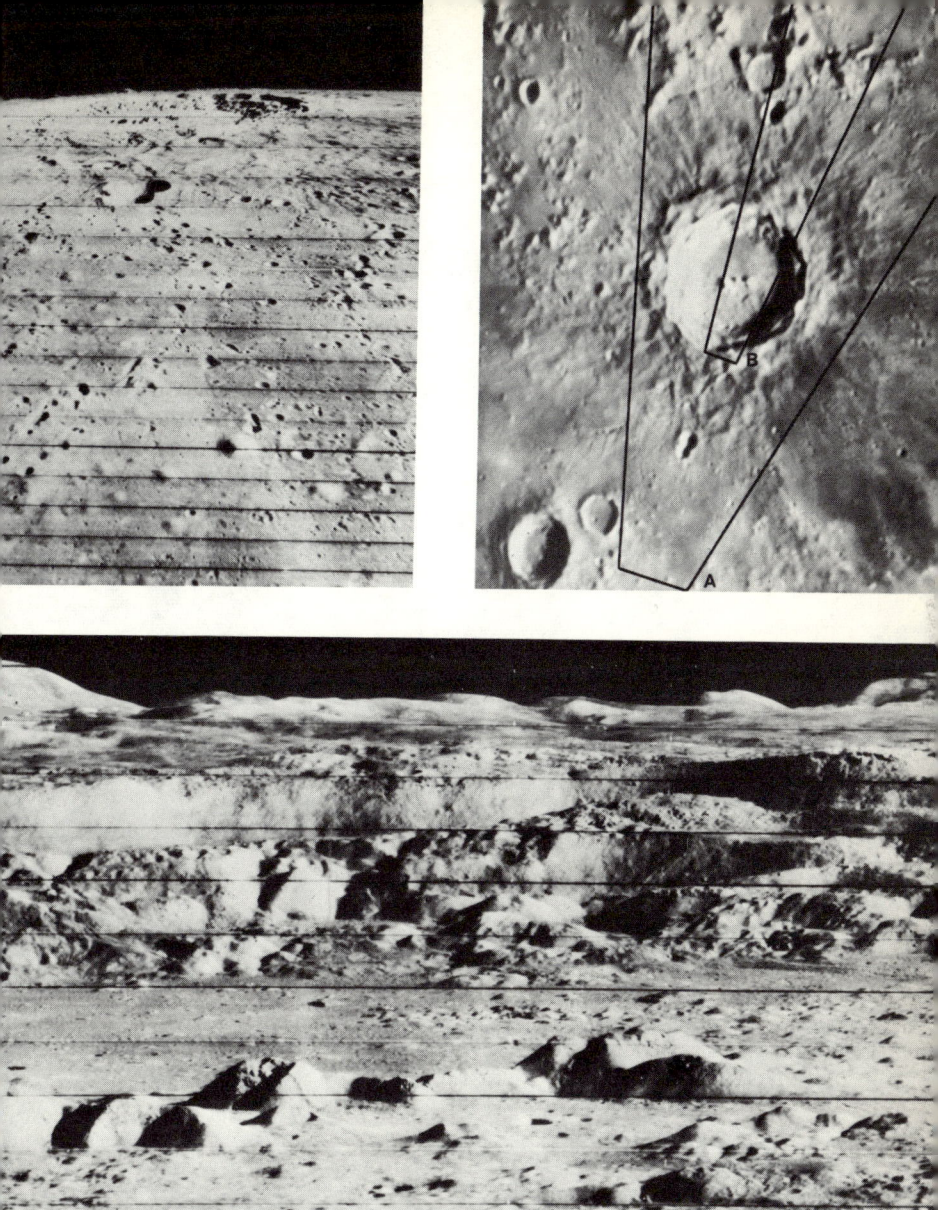

Plate 13 A view of the lunar crater Copernicus, as photographed from the Earth (upper right), in comparison with views of the same formation as recorded by U.S. Lunar Orbiter 2 on 23 November 1966 closer to the target. Photograph on the upper left shows an oblique view of Copernicus (with camera pointed 17° below the horizon) as recorded by the Orbiter's wide-angle camera; while the photograph below shows a high-resolution view of the interior of the crater. (The Orbiter photographs are reproduced by courtesy of NASA.)

Plate 14 (above) Lunar terrain view. This excellent view from the right window of the Apollo-11 Lunar Module on the surface of the Moon shows numerous rocks and craters in the Sea of Tranquillity. Reproduced by courtesy of NASA.

Plate 15 (right) Man's footprint on the Moon. Closeup of one of the footprints left by Apollo-11 astronauts Neil Armstrong or Edwin Aldrin on the surface of the Moon during their historic visit, 20–21 July 1969.

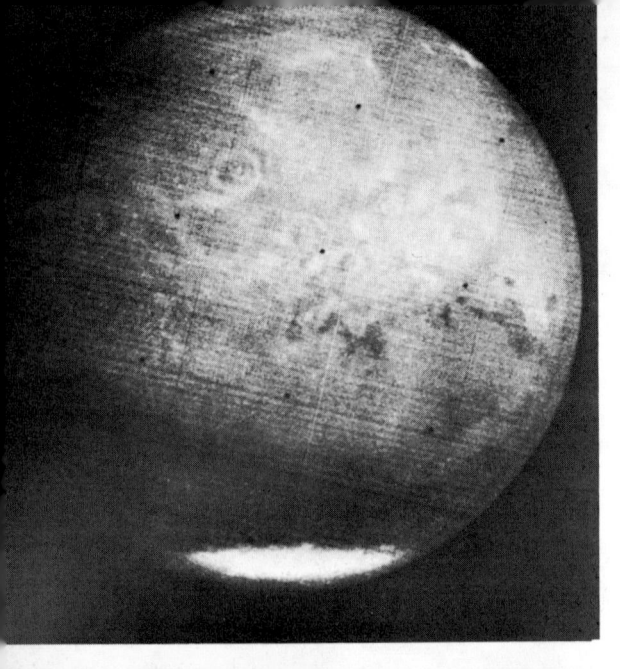

Plate 16 Far-encounter picture of Mars, taken by the Mariner 7 spacecraft on 4 August 1969 from a distance of 471,750 km from the planet (top). Near-encounter picture of Mars, taken by Mariner 6 on 30 July 1969 at the time of its closest approach to the surface of the planet. The size of the field is approximately 690 × 890 km on the Martian surface. This photograph recorded more than 100 individual craters, the largest of which is about 260 km in diameter.

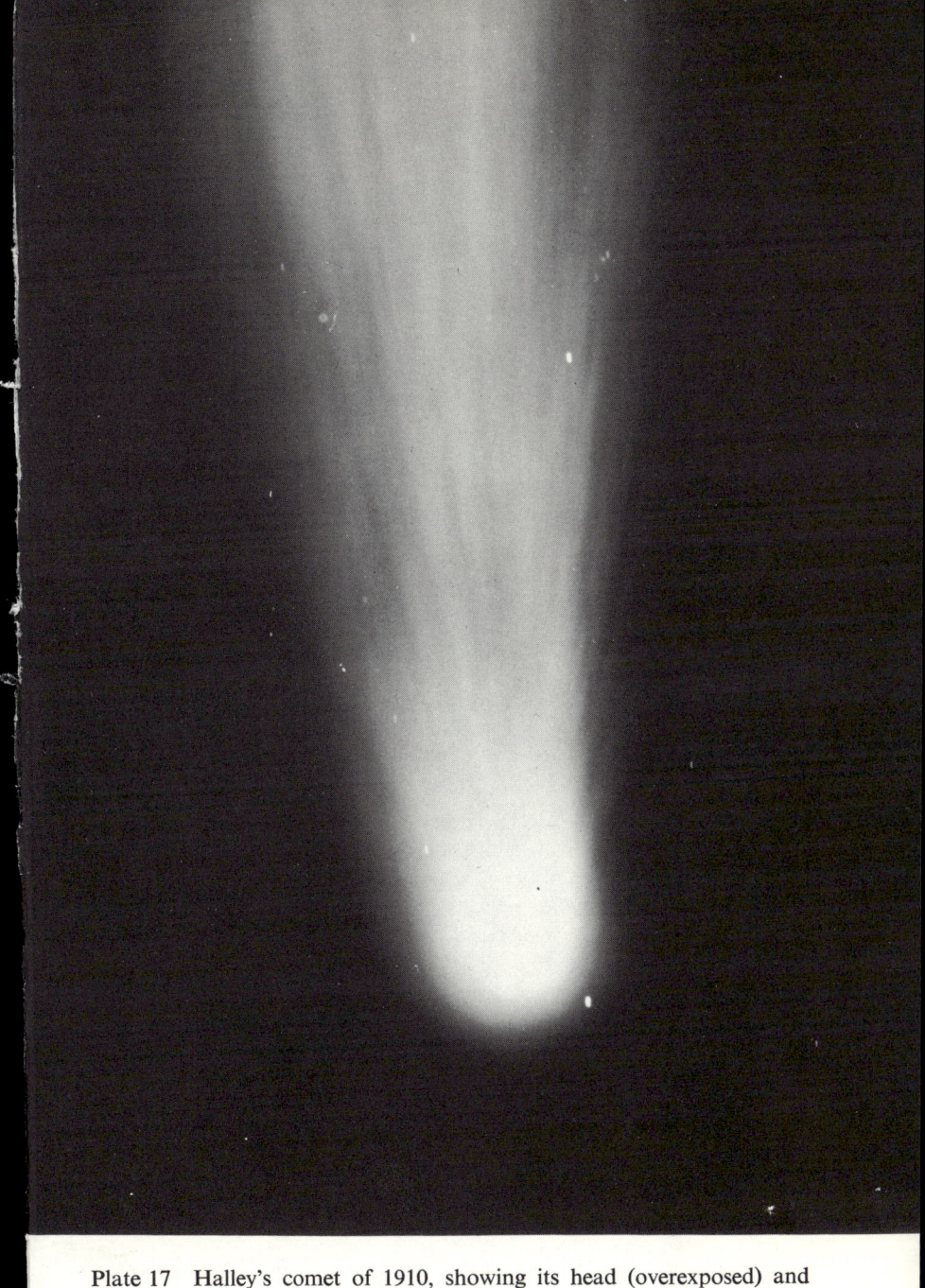

Plate 17 Halley's comet of 1910, showing its head (overexposed) and part of its tail, as photographed with the 60-inch telescope of Mount Wilson Observatory. The trails of the background stars disclose the proper motion of the comet during the exposure (reproduced by courtesy of the Hale Observatories, California Institute of Technology).

Plate 18 (above) The double cluster χ and h Persei, a young association of bright stars in the Perseus arm of our galaxy (approximately 2,300 parsecs away), probably not more than 20 million years in age. Photograph taken by 40-minute exposure with the 60-inch reflector of Mount Wilson Observatory, and reproduced by courtesy of the Hale Observatories, California Institute of Technology.

Plate 19 (right) The globular cluster Messier 3 in the constellation of Canes Venatici, containing one of the oldest known stellar populations in our Universe – as photographed with the 200-inch Hale Telescope at Palomar Mountain (reproduced by courtesy of the Hale Observatories, California Institute of Technology).

Plate 20 The Magellanic Clouds in the southern sky (with the star α Eridani near the lower left corner of the field), photographed with a wide-angle telescope at the Boyden Station of Harvard Observatory, Bloemfontein, South Africa (reproduced by courtesy of the Harvard Observatory).

Plate 21 The Great Nebula in Andromeda with its companions – one of the two neighbouring spiral galaxies at a distance of a little more than two million light years, a close twin of our own galactic system, indicating what we should look like to an external observer in space (reproduced by courtesy of Lick Observatory).

Plate 22 A photograph of the spiral nebula Messier 33 = NGC 598 in the constellation of Triangulum, taken with the 60-inch reflector of Mount Wilson Observatory, and reproduced by the courtesy of the Hale Observatories, California Institute of Technology.

Plate 23 The central part of the Great Nebula in Andromeda with its nucleus and dark lanes surrounding the centre. Photograph taken with the 60-inch reflector of Mount Wilson Observatory and reproduced by courtesy of the Hale Observatories, California Institute of Technology.

Plate 24 (above left) The Andromeda Nebula photographed in blue light, showing giant and super giant stars of Population I in the spiral arms. The hazy patch at the upper left is composed of unresolved Population II stars. (above right) NGC205, companion of the Andromeda Nebula, photographed in yellow light, showing stars of Population II. The brightest stars are red and 100 times fainter than the blue giants of Population I. Photographed with the 200-inch Hale Telescope of Palomar Mountain and reproduced by courtesy of the Hale Observatories, California Institute of Technology.

Plate 25 (right) The spiral nebula M51 (NGC 5194-5) in the constellation of Canes Venatici, photographed with the 100-inch reflector of Mount Wilson Observatory and reproduced by courtesy of the Hale Observatories, California Institute of Technology.

Plate 26 The spiral nebula M81 (NGC 3031) in Ursa Major, photographed with the 200-inch Hale telescope of Palomar Mountain and reproduced by courtesy of the Hale Observatories, California Institute of Technology.

Plate 27 The spiral nebula NGC 4565 in the constellation of Coma Berenices, photographed with the 60-inch reflector of Mount Wilson Observatory and reproduced by courtesy of the Hale Observatories, California Institute of Technology.

Plate 28 (above) A cluster of external galaxies in the constellation of Coma Berenices containing at least 1,000 individual galaxies at a distance close to 20 million parsecs, photographed with the 200-inch Hale Telescope of Palomar Mountain and reproduced by courtesy of the Hale Observatories, California Institute of Technology.

Plate 29 (right) The cluster of external galaxies in the constellation of Hercules (negative print), photographed with the 200-inch Hale Telescope of Palomar Mountain and reproduced by courtesy of F. Zwicky, California Institute of Technology.

5'

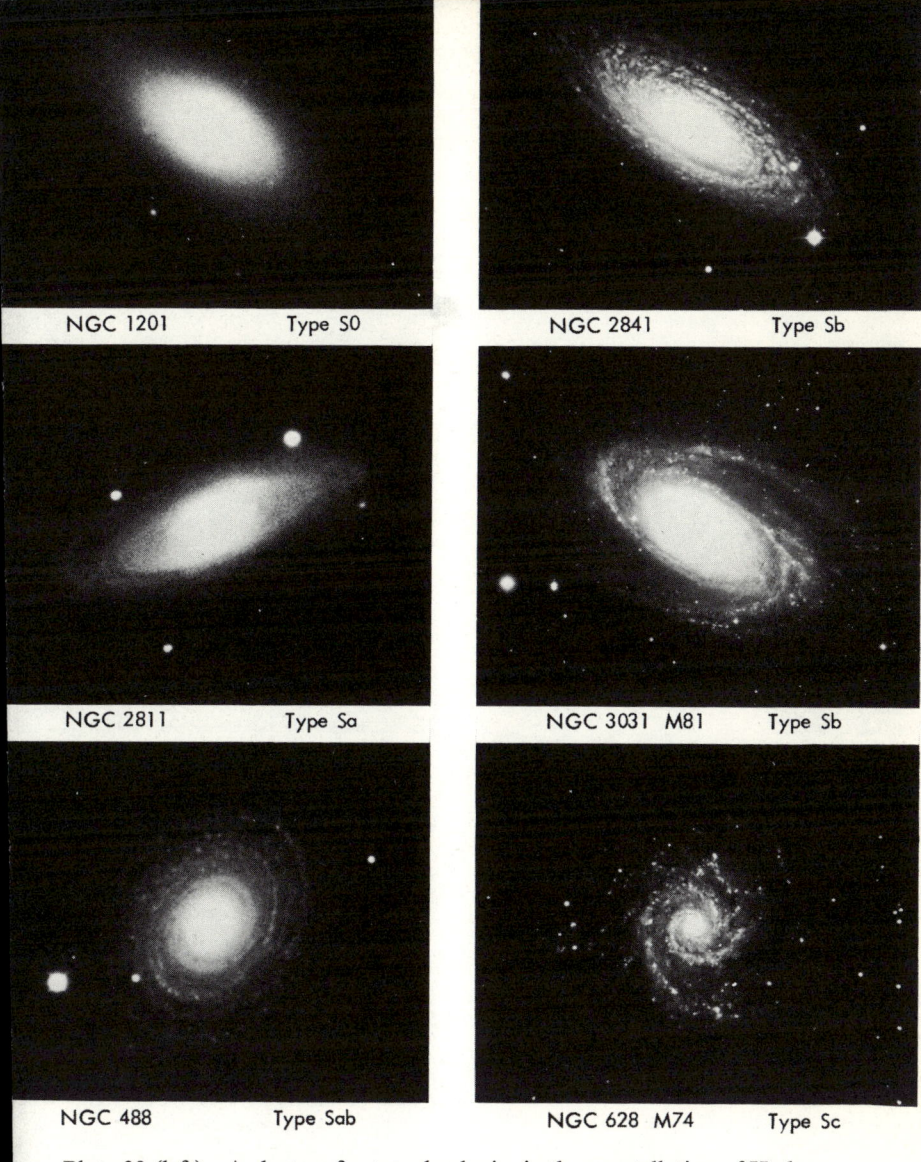

Plate 30 (left)   A cluster of external galaxies in the constellation of Hydra, at a distance of about 600 million parsecs. The faintest galaxies shown on this photograph represent the most distant objects which we can discern at optical frequencies in our Universe. Photograph taken with the 200-inch Hale Telescope at Palomar Mountain and reproduced by courtesy of the Hale Observatories, California Institute of Technology.

Plate 31 (above)   Photographs of different types of external galaxies, documenting the probable evolutionary sequence of such objects from spirals to elliptical galaxies (reproduced by courtesy of the Hale Observatories, California Institute of Technology).

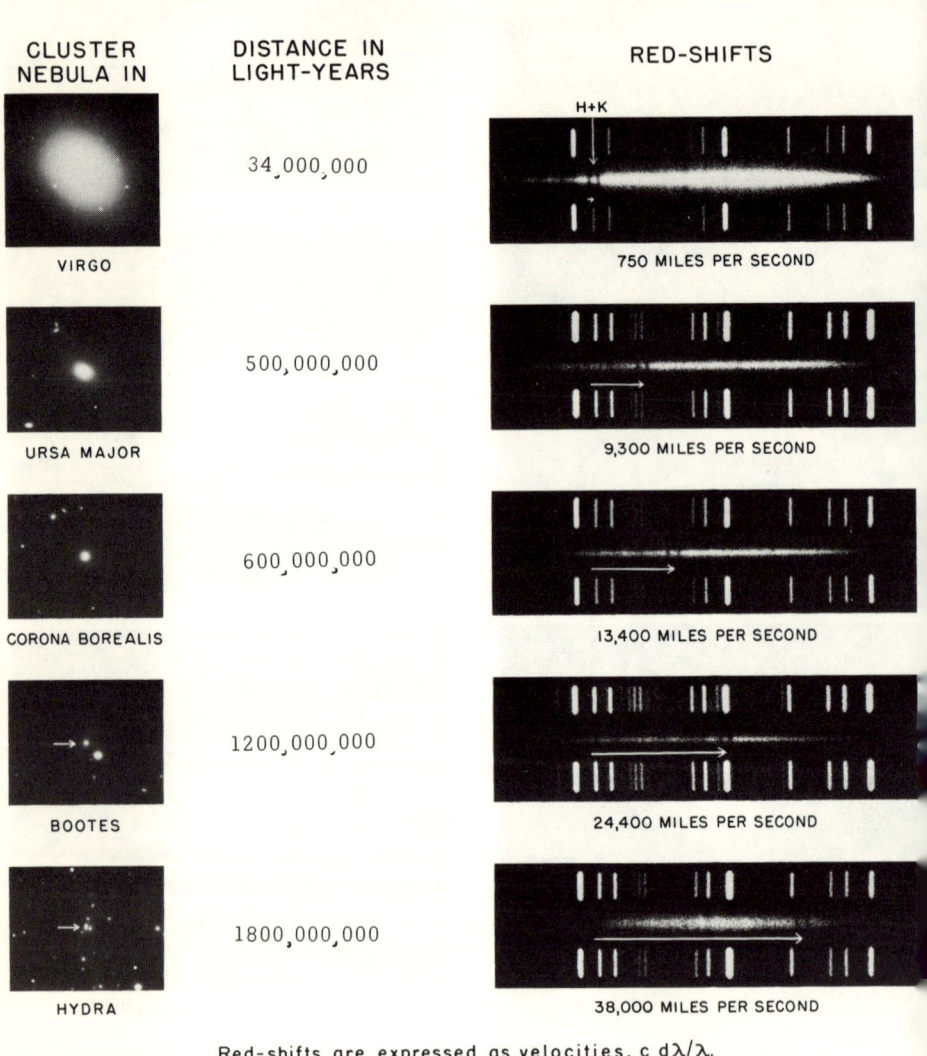

Plate 32 Relation between red-shift and distance for extragalactic nebulae. (Reproduced by courtesy of the Hale Observatories, California Institute of Technology.

successful than the alternatives; and staked the future evolution of life on the Earth upon them.

It is probable that the earliest plant life on the Earth developed in water under anoxygenic (reducing) conditions—before green plants provided (by photosynthesis) for the oxygen now constituting about 20% of our air. Moreover, the chemical composition of the aboriginal seas may likewise have been different from what it is now. Their water probably lacked its present content of sodium, magnesium and calcium—in brief, the present difference between marine and freshwater conditions may have developed only in the course of time.

Hydrocarbons with compositions suggestive of biological origin which are about $3 \cdot 1 \times 10^9$ years old have been found in South Africa; and structures claimed to be bacterial appear to be associated with them. Petrified multi-cellular algae and fungi found in the central part of the Canadian shield are dated at approximately $1 \cdot 9 \times 10^9$ years; and reef limestones of supposed algal origin in the Sahara desert may be almost equally old.

At about this time primitive organisms were slowly developing a very useful substance called 'chlorophyll' to decompose the carbon dioxide present in the air, and using the carbon thus reduced to build up the organic substances necessary for their growth. This possibility of 'feeding on the air' opened up new horizons for the development of organic life; and led eventually to the outgrowth of the present highly developed and complex forms of the plant kingdom. But some of the primitive organisms had adopted another way of development: instead of getting their food directly from the air (of which there was plenty for everyone), they preferred to obtain their carbon compounds in a 'ready-to-use' form as produced by the sedate hard-working plants; and this led, in time, to the rise of the *animal kingdom,* following that of the plants. Since this parasitic way of feeding was considerably simpler, the surplus energy of such organisms went into the development of an *ability to move,* which was indeed necessary to get to the food. Moreover, not being satisfied with a purely vegetable diet, a branch of parasitic creatures began to eat one another; and the necessity of catching the game or of running away from pursuit developed the locomotive ability of carnivorous animals (as well as of some of their victims) to their present high degree.

If the basic mechanism of the evolution of species is the random failure of exact self-reproduction, then we should expect that creative failures of this type (i.e., those which, under favourable conditions, can become progenitors of new species) will occur the less frequently, the more complicated the respective organism. The actual biological evidence we possess seems to bear out this expectation in a very convincing manner. The total number of distinct species of animals living now on our planet exceeds three million. Of these, however, an overwhelming majority are evertebrates at lower levels of the evolutionary ladder. More than 800,000 of these are insects—many species of which are painfully familiar to us in different parts of the world. Fish—the lowest class of vertebrate animals—account for only about 25,000 different species; mammals, for less than half that number; while the primate apes—our closest relatives in the natural kingdom—survive in barely half a dozen species which are all doomed to early extinction.

To return to the beginnings. With advancing time the geological record gradually became more complete as well as more readily legible to the paleontologists; and in the course of the past 500–600 million years—since the beginning of the paleozoic era—it becomes almost uninterrupted in many parts of the world. And it is fascinating to see what it discloses—with all the evolutionary twists and turns that read like a fairy tale.

At the commencement of the paleozoic era some 600 million years ago, we see organisms already as complex as various brachiopods and trilobites dominating the shallow waters of the Cambrian and Ordovician times and venturing to take the first tentative steps in the direction of dry land. With the commencement of the Silurian epoch (some 440 million years ago) evertebrates begin, however, to lose their exclusive position on the evolutionary ladder. The first fish begin to appear in the waters at the same time as green plants gain a foothold on land. True seed plants appear in the subsequent Devonian period (extending over 350–400 million years before our time), together with bony fish, including air-breathing forms, abundant in fresh water. Amphibians evolve from air-breathing fish towards the end of the Devonian period; and the first insects and spiders develop on dry ground.

At the next wave of the fairy wand the scenery changes profoundly; and during the period called Carboniferous (280–350 million years ago) the landscape turns into swamps dominated by giant ferns and vegetation which offer ample homes not only to abundant insects, but also to the amphibians and first reptiles. Petrified forests of luscious vegetation produced, in time, extensive seams of anthracite and hard coal which have given this period its name. The following Permian period (230–280 million years before our time), which closes the Paleozoic era, again saw rapid desiccation of climate, followed by an 'ice-age', which brought to an end the long line of trilobites on the Earth and greatly reduced the life in shallow waters in numbers and species.

On the other hand, the commencement of the Mesozoic era, with the onset of the Triassic period some 220 million years ago, once more brought the efflorescence of life on this planet and ushered in the age of the gigantic reptiles. The subsequent Jurassic and Cretaceous periods saw the development of dinosaurs—the largest living creatures that ever walked on the solid ground of this Earth—to populate the tropical forests and feed on vegetation that was rapidly approaching our contemporary plants and trees. Plane-trees, sycamores, oak, walnut, and palm trees offered food and nesting places to the first birds; and the first small mammals made a furtive appearance as nocturnal creatures in the darkness of night.

A change in global temperature, heralding the advent of a cooler climate towards the end of the Cretaceous period, led to the extinction of dinosaurs and of other large reptiles. The commencement of the Tertiary era in the Paleocene some 60–70 million years ago introduced on this planet the age of the mammals and of modern vegetation differing little from that which we know today. The climate became warmer in Oligocene (26–38 million years before our time), but grew temperate again in Miocene (5 to 25 million years ago). By that time, the terrestrial continents had more or less assumed their present shape, and the grasslands increased markedly in the world at the expense of forested areas. And the tropical forests of the Old World abounded with many kinds of monkeys and apes, some of which became the distant ancestors of the human race which dominates the face of our planet today.

The roots of this story in the Miocene period are indistinct and based on very fragmentary information—though anthropologists claim now that no essential link of the whole evolutionary tree of the human race is any longer missing from our records. The story assumes more definite outlines in the Pliocene period (1·5 million years before our time), concluding the Tertiary era before the onset of the last ice age; and the subsequent history of the human race falls within the Quaternary period.

Before concluding this chapter on the development of life on Earth, in which our race has played such an important part, let us try to explain some of the facts, inherent in our preceding outline, which preceded the emergence of man as the central figure of our narrative. The way in which the previous history of life can be provided with an absolute scale of time was explained in Chapter V–2; the clocks which measure this time are atoms of radioactive elements disintegrating spontaneously at a known rate; and the proportion of the decay products to their mother substances represents the hand on this cosmic clock which never needs repairing, and which we have learned to read of late by reliable laboratory methods with considerable accuracy. How do we know, however, anything about the climate and temperature which prevailed at different geological periods of the past? For more recent times we can infer this from the occurrence of fossil animals or plants still living today, whose thermal habits and preferences we know from our own observations. But even for time intervals too great to leave any direct link of this type, methods exist which enable us to measure the paleo-temperatures of remote geological eras—especially those of the seas—almost as well as if we could place a thermometer in their waters and read its scale.

For instance, it has been established by biological experiments with several living species of crustacea that the rate at which different isotopes of calcium are absorbed in their shells depends on the temperature of the water in which these animals grow their shells; and their proportion can be calibrated against ambient temperature. Now if we assume—reasonably enough—that these proportions remain unaltered throughout the ages for the same species (and some of them possess distinguishable ancestors in very remote geological epochs), modern determinations of the isotopic composition of the fossilized shells permit us to ascertain the mean temperature of the waters in which these extinct creatures have grown up during their lifetime. In this way, modern methods of nuclear physics once more come to our aid in offering important clues by which we can decipher the stony records engraved in the book of life on our Earth.

Before we introduce our human ancestors to the stage of our narrative, let us cast a retrospective glance at the past course of the evolution of life on the Earth accomplished in the 2–3 thousand million years before the onset of the last ice-age and the commencement of the Quaternary era. This course must appear to us like that of a river whose sources are beyond our view, and which slowly gathers strength while it meanders through ever-changing landscapes and climates. Sometimes it enters rapids so fast as to create an impression that life on the Earth has changed almost suddenly from one type to another—an impression which earlier generations of paleontologists used to explain by catastrophic upheavals that may now and then have played havoc with the further evolution of the preceding forms of life.

Whether they were actual interruptions in the evolution of species caused by catastrophic events that suddenly changed conditions for life over large areas of the Earth's surface; or whether changes (such as the disappearance of luscious vegetation at the end of the Carboniferous period, or the extinction of the dinosaurs towards the close of the Cretaceous epoch) occurred more gradually and appear sudden only when seen from a distant perspective, constitutes a problem which will have to be elucidated by paleontologists. However, the astronomer may observe that sudden cosmic events which would have exerted far-reaching influence on life on the Earth not only could, but probably did, occur in the past. By this we do not necessarily mean such slow-acting phenomena as secular changes in elements of the orbit of the Earth around the Sun, or the gradual increase in solar luminosity; nor even mountain-building periods or ice-ages on the Earth which occurred repeatedly in the course of the long geological past of our planet. But consider an event as sudden and unexpected as the impact of a large meteorite on the Earth—of the size that produced (see Chapter VII) the craters that we still see on the face of the Moon in large numbers.

The impact of a cosmic body—a stray asteroid, a meteorite or a comet like those which still wander through space today, capable of producing craters 100–200 km in size—would have released an amount of energy between 10^{29} and 10^{30} ergs. The face of the Moon bears mute witness to more than a hundred such events which it must have experienced in the past 4½ aeons of time; and since the Earth has a surface 16 times as large as that of the Moon, there can be no doubt that our Earth must have suffered many similar hits in the past; and if its surface is not as greatly pockmarked by them as is the face of the Moon, we have to thank erosion by our air and water.

Our atmosphere can offer next to no protection against actual impacts of this magnitude; but jointly with water it can erase the surface scars caused by such cosmic injuries so rapidly and so well that no trace of them remains apparent to anyone but a trained investigator after a lapse of time which is very short in comparison with the average time-interval to be expected between such events. On the Moon—because of a well-nigh complete absence of any air or water—its surface acts as a cumulative scoreboard for this celestial target-practice. It discloses to us the full intensity which such bombardment must have attained in the past; and of which the surface of our Earth must have been a similar recipient. On the Moon, the result of each such impact was the formation of a crater on the ground; but what would it have been on the Earth?

In order to attempt an answer, consider the impact of a cosmic intruder with a kinetic energy of (say) 10^{30} ergs—such as, on the Moon, would produce a crater some 100 km in diameter. On the Earth, however, three-fifths of the surface is now covered with oceans—and this fraction may have been even larger in the past. Therefore, the majority of cosmic impacts on the Earth must have been scored in deep water rather than on solid ground; and the consequences of such an event would be much more dramatic than anything that ever occurred on the Moon. The ocean floor would have been largely cushioned by water from direct mechanical effects of the impact. But the tidal waves generated by such an event would have flooded vast areas of low-lying shallow ocean shores; and the destruction of life—both plant and animal—caused both by its mechanical effects as well as by injecting salinity into inland fresh waters would have been enormous. If such an event were to occur today in the Atlantic, not only would countries like the Netherlands be completely wiped out from the face of the Earth, but large parts of Britain, France and Germany would suffer damage so extensive that life in them would never be the same;

and the same would be true of large areas adjacent to the East coast of North America.

And more than that; for some of the effects of such a catastrophic event could be felt all over the world for a long time. The partition of the energy of an impinging meteorite is such that about half of the original kinetic energy of the intruder should be converted into heat. Of the amount of 10^{29} ergs of kinetic energy which we ascribed to our hypothetical meteorite, about a half would be converted into heat equivalent to approximately 10^{21} calories, capable of vaporizing some 10,000 cubic kilometres of sea-water of a total mass of 10^{19} grams. The total mass of the terrestrial atmosphere is close to 5×10^{21} grams (cf. Chapter V–2), and of this about one per cent or less is water vapour. Therefore, an injection of 10^{19} grams of water by meteoritic infall could easily double—at least temporarily—the total atmospheric water content. An increase in the total air mass arising in this way would be marginal. But in spite of its relatively small contribution to the total mass of the atmosphere, water vapour, by its heavy absorption of the infrared thermal radiation of the terrestrial surface, makes an important contribution to the atmospheric 'greenhouse effect' which controls the global temperature of the Earth.

Increased moisture would probably lead also to the formation of more complete global cloud cover, and thus to an increase of the mean terrestrial 'albedo' which would back-scatter more of the illuminating sunlight and thus prevent it from warming-up the surface. If the thermal equilibrium of our atmosphere happens to be precariously balanced near instability at the time of a major meteoritic impact it is possible that such an event could alter the global climate of the Earth for thousands, or even millions, of years; and affect irreversibly the evolution of its fauna and flora. Since the occurrence of such events must be regarded as fairly probable in the light of independent astronomical (mainly lunar) evidence, repeated catastrophic interventions which may—now and then—have clipped the growth of the tree of life are a distinct possibility.

Another cosmic phenomenon which may have suddenly influenced the global climate of the Earth at times is cometary impacts. Comets of masses comparable with those of the solid asteroids are, in fact, more frequent now in space than the latter; and may have been even more so in the past. Now it is known (*cf.* Chapter IX) that cometary heads—the only part of their anatomy which really matters in the case of collision with as small a cosmic body as the terrestrial globe—consist of a loose conglomeration of frozen hydro-carbons which during collision would be rapidly converted into gas even before the object could strike the solid surface. The mass of an average cometary head is estimated to be between 10^{17}–10^{18} grams—i.e., a few hundredths of a per cent of that of the terrestrial atmosphere—so that the mass of air above our heads would again be barely altered by such an event.

However, some hydro-carbons which would thus be injected into our air possess optical properties which could affect a sensitive climatic balance of the solid ground beneath. If the Earth suffered in the past any collisions with comets of substantially large masses (10^{19}–10^{20}g), the consequences of such events could have been even more disastrous to our climate. Such comets are very rare in interplanetary space today; but in the past $4\frac{1}{2}$ aeons—who knows? Thus it is at least possible that, throughout the long astronomical past of our planet, its global climate may have undergone not only gradual alterations following in the wake of changes in the elements of the terrestrial orbit around the Sun (which would cause fluctuations in the amount of solar heat we receive on the Earth), but also suddenly by transient cosmic events of finite probability—like meteoritic or cometary impacts—with consequences which could appear catastrophic in geological perspective. And perhaps the petrified log-book of the rock strata as read by geologists in different parts of the world contains evidence that this has actually happened—not once, but several times during the long astronomical past of our mother planet.

VI–1: The Evolution of Man on the Earth

If we pause to look back at the growth of the tree of life and the diverse ramifications of its branches up to mid-Tertiary times, as its shape has been reconstructed by the paleontologists so far, we cannot escape the impression that the past evolution of life on the Earth appears to represent an essentially *haphazard* process, with little or no indication of any grand design. Indeed, life—both animal and plant—seems to have meandered throughout the ages without much purpose, responding opportunistically to the changes of climate and setting, which themselves have been under the control of physical processes that could almost be described as accidental. However, this complex situation contains one element which in the most recent stages of the evolution of life turned out to prove its guiding spirit: namely, the seat of the higher organization of a living body, called the *nervous system,* representing the organs of memory and control. The seed of this development was sown a long time in the past—for the rudiments of the nervous system can be traced to evertebrates whose ancestors had already appeared on the Earth in the early Paleozoic times some 600 million years ago; but the seed did not begin to develop its latent possibilities more fully till the Quaternary era, with the advent of *man.*

This event—so fraught with portent for the future history of the Earth, and indeed of the Solar System—occurred almost through the back door of the main evolutionary process; and none of the mastodons or sequoia trees of the late Tertiary period had any inkling of what was in store for them and the world with the emergence of that particular hairy ape from the shadows of the Miocene forests. For such evidence as we possess shows that distant ancestors of modern men were then living lives akin to those of primate apes which still survive in small parts of our world (though none of those now living are more than very distant cousins of ours, deriving common ancestry from forms that developed in the Tertiary era). They did not descend to the ground to walk erect till about a million to half a million years ago.

As is suggested by the names of Australopithecus, Sinanthropus, or the Javanese Pithecanthropus erectus—given by anthropologists to various forms of primitive men living between 500,000 and 700,000 years ago—the region where man originated was the tropical belt of south-east Asia and the adjacent parts of its temperate belt. No remnants of men as primitive as these earliest known representatives of the human race have been found in those parts of the world which we now call Europe or America—south-east Asia and the adjacent parts of Africa and Australia were the real cradle of our race on this planet for hundreds of thousands of years. From the scarcity of any traces or remnants of the species (not a single skeleton of them came down to us intact) we surmise, moreover, that these early men were relatively rare creatures.

However—no matter how small his numbers—the primitive man who descended from the trees to walk on solid ground some half a million years before our time already carried within him the essential instrument of his future ascendancy: namely, the human brain. The cranial capacity of the Pithecanthropus erectus of half a million years ago was already equal to some 1100 ccm (compared with an average of 500 ccm for present-day gorillas, or 370 ccm for the chimpanzee); and it has continued to grow (with small detours) ever since. Neanderthal man, whose ancestors drifted into Europe from the East during the inter-glacial periods of the last 100,000 years, already possessed a brain of 1,300 ccm in volume; and Cromagnon man—a race which populated western Europe between the last 10,000 and 30,000 years, and left behind the wonderful paintings of contemporary wildlife in the Altamira and Lascaux caves—already possessed a cranial capacity of 1,600 ccm, which is actually more than the average for men who have lived since.*

Between 500,000 and 100,000 years before our time (a period to which anthropologists generally refer as the 'Lower Paleolithic'), thanks to the development of his brain, the primitive man of the genus Homo sapiens was already beginning to differ significantly and unmistakably from any animal forms that shared with him life on Earth. He started to develop tools—first from stone, and later from bones—to help him overcome the limitations of his anatomy. He mastered the use of fire. And—perhaps the most remarkable fact, suggestive of the development of memory—he began to *bury his dead*. The reverence which this reflects is the first sign of *spiritual life* and was totally alien to all instincts of creatures living before that time.

Paleolithic man was still a rare sight on the terrestrial landscape; and to facilitate his survival, he developed a way of life in packs—those distant forerunners of later tribes and modern nations. In spite of their relatively small numbers men continued, however, to proliferate and gradually drift into all parts of the world. North Africa and such parts of Europe from which life was not driven out by recurrent ice ages were populated (or at least visited) by

---

*Probably because the Cromagnon man was larger and heavier than the present Homo sapiens.

men already during the Paleolithic times. When the Bering Straits separating northern Asia from Alaska became temporarily ice-bound, permitting foot traffic across, primitive men from eastern Asia gradually drifted into the American continent; and in the course of several thousand years penetrated it from northern Alaska to southern Patagonia. As the umbilical cord of ice connecting Asia with America melted with the advance of the warmer climate, these first Americans became stranded in the New World; but their numbers never became as large as the population of their parent Eurasia. Anthropologists conclude that, by the time of Columbus, the territory of the present United States and Canada was a home to scattered Indian tribes of a total population of no more than half a million.

With the recession of the last ice period in the northern hemisphere some 10,000 years ago, we arrive at last at the commencement of the 'modern' age. The record of human fortunes and achievements during this time becomes almost uninterrupted; and its principal scene became the shores of the Eastern Mediterranean, with the adjacent lands of the Near East. It is easy to see why this should have been the case. While most parts of Europe were still recuperating biologically from the privations of the last glacial period—and the retreating glaciers gave way to swamps followed by dense forests—the Mediterranean basin enjoyed a relatively mellow climate, favourable to agriculture and conducive to the development of a higher form of life. The African shores of the Mediterranean and the Sahara were not the deserts they later became with the gradual progress of climatic desiccation. The need to feed populations of increasing size almost predestined the first civilizations worthy of that name to develop in the valleys of the rivers which provided ample supplies of water for agriculture: in particular, along the river Nile in western Egypt, and in the valley of the Euphrates and the Tigris in Mesopotamia; to which we should probably add the Indus valley in eastern Kashmir. These were the first cradles of human civilization, the indigenous sources of which can be traced to a time 3,000 to 4,000 years before the birth of Christ.

The principal cause underlying the development of any civilization—old or new—is the requirement that at least a part of the community in question should be freed from perpetual struggle to eke out a bare living, and enjoy a certain amount of leisure to enable them to turn their minds to tasks and problems other than those necessary for day-to-day survival. In ancient Egypt, just as in Mesopotamia or the Indus valley, this leisure was the gift of the great rivers to the populations settled on their banks—of the water and silt carried in their streams which brought fertility to the land; and the principal dividend of this gift in all three different parts of the world proved to be the discovery and development of *writing*. With the discovery of writing, speech ceased to be the only form of human communication. The hieroglyphic signs of the ancient Egyptians, the cuneiform script used in the land of Sumer and Akkad, and the proto-Indian symbols (as yet undeciphered) found in Mohenjo-daro were invented at about the same time and independently of each other, but for the same purpose: namely, to supersede oral tradition by written records with a far greater degree of permanence; and the history of mankind—as distinct from its pre-history during which archaeology and anthropology are our only guides—dates back to that time. The development of writing and information storage, from the carvings in stone and sun-baked clay tablets to records written down on papyrus, parchment, or paper to the magnetic tapes of modern computers, forms a continuous story which is still far from having attained a final stage; and the entire future development of human civilization will be intimately connected with its continuation.

What kind of human civilization is reflected in the oldest extant records carved out in stone or clay at the dawn of written history of mankind? When the deciphering of ancient scripts raised the curtain on the first act of this story, people were still living in the Neolithic age, when the principal tool of man still remained the stone. However, the days of nomadic hunters or shepherds were long gone. In the valleys of great rivers people settled down to cultivation of the land with the aid of domestic animals already tamed for this purpose by their distant ancestors. Moreover, an adequate supply of food, provided by agriculture which mastered the methods of husbanding a seasonal water supply by irrigation, made it possible to support a population which became very large in comparison with the size of the tribes of the nomadic past. As a result, with the commencement of the fourth millenium B.C. we see the emergence of the first large units of human population called 'kingdoms', ruled absolutely by a small oligarchy headed by a 'king' for whom an early alliance with the priesthood safeguarded the support of the local gods.

The state of civilization attained under some of these early kingdoms—especially in Egypt or Mesopotamia—is truly astonishing. The mastery of work in stone in the last centuries of the Neolithic era reached heights—both technological as well as artistic—which evoke our admiration after the lapse of almost fifty centuries; and the great pyramids built at the time of the fourth dynasty of the Egyptian 'Old Kingdom' (around 2900 B.C.) to preserve for posterity the mummies of its ruling pharaohs are remarkable accomplishments for people who lacked any metal tools and whose hands were aided by mechanical contrivances of only the most rudimentary kind. With these they managed (apparently within not more than 20–30 years) to erect pyramidal stone structures as tall as the spires of the largest medieval cathedrals, and consisting of some million blocks of stone so large (and so precisely cut) that if they were lined up with each other they would form a row extending from New York to San Francisco, and back again across the Rockies to Denver!

The Egyptian pyramids represent the final apotheosis of the Stone Age, which had commenced hundreds of thousands of years before, when Paleolithic man began to sharpen his rudimentary flint tools. They are monuments which have survived the advent of the age of bronze and, later, that of iron—monuments which were already old when Alexander the Great, Julius Caesar, or Napoleon Bonaparte stood in front of them to gasp in awe. Less spectacular, but no less important developments of that time for the future of the human race, were the development of mining, which gradually made the bowels of the Earth surrender to man their mineral wealth; and the commencement of coastal seafaring which supplemented caravan transport on land. And—most important of all for the future of the human race—the extant records of the closing centuries of the Stone Age already contain the seeds of future development of sciences—medicine in Egypt, mathematics and astronomy in Mesopotamia—which, in due course, were not only to completely transform the material aspects of human life on the Earth, but also disclose our true position in the Universe.

These early sciences bore as yet little resemblance to the severe intellectual disciplines which they became at later stages of their developments; but they contained empirical elements of truth like seeds which required centuries and millenia to hatch and bear fruit. The early scientific efforts invariably grew out of a need to satisfy certain practical requirements—such as setting the bones of an injured man or trepanning his skull; mathematics to facilitate the administration of property or collection of taxes; astronomy to maintain the calendar and for setting the dates at which local deities could be most successfully propitiated. Yet it was almost inevitable that such knowledge, cultivated for centuries by priests and scribes whose task was not only to apply it but also to teach it to others, was bound in the end to be studied for its own sake; and this opened the road to the growth of science as we know it today.

CHAPTER VII

Our Nearest Celestial Neighbour—The Moon

IN THE last chapter we introduced our Earth as an astronomical body, and gave an account of its principal physical properties. But the Earth is not alone in space. In its relative proximity, at a mean distance of only some 60 terrestrial radii, we find its faithful attendant and our nearest celestial neighbour—the Moon —which still waits to be brought to the scene. We wish to do so now, for several reasons. First, because the Moon interacts with our Earth gravitationally and forms with it a dynamical couple— a tiny 'double star'—influencing the motion of our planet through space, as well as about its centre of mass—including its axial rotation. The present length of our terrestrial day and its secular changes throughout the past are largely governed by the presence of the Moon; and so is the wobbling of the terrestrial axis of rotation in space which gives rise to the 'precession of equinoxes'.

The Moon is also the 'guardian of antiquities' in the solar system—a role for which, as we shall see, our satellite is particularly suited by its physical properties. In the preceding chapter we mentioned that the earliest part of the history of our Earth is largely shrouded in mystery, as no direct testimony in the form of rocks has survived on it from the first billion years of its existence; and the early evolution of our atmosphere and oceans likewise remains largely subject to guesswork. On the other hand, the stony face of the Moon—undisturbed by water, and unprotected by any atmosphere—contains an uninterrupted record of all the major events which have taken place on its surface since the time of its formation. Surface features have now been identified on the Moon which have thrown light on the initial 'dark aeon' in the history of the Earth-Moon system, and provided information of unique value to the astronomer and geophysicist alike.

Last—and most important for us at the present time—the

proximity of our satellite has destined it to become the first celestial body (other than the Earth) to become at least a temporary host to life. On 24 December 1968, three American astronauts (William Anders, Frank Borman and James Lovell), who on 21 December disengaged themselves from the gravitational field of the Earth, reached in their spacecraft (Apollo 8) the proximity of the Moon and allowed themselves to be gravitationally attached to the Moon for almost twenty hours. While in orbit around the Moon, these intrepid men could have considered themselves 'lunar' in the same sense as the Earth-circling astronauts remain terrestrial. In May 1969—barely five months later—another three Americans manning the Apollo 10 spacecraft managed to spend a total of some 120 man-hours in the lunar orbit—a feat which earned its crew of Eugene Cernan, Thomas Stafford and John Young the right to claim citizenship of the Moon at least by temporary naturalization.

None of these six men who came from the Earth to pay close calls on the Moon up to the first half of 1969 descended on to its surface. The first actual descent on to this surface was accomplished on 20 July 1969—an even more memorable date for all times—when two American astronauts of Apollo 11 mission—Neil Armstrong, and Edwin Aldrin—set foot on the vast plains of the lunar Mare Tranquillitatis (see Plate 12), while the third—Michael Collins—piloted around the Moon the spacecraft in which all three would eventually return to Earth. Their feat was repeated only four months later by Alan Bean, Charles Conrad and Richard Gordon of the Apollo 12 mission, who on 19 November landed with equal success in the central parts of Oceanus Procellarum.

As ill luck would have it, no manned landings took place on the Moon throughout 1970; but in 1971 this achievement was accomplished twice more. Alan B. Shepard and Edgar D. Mitchell of Apollo 14 mission landed on 31 January near the Fra Mauro crater in the Oceanus Procellarum while Stuart A. Roosa—the third member of the team—stood by in the mission's command module in orbit; and on 31 July the Apollo 15 astronauts David Scott and James Irwin (backed up by Alfred Worden in orbit) planted human foot near the Hadley Rille in the shadow of the lunar Apennines. Thus up to the end of 1971, astronauts of the Apollo 8–15 missions spent a total of 29 days in lunar captivity; of which over 300 man-hours were actually spent on its surface.

Material traffic in the Earth-Moon system is nothing new in the world; for lunar debris must have fallen on the Earth from time to time in the past. As we shall detail later in this chapter (VII–2), the impact of every major meteorite on the bare surface of the Moon is bound to cause a 'kick-off' and spill-over of relatively large amounts of lunar rocks into space. Most of these will eventually be swept up by the broom of terrestrial attraction on to the Earth, where they may reappear in various guises. While the Earth-bound transport from the Moon can thus be kept alive by intermittent natural processes, the traffic in the opposite direction is much more difficult to accomplish—not only because of the six times greater terrestrial gravity and thus higher velocity of escape, but mainly because of the presence of our overprotective atmosphere, whose resistance makes the escape of solid material beyond the gravitational confines of the Earth virtually impossible by the natural processes already mentioned. It was not till the advent of man with all his technological ingenuity that this age-old situation at last began to change. And in December 1968, man of the genus *Homo sapiens*—a species born and developed on our planet—left his terrestrial cradle to take the first steps towards his proliferation in the solar system.

Then, in 1969, the first men who landed on the Moon brought back with them not only a first-hand knowledge of the environmental conditions prevailing on the surface of our satellite, but also invaluable samples of lunar rocks for an analysis in our laboratories. Most of these proved to be older than anything we have found on the Earth so far, and to mirror in their structure an echo of events which happened so long ago that nothing on the Earth—man, animal, or stone—remembers them any more. In this chapter we shall attempt to bring home to the reader some of the principal results derived from study of the Moon, as well as to outline the vistas which are opening up to us—figuratively as well as literally—when we use our Moon as a base for exploration of the Universe around us in space and time.

VII–1: Some Facts and Figures

To the astronomer in particular—and not only to him—the Moon has been a friend of long standing; and at least a rudimentary knowledge of its motion goes very far back in the history of mankind on this planet; for since prehistoric times the waxing and waning of the lunar phases and the light changes accompanying them provided the first astronomical basis for the reckoning of time. Whenever we go sufficiently far back in the history of almost any primitive civilization, we invariably find it dependent on the lunar, rather than the solar, calendar: the month became a unit of time long before the concept of the year emerged from accumulating observations; and the Moon as the graceful carrier of this knowledge thus gained entrance, as a female deity, to the pantheons of most ancient nations—the semitic goddess Ishtar, Tanit of Salammbo, or the nimble-footed Artemis of the Greeks, all bear witness to its cult.

The orbit of the Moon around the Earth is approximately an ellipse (distorted somewhat by the attraction of the Sun), inclined by a little more than 5° to the ecliptic. The mean period of revolution of the Moon is equal to 27 days, 7 hours, 43 minutes and 11·5 seconds before the Moon returns to the same place in the sky (the so-called 'sidereal month'); though (because the Moon shares in our annual revolution around the Sun) it takes our satellite 29 days, 5 hours, 5 minutes and 35·8 seconds before it will attain the same phase (the 'synodic month').

How far is it to the Moon? The size of the relative lunar orbit around the Earth was already known approximately to the ancient Greeks (from the relative durations of different phases of lunar eclipses) to be equal to about sixty times the terrestrial radius. More recently, astronomers have determined this distance much more accurately by triangulation (and, still more recently, from the measured time-lag of radar echoes reflected from the Moon). The results show that the Earth-Moon distance varies in the course of each month between 356,000 and 407,000 kms. The mean distance amounts to 384,400 kms, and is equal to 60·267 times the Earth's equatorial radius, or 0·00257 times the mean distance separating us from the Sun. It represents less than one per cent of the distance separating us from our other two nearest celestial neighbours—the planets Venus and Mars—at the time of their closest approach. Many a terrestrial traveller has probably averaged a greater mileage by car during his lifetime than would be involved in a round trip to the Moon! Light traverses this distance in 1·28 of a second; and an average spacecraft will traverse it in 65–70 hours. The mean velocity of the Moon in its orbit around the Earth averages 3,681 kms per hour, or about 1,023 m/sec—corresponding to a mean angular velocity in the sky as seen by us from the Earth of about 33 minutes of arc per hour (which is just a little greater than the apparent diameter of the Moon itself).

The mean apparent diameter of the lunar disc in the sky amounts to just over half a degree which at the mean lunar distance of 384,000 kms corresponds to a radius of an essentially spherical globe of 3,476 kms in diameter. The Moon is, therefore, about one quarter of the Earth in size; and so far from it that if we were to regard the Earth as a sphere 10 cms across (i.e., the size of a grapefruit), relatively to it the Moon would appear like a tangerine not quite $3\frac{1}{2}$ cm in size, revolving around us at a mean distance of some three metres.

We may add that, just as the Earth rotates around its axis once each sidereal day (equal to $23^h\ 56^m\ 4.09^{sec}$ of mean time), the Moon rotates about an axis inclined a little ($1°32'$) to its orbital plane as well, in the direction in which it revolves, and with exactly the same period—thus showing us each month always the same face, or almost so; for 'libration' of the apparent lunar disc (due to the fact that the Moon revolves around us in an eccentric orbit, inclined to the ecliptic) enables us sometimes to see more behind the hump of one limb of the Moon, and sometimes more behind the other. No less than 59% of the entire lunar globe can be seen from Earth at one time or another; only 41% remains permanently invisible to all but the lunar astronauts, while an equal area is always visible; the remaining 18% is alternately visible and invisible.

The *mass* of the Moon—like that of any other celestial body—can be determined only by the effects of its attraction on another body of known properties. In the case of the Moon, this was first our Earth, and more recently, fly-by or impinging spacecraft. As such spacecraft approach the Moon, the lunar attraction is bound gradually to accelerate their motion; and accurate tracking of such accelerations led recently to a determination that the Earth's mass bears a ratio of 81.302 to that of the Moon. Since, moreover (cf. Chapter V–1) the mass of the Earth is known to be equal to 5.978×10^{27}g, the mass of the Moon results as 7.353×10^{25}g.

This mass of over 73 trillion tons may loom large by terrestrial standards; but on cosmic scales it constitutes a relatively tiny speck. And neither is the *mean density* of the lunar globe at all unusual; for dividing the mass just found by the lunar volume of $2 \cdot 199 \times 10^{25} cm^3$, we find its mean density to be $3 \cdot 34$ g/cm^3—i.e., only a little more than the density of common granitic rocks of the Earth's crust ($2 \cdot 78$ g/cm^3), and considerably less than the mean density of the terrestrial globe ($5 \cdot 52$ g/cm^3). The gravitational acceleration on the lunar surface is, therefore, only some 162 cm/sec^2 (i.e., less than one-sixth of the terrestrial one); and the velocity of escape from the lunar gravitational field is close to $2 \cdot 38$ km/sec —in comparison with its terrestrial value of $11 \cdot 2$ km/sec.

This much-reduced gravity prevailing on the lunar surface is the reason why the Apollo astronauts were able to swing their heavy back-packs containing the life-support systems with relative ease; and why the periods of close lunar orbiting satellites ($3\frac{1}{2}$–4 hours) are so much longer than those of comparable circum-terrestrial spacecraft (2 hours and less). However, low gravity entails also some disadvantages. Although much less muscular work is required on the Moon to lift weights or throw stones at a distance, our own weight would work less effectively for us if we wanted to use it to compress anything, or to drive a shovel into the ground by stepping on it.

The relative smallness of the mass of the Moon and the low velocity of escape from its gravitational field entail several further consequences; and perhaps the most important one for an understanding of lunar surface features and of their history is the well-nigh complete *absence of any atmosphere,* which would protect this surface from a direct contact with outer space. Why should a self-gravitating astronomical body of lunar or planetary size possess an atmosphere? The present atmospheres of the terrestrial planets with masses comparable to that of the Earth may constitute mixtures of primordial gases with those liberated from their interiors by essentially thermal processes in the course of their long cosmic past. But it is most unlikely that a body as small as the Moon could have permanently retained any primordial gas; any atmosphere which it could possess would be regenerated (or possibly accreted).

In order to appreciate the reason why this should be so, let us recall that the continued existence of an atmosphere around any celestial body, and its composition, testify to a stalemate between two opposing tendencies: the attraction of the central body which weighs on each gas molecule in the same way as on any stone or other macroscopic object, and will prevent the escape of all those whose velocity is (for the Moon) less than 2·38 km/sec; while, on the other hand, the heat pumped into our gas by the Sun (as well as by the surface of the respective planet) maintains the kinetic energy of the gas particles and thus keeps the atmosphere distended.

In general, the velocity of the molecules constantly bouncing against each other will be the greater, the higher the temperature of our gas; though heavier molecules will require higher temperatures to acquire the escape velocity than the light ones. A simple application of the kinetic theory of gases discloses that, under temperatures prevailing on the lunar surface (ranging, as we shall see, between some 130°C at noontime in the lunar tropics, and −200°C in the second part of the lunar night—roughly a range between the temperatures of boiling water and liquid air), any hydrogen or helium atmosphere would dissipate from the Moon in a matter of days. Water vapour would escape more slowly, but still would be lost in a (geologically speaking) very short time. At noon temperatures, oxygen and nitrogen, as well as carbon dioxide, would also completely escape in a relatively short time. In fact, the rate of dissipation into space of all but the heaviest gases (which are cosmically very scarce) is so high on the Moon that we should not expect to find any appreciable permanent atmosphere around it; and this expectation has been borne out by all aspects of the observational evidence available to us so far.

If, therefore, the Moon possesses no detectable atmosphere because of its low gravitational field and relatively high daytime temperature it cannot, of course, maintain any liquid on its surface. Near its poles depressions may exist which are never reached by direct sunlight (or which are illuminated, at best, by sunlight scattered from neighbouring landscape). In such regions, condensed volatile substances may possibly be present in the form of some kind of a permafrost; but should they ever evaporate, they would be irretrievably lost to the Moon in a very short time. Hence, no water or ice could be present anywhere on the Moon's exposed surface which can be reached by sunlight. The surface of our satellite must, therefore, be regarded as bone dry; and to have been so, very probably, from time immemorial. No feature visible there today could have been formed, or modified, by the effects of running water, or by repeated freezing and melting of water entrapped in surface rocks. Thus one of the most important agents responsible for geological changes on the Earth's surface seems to have been absent on the Moon, and cannot be invoked to explain any common structural characteristics on the surface of our satellite (which we shall describe later in section VI–2). Likewise, one cannot expect to find on the Moon any rocks which originated by sedimentation, and which cover such large areas of the surface of our own planet—an anticipation fully borne out by the results of the Apollo 11–15 missions.

Before we turn to the interpretation of those results, let us leave no stone unturned in our quest for possible atmospheric phenomena on the Moon—now or in the past. If the Moon does not possess any atmosphere to speak of at the present time, could it—perchance—have acquired at times a *transient* atmosphere which could have temporarily shielded its surface, and thus enabled fluid flow to exist on it for limited periods during the long lunar past? The answer to this question cannot as yet be an unqualified 'no'; for—regardless of any possible past period of temporary volcanism or any other kind of degassing—a transient atmosphere could also have been 'imported' from outside whenever the Moon suffered a collision with a comet.

That comets—like meteorites or an occasional small asteroid which strayed too far from its customary beaten track—must have occasionally run into the Moon and collided with its surface is incontestable, because they have had ample opportunity to do so in the long past. The mechanical aspects of such collisions will be taken up in the next section of this chapter, when we come to consider the origin of the lunar craters. What interests us at present is not the type of scars which such events may have left on the Moon's surface, but rather the subsequent fate of the gas imported in frozen state from cooler parts of the solar system by the nuclei of cometary heads. The nucleus of a comet—the only part of their anatomy possessing any kind of permanence—constitutes an iceberg of frozen hydro-carbons and other compounds of moderate molecular weights, which remain in solid state as long as the comet floats in space sufficiently far from the Sun; and whose gradual evaporation in more moderate zones of interplanetary climate gives rise to the beautiful—though ephemeral—phenomena of cometary heads and tails. When, however, a cometary nucleus strikes a solid obstacle—such as the surface of the Moon—a conversion of its ice to gas should be virtually instantaneous. Cometary impacts on the Moon must have occurred many times during the long astronomical past of our satellite. Therefore, the question arises as to the fate of the gas which must have been let loose over the lunar surface each time a comet committed suicide in this manner.

The total amount of gas which can be acquired by the Moon by such catastrophic encounters is far from negligible. The average mass of a cometary nucleus is of the order of 10^{18}g; though comets that may have been 10 or even 100 times as massive are known from history (the most recent being the comet Arend-Roland 1956h). The total mass of our terrestrial atmosphere (generated essentially by degassing of the Earth's interior) is known to be about 1,000 times that of an average comet; 3×10^{20}g would thus be sufficient to provide the Moon with a gaseous envelope containing about 1% of the terrestrial air mass above each unit area of the surface; and a larger comet could import proportionally more.

What is the chemical composition of the gas that could be acquired by cometary impacts? An analysis of the spectra of cometary tails has disclosed in them a number of molecular constituents* in neutral as well as ionized state. No one knows for sure the actual composition of the cold cometary nucleus, which is the sole source of gases evaporated from it by sunlight. Since, however, many of the observed gaseous constituents of cometary tails may have originated by photo-dissociation of more complicated parent molecules present in the nucleus, the latter may well contain constituents of molecular weight well in excess of 50.

Now the kinetic theory of neutral gases discloses that constituents of molecular weights close to 25 could remain gravitationally attached to the Moon for time intervals of the order of 10^3 years of daytime (indefinitely long at night), and those of molecular weight of 40–50 could remain so attached for 10^8–10^9 years. Time intervals of this order are comparable with the total age of the Moon, and certainly long in comparison with an average time-lapse between successive cometary impacts on its surface. Since, moreover, each such impact could have provided the Moon with an atmosphere of mass of the order of 1% of the

---

*Such as C_2, C_3, CN, CO, or CO_2.

terrestrial air mass, giving rise to air pressure on the Moon of the order of a few millibars. Why is it not there?

The absence of any noticeable twilight phenomena on the Moon leaves no room for doubt that the actual amount of gas around the Moon now must be smaller by several orders of magnitude to escape detection. On the other hand, it is equally certain that comets must occasionally strike the Moon; and the only way to reconcile this with the apparent absence of gas on the Moon now is to admit that cometary gas can be removed from the lunar environment faster than predicted by the kinetic theory of neutral gases—so that a complete dispersal can occur within time intervals which are short in comparison with the mean interval between cometary impacts.

Such a mechanism indeed exists as soon as imported cometary gas becomes ionized by energetic solar radiation; for as soon as this is accomplished, electrostatic repulsion takes care of the removal of cometary gases as effectively as of any lunar indigenous gas. The speed of removal is, in effect, then identical with the speed with which the gas can be ionized, and depends essentially on its transparency. If the respective mass of gas is small enough for the entire atmosphere to be optically thin in the ultraviolet, a virtually total dispersion of the corresponding atmosphere by electrostatic action can be accomplished in a time-span of 10–100 days. If, on the other hand, the mass is large enough to protect the bulk of its gas from hard radiation of the Sun by self-absorption, only in the outer fringe of semi-transparence can gas be removed electrostatically; while dissipation of the rest follows the kinetic theory of neutral gases. Should this latter regime comprise the bulk of the atmospheric mass, its mean lifetime could be increased from days to years and even centuries.

This is, indeed, likely to be true after impacts of comets whose masses happen to be large. Even then, however, the mean lifetime of such an atmosphere would be fleetingly short in comparison with the age of the Moon; and, consequently, the likelihood that we find gas left at any particular time is correspondingly minute. But, while it lasts, it may permit processes to occur which—even though short-lived—leave a more permanent imprint on the stony face of the Moon for posterity to decipher. With enough comets all around us in interplanetary space, it is thus impossible to be sure that it never rained on the Moon, or that its landscape was never swept by winds. However, such evidence as we now possess suggests that the role of such processes in shaping the lunar surface—if not altogether negligible—must have been very small or highly localized. With both the 'hydrosphere' as well as 'atmosphere' effectively absent from the lunar environment, the fossil record of its surface should possess a vastly greater degree of permanence than anything known to us on Earth; and in section 3 of this chapter we shall find that this is indeed the case.

In the meantime, a quest for the processes which could have influenced this surface should lead us to consider the state of the *interior* of the lunar globe which contains the bulk of its mass; for, as is true of every celestial body—be it a star, a planet, or its satellite—this interior is the 'engine-room' which controls the large-scale structure and cosmic evolution of the body. The visible surface represents only the 'boundary condition' of all thermal and stress processes going on in the interior—as well as an 'impact counter' of external events which our satellite must have experienced since the days of its formation.

If we wish to examine the essential properties of the lunar interior, the primary clues are already in our hands: namely, the observed mass and the size of our satellite, combining as they do in a mean density of 3·34 g/cm^3. What is the pressure prevailing inside this mass? Even in so small a celestial body existing under the influence of its own self-attraction, the internal pressure is essentially hydrostatic throughout most of the interior—in other words, the strength of the material is unable to withstand its weight anywhere except, possibly, in the very outer part of its crust. If so, however, application of the theory of hydrostatics reveals that the internal pressure in a globe of the lunar mass and size cannot exceed some 50,000 atmospheres even at its centre—a pressure exceeded at a mere 150 kms below the surface of the Earth—regardless of the kind of material of which the Moon consists. Pressures of this order of magnitude are readily attained in terrestrial laboratories today; and the changes in density exhibited by common rocks under such pressures have already been measured. On the basis of all the evidence we now possess it is reasonable to conclude that the average density of the lunar sub-surface material is very approximately equal to 3·28 g/cm^3, and increases by compression to 3·41 g/cm^3 near the Moon's centre.

Such a model fits in satisfactorily with the observed mean density of the lunar globe as a whole, and leads us to believe that the Moon consists of material which is very similar to that constituting the outer crust of our own planet.

Does the Moon represent, then, a solid and nearly homogeneous spherical rock, or is it partly molten in its interior? The answer to this question depends essentially on the sources of heat which would have been available for this purpose; and which until quite recently could only have been guessed at. Since 1966, however, considerable new light has been thrown on the problem of the actual rigidity of the lunar globe by lunar orbiting spacecraft and these have been so original as well as interesting that we must describe them in more than a few words.

Perhaps the most interesting—because unexpected—was the discovery of relatively large and severely localized gravitational anomalies on the Moon, which accelerate the motions of over-flying satellites. Such accelerations can be produced only by anomalous mass concentrations ('mascons', for short) in the respective areas, and none are apparent on the surface; moreover, the large rates of change observed in orbital motion indicate that the 'mascons' responsible for them must be located at a shallow depth below the surface, and be relatively small in size (50–200 kms).

Muller and Sjogren analyzed in 1968 the distribution of 'mascons' over the lunar surface, and found them to coincide largely with the so-called 'circular maria' on the Moon—a term which we shall describe more fully in the next section. Let us suppose—and this we shall discuss again later—that these 'mascons' represent leftovers of asteroidal bodies whose impacts created the circular maria—i.e., cosmic 'bullets', possibly metallic, which hit the Moon in the distant past and became embedded in its crust at a shallow depth below the surface (the maria being comparable, in general, with the original dimensions of the impinging missiles).

How long could these 'bullets' remain embedded in a layer of finite rigidity defying persistent efforts of gravity to pull them down? A simple analysis of the mechanical aspects of the problem shows that if the Moon possessed the same rigidity as the terrestrial mantle the 'mascons' would be bound to sink to depths at which orbiting satellites could no longer sense them within 10 million years—i.e., within less than one per cent of the probable age of the Moon. This explains, incidentally, why there are no 'mascons' akin to the

Our Nearest Celestial Neighbour—The Moon

lunar ones on the Earth (which should have intercepted a comparable number of cosmic impacts, per unit area) at the present time; for they could linger near the surface for only a relatively short time.

Since, however, they appear to be present on the Moon, the only conclusion we can draw is that *the lunar globe as a whole must be very much more rigid than the Earth*—in effect, about 1,000 times more so if the ages of the lunar mascons are to be of the order of 10^9 years. On the other hand, we now know (cf. chapter VII-3) that the chemical (basaltic) composition of the lunar crust does not differ greatly from that of the terrestrial mantle. So the only way to endow our Moon with a rigidity sufficient to support its mascons for astronomically long intervals of time is to cool its material, globally, much below the level of temperatures encountered in the terrestrial mantle. The crust of the Moon appears to be capable of tolerating much greater departures from hydrostatic equilibrium than does our Earth; and this can be so if it is much cooler than the mantle of our own planet.

This result is, moreover, in agreement with recent measurements (by the U.S. Explorer 35 satellite) of magnetic interaction between the lunar globe and the 'solar wind'—or rather, the lack of one. For it appears that the Moon simply casts a geometrical shadow behind it in the solar plasma—thus behaving like an insulator rather than a semi-conductor. This can, however, be true for silicate material, of which the Moon appears to consist, only if *the mean temperature of the lunar interior is less than about 1,000°C*. This is a much lower temperature than that prevailing in most parts of the terrestrial mantle. It is sufficiently low to endow the lunar globe with the requisite degree of rigidity; but gives very little encouragement to anyone expecting to find on the Moon any source of large-scale volcanism. The existence of local volcanic 'pockets' can never be ruled out by such 'global' arguments as we have advanced so far. Nevertheless, such arguments lead us to expect that volcanic activity on the Moon—if any—should have been present on a much smaller scale than on the Earth.

Incidentally, the recent work of Explorer 35 provided us with one additional bit of information characterizing the physical properties of the lunar globe: namely, a well-nigh complete absence of any magnetic field on our satellite. That the magnetic field of the Moon—if any—is very weak had already been indicated by experiments performed by the Russian Luna 2 in September 1959. As a result of more recent work by Explorer 35 we know now what the magnetic field of the Moon—if any—does not exceed 10^{-5} gauss in strength; and that the magnetic moment of the lunar globe is less than one-millionth of that of the Earth if it is to escape detection. This result confirms that the Moon does not possess any metallic core; and that iron present in the Moon's mass has not been thermally extracted from it.

VII–2: Lunar Landscape and its Formations

In the preceding section of this chapter we got acquainted with some of the fundamental physical properties of the lunar globe. The aim of the present section will be to look more closely at the diverse surface features visible on the face of the Moon, and to try to understand the nature of the principal forces which have been shaping the face from time immemorial.

What is so arresting about this face, and what can we learn from it? The Moon is a very old body, and has probably been a close companion of the Earth since the days of its formation. The permanent absence of any air or water on the Moon makes it, moreover, virtually certain that most of the composite fossil record exhibited by its familiar features must be of very ancient date—its oldest landmarks being, perhaps, not far removed in time from the days of the origin of our whole solar system. On the Earth or other nearby planets, all landmarks of comparable age must have fallen prey to and been completely obliterated by the joint action of their atmospheres or oceans aeons of time ago. However, as any changes on the lifeless Moon can proceed only at an exceedingly slow rate, its present wrinkled face must still bear scars and traces of many events which have taken place in the inner precincts of our solar system since the days of its formation; and if so, their correct interpretation holds a rich scientific prize.

Even to the naked eye the Moon is a beautiful object, covered with markings which have been associated with numerous popular myths. If we take a cursory glance at its wrinkled, pockmarked face through a telescope, we can see that the lunar surface consists essentially of two different types of ground. One type, rough and broken, is comparatively light in colour (reflecting, in places, as much as 18% of incident sunlight), the other is darker (reflecting, on the average, 6–7% of light), much smoother, and frequently so flat as to simulate the surface of a liquid. The first type of ground we shall generally call the 'continents'. They occupy large continuous areas—particularly on the far side of the Moon—and cover a little less than two-thirds of the entire visible face of our satellite. The flatlands—or 'maria' as they were misnamed by early observers of the Moon, before the true nature of its surface was properly understood—occupy the rest. They are, on the whole, remarkably uniform in reflectivity and general appearance—be they small or large.

A closer look at the Moon with the aid of a telescope, or at any photographs of the lunar surface, reveals an almost bewildering array of formations and structures, no two of which are exactly alike. However, the dominant type of formation among them is the ring-like walled enclosures commonly called the 'craters' (see Plate 13). They occur almost everywhere on the Moon—in continental regions as well as in the maria—in truly prodigious numbers, giving the lunar surface the appearance of a pockmarked face. The largest (mostly on the Moon's far side) are 300–400 kms across; the number of craters with diameters of more than 1 km is in excess of 300,000 on the visible hemisphere of the Moon alone (many more on its far side); and those smaller still are too many to be counted.

No two craters on the Moon are exactly alike, but they possess many characteristics in common. Their distribution over the lunar surface appears to be essentially random; the heights of their ramparts are, in general, very small in comparison with their dimensions; and their floors are depressed below the level of the surrounding landscape (cf. Plate 13).

The origin of, if not all, at least the large majority of such crater formations is now thought to be due to *impacts* on its surface by other celestial bodies moving through interplanetary space, which the Moon happens to run into in the course of time. The interplanetary space through which the Earth and the Moon continue to circle around the Sun is not entirely empty. Far from it; for it contains a wide variety of ingredients of all weights and sizes: from the ubiquitous gas of free electrons escaping from the Sun and extending well beyond the radius of the terrestrial orbit, through microscopic specks of dust and larger meteoritic debris (representing probably the left-overs from the time of formation of the solar system), to major meteorites, asteroids, or comets whose orbits through space may intersect the path of the Moon and occasionally collide with it. The frequency with which the Moon—like the Earth—suffers direct hits by major meteorites, asteroids, or comets is known approximately from terrestrial evidence of such impacts in more recent geological times, which are unlikely to have been less in the more distant past. However, even at the impact frequency no greater than that attested by terrestrial geology the Moon could have acquired most of its surface marking—not only the craters, but also the circular maria—in this way; the simplest (though possibly an oversimplified) way of interpreting the enigmatic stony hieroglyphs of the lunar face is to regard it as a scoreboard of this celestial target practice, which no processes of Nature have managed to wipe out from the time of the formation of our satellite.

The effects of celestial impacts on the Moon of bodies capable of producing craters visible through a telescope can be devastating almost beyond imagination. In order to try to visualize them at least to some extent, consider a moderately large meteorite—of the size of a rock weighing one million tons, and impinging on the lunar surface with a velocity of (say) 30 km/sec—equal to that of the Earth in its relative orbit around the Sun. The kinetic energy of such a missile would be of the order of 10^{25} ergs, and would enable it to penetrate the lunar crust like a bullet—regardless of whether it were a metal or stone—and get buried well underneath the surface before coming to a complete stop. The kinetic energy which the meteorite possessed before impact must, however, be conserved; and its entire amount would reappear in other guises—mainly as mechanical energy of shock and fracture, thermal energy, and seismic energy of 'moonquake' waves, to which it would be converted in accordance with the laws of physics. Actually rather less than one-third of the total energy would go into heat; but even this fraction should be sufficient to volatilize the entire mass of the intruder, and convert it for a short time to a gas bubble of a temperature of a few (and possibly several) hundred thousand degrees.

So hot a gas bubble could not be contained very long by the weight of the overlying debris. It would explode immediately with great violence, and this explosion would give rise to the crater that can be seen on the surface. A large amount of rock would be thrown out by this process—some of which (if accelerated to a velocity in excess of 2·4 km/sec) could disengage itself from the lunar gravitational field altogether and float freely in space, until most of it was picked up by the Earth; while more rock (moving more slowly than 1·6 km/sec) would fall back on to the Moon and produce, on impact, a family of 'secondary' craters around the parent 'primary' one. Lesser debris could be splashed out to great distances, and form 'bright rays' around the parent formation, easily visible from a distance until they get bleached out by the Sun after hundreds of millions of years.

Terrestrial experiments with impacts of metallic or stony particles in brittle media—or with explosive charges ranging from microscopic dimensions to nuclear detonations in the megaton range of TNT—are found to produce effects that simulate to an astonishing degree the ramparts and other features of many lunar craters. Moreover, since the total energy needed to produce terrestrial craters of a given size by aerial bombardment or nuclear explosions is known, an extrapolation of the size-energy trend indicated by such experiments permits us to estimate the energies likely to be involved in the formation of much larger craters on the Moon by impacts of meteorites and other cosmic bodies.

In doing so we find that an intruder impinging on the Moon with a kinetic energy of the order of 10^{25} ergs would have marked its burial place with a crater barely $2\frac{1}{2}$ kms in size. In order to produce by impact a crater 20 kms in diameter, a kinetic energy of 10^{28} ergs would have to be expended; and to double or quadruple its size, energies 10 or 100 times as large would be necessary. The mass of such a body impinging with a velocity of (say) 30 km/sec would be of the order of one billion tons for a total energy of 10^{28} ergs; and the diameter of a solid sphere of such a mass would, moreover, be about 1,200 metres if its material were stony (of density close to 3 g/cm^3), and about 900 metres if its principal constituent was nickel-iron.

The impact production of the largest craters—like Clavius, or Deslandres—seen on the lunar hemisphere visible from the Earth would call for an expenditure of energies of the order of ten million megatons of TNT to raise their ring walls more than 200 kms across, and to dig out their floors (by throwout) to a level some thousands of metres below that of the surrounding landscape. Such energies can be associated with high-velocity impacts of small asteroids—of the size of Adonis, Hermes, or Eros (to mention a few of those which paid rather close calls on the Moon in recent decades)—whose dimensions are of the order of 10 kms; and masses, 10^{13} tons.

Is it possible that proportionally larger impacts are responsible also for the 'circular maria' on the Moon—such as Mare Crisium, Nectaris, Serenitatis, or even the two largest of them known as Mare Imbrium or Orientale which attain dimensions of almost 1,000 kms? That these may indeed represent huge 'impact craters', produced by nearly grazing low-velocity collisions of the Moon with planetesimals (which constituted the 'building bricks' of planetary bodies in the early days of the solar system) was a view proposed in 1893 by the American geologist Gilbert, and more recently elaborated by Harold C. Urey. According to Urey, Mare Imbrium originated in a collision occurring in the early days of lunar history, when a solid planetesimal about 200 kms in size, and weighing some 5×10^{16} tons, made a nearly grazing plunge into the region of the present mare with a velocity no greater than 5–6 km/sec. The kinetic energy of the impinging body would have been of the order of 10^{33} ergs, equivalent to some thirty billion megatons of TNT. The heat produced by the sudden stoppage of such a body would have been sufficient to melt enough rocks into lava to flood the entire crater and obliterate the initial scar. The gravitational anomalies, discovered by Muller and Sjogren in 1968 from irregularities in the motion of lunar orbiting satellites in the region of Mare Imbrium and other circular maria (Orientale, Serenitatis, Crisium, Nectaris, etc.), can be traced to anomalous sub-surface mass concentrations ('mascons') which could constitute a remnant of the mass of the cosmic intruder (or a high-density modification of lunar rocks brought about by pressure generated on impact). These anomalies lend powerful—though not yet decisive—support to the view that lunar maria too are simply gigantic impact craters, differing from their lesser brethren in size rather than in kind.

On the Earth, recent examples of some cosmic impacts—of meteorites as well as of comets—are sufficiently well preserved to give us an idea of their consequences. The well-known Arizona Crater near Canyon Diablo by Flagstaff was undoubtedly produced by the impact of a large metallic meteorite in the past 10–50 thousand years (and a few scores of similar formations are now on record in other parts of the world); while the Siberian Tunguzka Crater was produced in 1908 by the impact of a small comet that exploded in the air before touching the ground. None of the known terrestrial 'astroblemes' of this kind are much older than one million years; erosion caused by air and water would obliterate any trace of such formations from the Earth's surface after much longer intervals of time. However, in rare instances—such as in the South African plateau—large sedimentary beds have come down to us from an age between $3 \cdot 0$ and $3 \cdot 5$ aeons of time ago; and these show no evidence of fractionation by impacts over areas which—if transplanted to the continental areas on the Moon—would be dotted by craters, small and large. From this fact we infer that *the principal period of cosmic bombardment which disfigured both sides of the Moon extended over less than the first thousand million years of its existence*—possibly half of this time —after which the principal supply of available ammunition in the form of planetesimals, meteorites and (possibly) comets became rapidly exhausted. Large craters on the Moon which are younger —such as Copernicus (Plate 13), Theophilus, or Tycho—are apparently few and accreted at long intervals of time, as is indicated by the differing brightness of their ray systems splashed out radially to great distances from the initial point of impact.

The strong probability—if not certainty—that most lunar craters and maria are of impact origin, and go back in time to the first aeon of the history of our satellite, does not preclude the existence of other craters that may be of internal ('volcanic') origin. Such craters probably exist on the Moon, but in limited numbers and relatively small sizes. There is no evidence that volcanism ever existed on the Moon on a scale larger than on the Earth (if anything, the opposite is likely to be true); and analogues to such well-known terrestrial cones as the volcanoes girdling the Pacific Ocean, or even cones of the size of the European Vesuvius, are conspicuous by their absence on the Moon. We see, however, other formations on the lunar surface—such as the so-called 'domes' or 'wrinkle ridges' in the plains of the maria—which are indubitably of internal origin, though they are quite unfamiliar to us on the Earth; but the more specific mechanism of their formation still remains largely unknown.

To conclude this brief guided tour of the principal types of formations characteristic of the lunar surface, let us point out other geological formations familiar to us on Earth which we have *not* found among them. The entire surface of our satellite shows no evidence of mountains which would have been formed by *folding,* or by any lateral motion of the Moon's crust. Such mountain chains as we do find on the Moon all border on large maria, and probably constitute partly destroyed walls of gigantic impact craters formed in the early part of lunar history. Thus folding—the most important orogenic process continuously active on the surface of our own planet—seems to be completely absent on the Moon; just as the principal types of formations apparent on the lunar surface lack any obvious terrestrial analogy.

That this should be so is only natural, and due in effect to the great disparity in mass between our own planet and its only natural satellite. We have already seen that the smallness of the Moon's mass has deprived our satellite of the possibility of generating or retaining (except, perhaps, for very short intervals of time) any air around it, or water on its surface. A complete absence of any effects which could be produced by air and water is obvious (on any scale); and accounts for the fundamental difference between the external appearance of the Earth and the Moon. Moreover, a globe as small as the Moon can generate, and retain, little internal heat; and thus is condemned to remain cooler in its interior than a planet of the size of the Earth. In consequence, the crust of the Moon should be solid rather than plastic down to a much greater depth than it is for the Earth; and the large-scale structure of the lunar surface bears this out by a total lack of any evidence of folding, or any lateral crust motions which on the Earth would be called 'continental drift'. The bulk of the Moon's mass is apparently too cold (and, consequently, too rigid) to allow any appreciable differential motions to arise in its globe—or, at any rate, near its surface; and the morphology of its entire surface —based now not only on telescopic evidence, but also on all information furnished by spacecraft—is entirely consistent with this picture.

VII–3: Structure and Composition of the Lunar Surface

Many definite facts about the structure of the lunar surface were established before the advent of lunar spacecraft, from observations made from the Earth with telescopes of moderate size—even with the naked eye. Perhaps the one piece of such evidence most directly obtainable is the 'light curve' of the Moon, representing the variation of its total brightness with the phase in the course of each month. The most astonishing feature of this curve is its steep slope—a rapid rise of light towards full Moon, and an equally rapid diminution after the full phase has been passed. For the full Moon has only twice as large an illuminated area as the Moon at the time of the first or last quarter; yet photometric measures disclose the full Moon to be not twice, but 19 times as bright as at the time of quadratures. Moreover, there appears to be a real surge in intensity of moonlight, more than doubling its brightness within only a matter of hours just before zero phase, and losing it with equal speed after full phase has been passed (the 'opposition effect').

These rapid light changes before and after full Moon would be quite inexplicable in terms of a diffuse scattering of light on a smooth surface of any composition; and have already driven our astronomical ancestors to the conclusion that *the structure of the lunar surface must be highly broken and vesicular; and the surface itself replete with innumerable pits which begin to cast appreciable shadows almost as soon as the Sun has ceased to stand directly overhead.* In other words, a rapid loss of the brightness of a sunlit landscape on the Moon in the course of a morning or an afternoon is due to *shadows* cast on itself by its own irregularities. This was the conclusion arrived at from photometric studies by the majority of astronomers at least 20–30 years before spacecraft at last subjected this surface structure to a more detailed inspection; and the reader can judge for himself the correctness with which astronomers anticipated the outcome.

These findings are also entirely consistent with the fact—noticed by Galileo Galilei in the early part of the seventeenth century—that the apparent brightness of every element of the surface attains a maximum at full Moon, regardless of its relative position on the lunar disc, be it a part of the continents or the maria. The apparent disc of the Moon indeed exhibits no 'limb-darkening'; and this photometric homogeneity of its face, attested to with considerable accuracy by more modern observations, also suggests the cause of the underlying surface roughness which gave rise to its honeycomb structure. For *what else but an external influence—such as the continued infall of micrometeorites* (against which the surface is in no way protected by nature) *and the 'cratering' produced by them could impress the same uniform kind of micro-relief on any type of ground all over the Moon?*

All these conclusions (confirmed in 1966 by soft-landing mooncraft) have been deducted from the observed photometric properties of the Moon in visible light, which represents sunlight incident on the Moon and scattered by its surface in the direction of the Earth. The Moon is, on the whole, a pretty poor reflector of sunlight; for only a little more than 7% of light incident upon it is scattered in all directions. When happens to the rest? The balance of it must obviously be *absorbed* and used up to *heat* the surface. But any body possessing a finite temperature must also *emit* radiation of its own; and its characteristics should depend essentially on its absolute temperature. For our Sun—whose effective temperature is a little more than 5,800°K—most of its radiation is emitted at optical frequencies, between the violet and the red end of the visible spectrum (with a maximum in the yellow), giving together an impression of what we call 'white light'. This is also the colour of reflected moonlight; but the lunar radiation proper is of a very different kind.

The sole—and sufficient—reason for this difference is the fact that the temperature of the lunar surface is so much lower than that of the Sun. The Moon—like the Earth—receives virtually all its heat by radiation from the Sun; but as the lunar surface's average distance from the Sun amounts to 214 solar radii, each square centimetre of lunar surface receives only about one $(214)^2$th or a 46,000th part of the heat flux passing through each square centimetre of the surface of the Sun. As this flux is proportional to the fourth power of the absolute temperature, it follows that the mean temperature of the Moon should be $\sqrt{214}$ or about 15 times lower than that of the Sun—or approximately +120°C. This supposes, of course, that the Sun stands in the zenith, and its light falls normally on the illuminated surface; should it fall obliquely, the radiation would be diluted, and the temperature maintained by it would be lower.

These considerations lead us to expect that the temperature of the Moon will not be more than 380°K; and if so, its radiation should be very different from the white light, most of it being emitted in the deep infrared, with the maximum around the wavelength of 0·01 mm. Light of this colour is, of course, quite invisible to the human eye, and incapable of impressing the photographic plate. It would, in addition, experience considerable difficulty in penetrating through our terrestrial atmosphere in between the interlocking absorption bands of water vapour and carbon dioxide. However, that part of it which does pierce through can be detected—and, in fact, measured quite accurately—by its thermoelectric effect.

Such measurements, performed extensively in the past ten years, have indicated that at the subsolar point in the lunar tropics—when the Sun stands directly overhead—temperatures as high as 130°C are reached each day. During the afternoon—as the zenith distance of the Sun is increasing—the temperature steadily declines to well below freezing at the time of sunset, and continues further to decline in the course of the night until an appalling minimum of between $-180°$ and $-190°C$ is reached before sunrise. The total range of day-to-night variation in temperature on the Moon is, therefore, a little more than 300°C, and ranges from a temperature above that of boiling water at noon down to that of liquid air at dawn. This is the maximum range encountered in the lunar tropics. Near the poles, where the Sun never rises high above the horizon nor sets completely for very long, the temperature variations become correspondingly smaller; but even there its range is rather frightening and apt to cool the enthusiasm of many a would-be space explorer!

Why does the Moon behave so differently from the Earth in this respect? For both the Earth and the Moon the principal source of heat is, of course, sunlight; and as our planet and its satellite are, on the average, equally far from the Sun, both are bound to receive equal shares. But the particular properties of their surfaces allow them to husband this energy in essentially different ways. The visible light of our satellite represents only a few per cent of the total energy actually received from the Sun. The bulk of incident sunlight is absorbed by the lunar surface and re-radiated as infrared light—far too red to be visible to the human eye, but measurable by its thermoelectric effect. The Earth does the same; but its own absorbing and protective mechanism is completely different from anything that exists on the Moon. The absence of any air there also precludes the existence of any liquid on the surface; and solid rocks possess a heat capacity which is very small in comparison with that of water. Their surface rapidly becomes hot during daytime, and then cools off. Their ability to store heat is so limited that the extremes of their temperature are great—though the mean temperature of the Moon is not so very different from that of our own planet.

In one respect, however, lunar climatic changes are not as drastic as the foregoing figures may indicate. Although the extremes are great, the duration of the lunar day—lasting 29·53 days or 709 hours of our time—is so long that the rate of change of the temperature is not actually so impressive: a drop from 110°C to −180°C in $14\frac{1}{2}$ days separating the lunar noon and midnight corresponds to a mean temperature gradient of less than 1° per hour—which is certainly not so out of the ordinary. It is its persistence over so many hours of rise and fall which makes the extremes in temperature so far apart. Much more rapid temperature changes occur on the Moon about once a year (i.e., once every 12th lunar 'day') during the relatively brief intervals of lunar eclipses, when the Moon passes through the shadow cast by the Earth into space. Such eclipses last only 2–3 hours of our time; but while they last, the Moon experiences almost as large a change in climate as it does between day and night. In particular, the egress of the Moon from the shadow is accompanied by a steep rise in temperature of almost 200° in less than one hour, or more than 3° per minute. Even so steep a temperature gradient should not, however, cause any thermal cracking of the rocks, which could contribute to their disintegration; the mechanical action of impacts is vastly more effective to this end.

The larger the rock, the more heat it can absorb in daytime without becoming too hot, and store for re-radiation at night. Wherever, therefore, boulders occur in profusion on the exposed surface, the local temperature of the region should remain lower in the lunar daytime, and warmer at night, than in the surrounding regions covered by finer debris. That this is the case has actually been observed. The nocturnal 'hot spots' discovered on the Moon by Shorthill and Saari during the lunar eclipse of 20 December 1964 are due to this cause, as has subsequently been verified by high-resolution photography of U.S. Lunar Orbiters, on which the respective fields of boulders 1–10 m in size came directly to light. With each boulder acting as an independent radiator, the night-time temperature of such regions can be as much as 40°–60° above that of their surroundings. With the latter at the temperature of liquid air, an excess of 40°–60° would make little difference to an astronaut on the exposed lunar surface; but the instruments will faithfully record it.

These large climatic changes are however limited to the exposed surface, and become very much reduced immediately beneath it. How do we know this? From the measurements of the thermal emission of the lunar globe in the microwave domain of the spectrum—i.e., at wavelengths longer than 1 mm—which has been opened up by observers from the Earth during the past 20 years, with truly revealing results. First, the range of temperature variations deduced from the measured intensities of thermal emission of the lunar globe in the domain of radio-frequencies (i.e., at millimetre to metre wavelengths) proved to be *less* than that measured in infrared light—becoming the more reduced, the longer the wavelength. Secondly, the maxima and minima of the temperatures deduced from the microwave measures did not prove to follow the altitude of the Sun above the horizon, but *lagged behind* the surface temperatures by a phase-shift increasing with the wavelength.

How can we account for such phenomena? Why, in particular, does the amplitude of diurnal temperature changes diminish so rapidly with increasing wavelength, and what causes the diurnal heat wave to lag increasingly in phase behind the surface insolation? The basic clue is the fact that radiation observed at different frequencies does not originate at the same depth; but is forthcoming from layers which, in general, are located the deeper, the longer the wavelength. In other words, the surface of the Moon—opaque to visible and infrared light—becomes partially transparent to microwaves; and the lower their frequency, the deeper inside we penetrate with their aid. In practice, a limit to this prospecting in depth will be imposed by the fact that the thermal emission of the Moon diminishes rather rapidly with increasing wavelength; and the lunar radiation at wavelengths in excess of one metre cannot be disentangled from the instrumental noise and that of the sky background. In the millimetre-to-decimetre wavelength range the readings are, however, significant and enable us to penetrate down to approximately one metre beneath the surface in tracing the flow of heat due to diurnal insolation.

If the variation of microwave temperatures is damped so rapidly with increasing depth, and continues to lag in phase behind the infrared (surface) temperatures as the observations appear to indicate, the only reason for it must be a very low thermal conductivity of lunar surface layers. The observations indicate that the daily variation in temperature at a depth of 30 cm already amounts to less than one-third of its surface range, and the effects of diurnal heat waves do not make themselves felt there till after a time lag of some 80 hours. Moreover, at a depth of about one metre any variation completely disappears and a constant temperature of about $-35°C$ obtains day or night. These data should make it possible for us to evaluate the coefficient of heat conduction of the lunar surface material, sufficient to retard the flow and attenuate it as is observed.

When such computations were made for the first time, the investigators received a considerable jolt: namely, the coefficient of heat conduction required to account for these phenomena turned out to be about a thousand times smaller than for any known terrestrial rocks. This was so, however, only as long as we compared the computed lunar conductivity with that of solid rocks, in which heat flows through their entire body. In a broken material, on the other hand, heat can propagate only through the actual areas of contact between the individual grains or pebbles—areas which diminish by loose packing. When the computed coefficients of lunar heat conduction were compared with those of loosely-packed powders of common terrestrial rocks, some disparity still persisted; but it was almost completely removed when the laboratory measurements were repeated in a vacuum (as otherwise heat would also propagate through air in between the dust grains).

Thus while photometric observations of the Moon in visible light produced adequate evidence of the fact that its surface must be rough and porous, observations of lunar thermal radiation in the microwave domain of its spectrum disclosed that the broken structure of the surface must extend to at least a foot or so under the visible surface. This we knew years before the first soft-lander—and, eventually, men—probed the surface on the spot. But even these findings were exceeded in depth by what we learned during the past quarter of a century by another method of active exploration of the Moon at a distance; namely, by means of *radar echoes*.

It is customary to date the commencement of the lunar space

age at 13 September 1959, when the first particles of terrestrial matter—in the form of the Russian spacecraft Luna 2—crash-landed on the surface of our satellite. Should we, however, wish to date the beginning of the space age from the day when the Moon was reached by electromagnetic radiation sent out from the Earth, it would be 10 January 1946 when scientists of the U.S. Army Signal Corps in Belmar, New Jersey, beamed onto the Moon a series of short radar pulses emitted by a mere 3kw transmitter operating at 110 Mc/sec; and approximately 2·56 seconds later echoes were recorded, demonstrating that within this interval the signals sent out from Belmar completed a trip of half a million miles to the Moon and back. The real triumph of the experimental technique was to amplify the echoes sufficiently to make them audible; for while the energy fed into the antenna of the transmitter was 3 kilowatts, the returning echoes carried an energy of little more than 10^{-17} of a watt.

This first radar contact with the Moon was repeated a month later from Hungary, and has never been lost since that time. In the past 25 years it has provided us with a wide range of valuable scientific data, of which only one aspect—directly relevant to the structure of the lunar surface in depth—will be mentioned here: the unexpected weakness of the observed radar echoes from the Moon. Ever since the first echoes of radar pulses sent out to the Moon were recorded in 1946, it has been found that these echoes were considerably weaker than they should have been for a globe of lunar distance and size, consisting of solid rocks. In order to reconcile theory with the observations it was necessary to assume that the effective dielectric constant of the lunar surface material was about three times smaller than that of common silicate rocks. Between 1946 and now, the same conclusion was arrived at by countless experiments with radar pulses at very different wavelengths, and reflected from surface layers of very different depth (equal, in most cases, to several multiples of the wavelength). It was not until pulses at decameter wavelengths were first reflected from the Moon in 1964 that the strength of the echoes began to point to dielectric constants approaching those of solid rocks.

The actual depth of the broken layer overlying solid bedrock cannot, unfortunately, be fathomed by radar alone. Certain features observed on the lunar surface—in particular, the so-called 'rilles'—suggest that its depth may amount in places to several hundred metres; and recent interpretations of seismic echoes produced on the Moon by impacts of spacecraft or meteorites, and lasting almost an hour, suggest that the fragmented layer through which the Moon borders on space may be kilometres deep. The lunar geologists call this fragmented layer a 'regolith', and seek its origin in the cumulative mechanical damage which the Moon must have suffered in the past by its countless encounters with the material flying loosely in interplanetary space.

The primary cause of this damage—high-velocity encounters with meteorites and comets—is not operative on the Moon alone; for every other celestial body is equally exposed to it. In particular, our Earth must have received a comparable bombardment, per unit area, in the same length of time; since our atmosphere provides next to no protection against cosmic bodies causing the greatest mechanical damage—intruders with masses greater than 10^6 g. However, the combined action of terrestrial air and water tends to obliterate any wounds caused by cosmic bombardment very much more rapidly than these are inflicted, so that our lithosphere shows no evidence of a global fragmented layer. The fact that our Moon does exhibit evidence of such a layer discloses not only that the 'healing agents'—air or water—are absent from the Moon now (as we know abundantly also from other sources), but that they were probably of no importance—even temporarily—during the long astronomical past of our satellite.

Thus we can now see that the outermost crust of the Moon consists of a stony regolith produced by cosmic abrasion of the surface of the Moon through external impacts. Its extent in depth may vary from place to place; but its global average is unlikely to be less than several dozen metres. It is also clear to us now that a cosmic body of the size of the Moon (or, for that matter, of Mercury; and to some extent, of Mars) must interface with outer space through such a regolith. The latter merely represents as natural a 'boundary condition' to a globe of the lunar size, as are the hydrosphere and atmosphere for planets like the Earth or Venus.

So much for the physical structure of the lunar surface and its regolithic layer; but what about the chemical and mineralogical composition of its material? Today, thanks to the recent contributions of the soft-landing Surveyors and of the manned Apollo missions, we can describe these properties almost as well as we could for any part of the Earth; and the advances in our knowledge—not only of the Moon, but also of the solar system as a whole—are truly epoch-making. An analysis of the samples brought back by the Apollo missions suddenly illuminated for us the earliest part of the history of our planetary system before the Earth solidified, and before the Sun became a star as we know it today. The wealth of the information thus acquired has already more than repaid the money and effort which were required to make the U.S. Apollo project a success.

By atomic contents, the most abundant constituent of the material brought back in July 1969 by Apollo 11 from its landing-place in the Sea of Tranquillity was oxygen (40–60% by weight), followed by silicon (17–20%), aluminium (4–7%), titanium (4–6%) and magnesium (4–6%)—to list only the elements present in amounts exceeding one per cent (the ranges indicated for each element refer to the respective abundances in different samples). The samples returned by Apollo 12 from the Oceanus Procellarum in November 1969 were found to be of a broadly similar composition with some differences (such as a lower titanium content). The molecular composition of lunar matter was found to consist predominantly of silica (38–43%) followed by FeO (16–21%), Al_2O_3 (9–13%), CaO (9–12%), TiO_2 (7–11%), MgO (7–10%) and other constituents amounting to less than one per cent by weight.

The bearing strength of the surface amounts to a few pounds per square inch—increasing rapidly with depth; and the bulk density of the fine-grain component of the material is between 1·5 and 1·6 g/cm³. Since the densities of the individual compact grains were found to range between 3·1 and 3·5 g/cm³, it follows that about half of the volume of the bulk of material lifted from the topmost layer of the surface is empty space. This accounts for the relatively low bearing strength of the material, as well as for its low effective dielectric constant. Therefore, the bulk of the material covering the lunar surface as we see it in the photograph reproduced on Plate 14, or in which the astronauts made imprints of their footsteps (Plate 15) consists of loosely-packed silicate material (predominantly silica).

How do these results compare with previous expectations? That the surface of the Moon is covered with loosely-packed material of very low thermal conductivity and radar reflectivity we knew before from observations made on the Earth; and its relatively low bearing strength had been previously disclosed by the Surveyors. However, prior to the return of the Apollo samples, there were two schools of thought on the chemical composition of lunar material. One expected the Moon to possess a chemical composition akin to that of the terrestrial mantle (which should have been the case if the Moon's mass ever came from the Earth); while the other—regarding the Moon as a primary object possibly older than our planet—anticipated a similarity between the composition of the Moon and that of the solar atmosphere, as the latter should approximate as closely as anything within observational (i.e., spectroscopic) reach to the unadulterated composition of primordial matter from which the solar system originated; unadulterated because, on the one hand, the large mass of the Sun would have prevented any selective escape of the elements from its gravitational field, while on the other hand, its temperature is too low to allow nucleogenesis by equilibrium processes on any appreciable scale.

The observational verdict delivered by the lunar spacecraft confounded both these views, and presented the Moon to us in a much more enigmatic light. The Moon proved to be quite different chemically from both the Sun and the Earth. For example, its content of titanium (and also chromium, zircon, and others) is very much higher than in the Sun or the Earth's crust; whereas other elements (like nickel and sodium, potassium, or europium) are again very much less abundant. In particular, the ratio of iron-to-nickel in the Moon appears to be larger than that encountered in any other sample of cosmic matter we know (the Earth's crust; solar atmosphere; meteorites); and the common elements like carbon or nitrogen appear to be conspicuously absent from the compounds found so far in the lunar crust.

What kind of rocks have been found on the Moon? All those brought back so far are *igneous,* of generally *basaltic composition;* and numerous minerals of this type well-known from the Earth—such as olivine, plagioclase, feldspar, ilmenite, and others—have been identified in many samples. In point of fact, only three new minerals, not known previously from the Earth, have so far been found in lunar rocks. Their crystalline structure and chemical properties indicate, moreover, that lunar rocks solidified rapidly (as crystals grown in them are small) at temperatures between $1,000°$–$1,200°C$ under highly reducing conditions (the partial pressure of available free oxygen had to be less than 10^{-13} of an atmosphere to account for the virtual absence of higher states of oxidation). Moreover, many rocks brought back from the Moon exhibit evidence of shock metamorphism, which is strongly suggestive of the effects of the passage of intense shock waves through solids—such as can be produced on the Moon by meteoritic impacts from space. All rocks returned from the Moon so far are, therefore, igneous; but we should not jump too readily to a conclusion equating 'igneous' with 'volcanic'. All rocks we call 'volcanic' on the Earth are igneous; but the converse is not necessarily true. Lunar rocks manifestly indicate the effects of heat treatment in the past; but no rocks of the same structure ever passed through the crater of any terrestrial volcano!

Perhaps the most important single result that we owe to the recent Apollo missions has been a determination of the *age* which elapsed since the solidification of the lunar rocks now in our hands. This age can be ascertained from the readings of atomic clocks present in most minerals, by the same methods used for determining the age of our Earth or of meteorites. When such methods were applied to the crystalline material which the Apollo 11 astronauts brought back from the lunar Mare Tranquillitatis, the radiative clocks indicated that *these rocks must have crystallized 3,000–4,000 million years ago*—with the average age close to 3,700 million years. Similar finds picked up by Apollo 12 at its landing-place in Oceanus Procellarum appear to be, on the average, some 200–300 million years younger. The dispersion in age of rocks within each group is no doubt real; and testifies to the fact that not all rocks found in the same place on the Moon actually solidified *in situ*. The local soil represents rather a mixture of rocks which may have been transported there by impact throwouts from different parts of the Moon. A difference between the average age of the majority of rocks brought back from Mare Tranquillitatis and Oceanus Procellarum may be due to a difference of a few hundred million years between the events which gave rise to these formations; Mare Tranquillitatis being slightly the older of the two.

However, perhaps the most interesting result which has emerged so far from radioactive dating of lunar rocks is that, on each landing site investigated by Apollo 11 and 12 so far, the smaller debris were found to exhibit substantially greater age. The time which has elapsed since the solidification of the small particles of the soil proved, in fact, to cluster around 4·6 billion years in *both* localities—making their ages virtually identical with those of the oldest known meteoritic material. The lighter colour of many of these small chips lends some weight to the conjecture that these chips solidified in the *continental* regions of the lunar surface, and were subsequently transported to their present localities by the mechanical action of meteoritic impacts.

Whatever may have been the case, however, such chips constitute an irrefutable testimony that *solid matter already existed on the lunar surface 4·6 billion years ago,* which has not been melted since; while the substantially younger age of dark rocks characteristic of the lunar mare ground from the plains of Mare Tranquillitatis or Oceanus Procellarum shows that later solidification of material in these localities must have been the result of subsequent but isolated events. This is indeed what we had already inferred before the Apollo flights from the stratigraphy of the lunar face; and the radioactive dating of the rocks collected at four localities so far has provided our previous time-scale with absolute calibration. Earlier we surmised the great age of the stony relief of the lunar surface from the number of its disfiguring pockmarks. Now we know that the continental land masses may have solidified while the Sun was in the last throes of its Kelvin contraction towards the Main Sequence.

What is the origin of the Moon as a whole? In the present state of research it is probably that the Moon—like most other bodies of the solar system—came into being by an agglomeration of *solid* pre-existing particles. It does not seem possible to envisage a workable process which could lead to the formation of planetary bodies —let alone bodies of mass as small as that of the Moon—by condensation of gas at moderate or high temperature. Therefore, the view prevalent today is that the Moon accumulated from pre-existing solid particles more than 4·6 aeons ago; and if so, it is at least possible that some of these particles may have been heated up to temperatures well above their melting point by the Sun which, at that time, may have been in the last stage of its contraction towards the Main Sequence, and very much larger than now— possibly of dimensions comparable with those of the present orbits of the inner planets.

At this stage the Sun would have been somewhat cooler than

today; but dust clouds exposed to it at a short range could have been heated to several hundred degrees or even more. If any particles evaporated during this heat treatment, the gas thus produced would have dissipated beyond retrieval; but particles which only melted could have cooled off again quite rapidly in a condensing swarm (in which the individual particles shield each other by their shadows from the scorching sunlight). It is, therefore, possible that not only the surface material, but the bulk of the Moon's mass may have acquired its igneous (basaltic) nature *before* the original swarm of solid particles coalesced into the lunar globe as we know it today; and that the source of heat responsible for this conversion need not have been any radioactively-heated sub-surface volcanic 'pockets', but radiant energy of the youthful Sun.

Nothing of comparable age, certainly, can be found anywhere on the Earth, or (as far as we know) elsewhere in the solar system. In contrast to the Moon, our mother Earth exhibits to the outside world a cosmic face of almost eternal youth—rejuvenated continuously by geological processes such as erosion and denudation of its land by the joint action of air and water; or (more important) by continuous continental drift operative in its mantle and driven by the internal heat engine of the Earth. Very few parts of the terrestrial continents or ocean floors are known to be older than a few hundred million years. In contrast, the Moon (on account of its small mass and heat capacity) can afford none of these means of cosmic cosmetics to make up her face. The latter, therefore, mirrors truly the ages gone by and preserves a reflection of events that occurred long before our own terrestrial continents were formed; and long before the first manifestation of life on Earth flickered in our shallow waters. As a monument to the past, the Moon constitutes the most important fossil of the solar system; and an interpretation of the hieroglyphs engraved by Nature on its stony face reveals a fascinating story.

CHAPTER VIII

Other Terrestrial Planets

IN THE two preceding chapters we got acquainted with the fundamental physical characteristics of the prototype of a terrestrial planet—our Earth—as well as with those of its faithful companion, the Moon. In the present chapter we shall now extend this acquaintance to other planets of the same general order of magnitude which include Venus, Mars, Mercury and Pluto.

The principal properties—both physical and kinematic—of these celestial bodies are listed in the accompanying Tables VIII–1 and 2, in which we have added those already known for the Earth and the Moon for the sake of comparison. Most properties of all other terrestrial planets are intermediate between those of the Earth and the Moon; so that the knowledge we have already gained about them will help us to understand those of other planets as well.

VIII–1: Venus

A glance at the basic data compiled in Table VIII–2 reveals that the planet most akin to our Earth in its vital statistics is Venus. This second innermost planet of the solar system—known since time immemorial as the evening or morning star of our sky—revolves around the Sun in a period of $224 \cdot 71$ days in a mildly eccentric orbit and inclined a little to the ecliptic which brings it at inferior conjunction within $40 \cdot 7$ million kms from the Earth. At such times, it becomes our nearest planetary neighbour—the planet Mars never approaches us within less than $55 \cdot 5$ million kms—though more than a hundred times as far as our Moon. A spacecraft which can nowadays reach our satellite after a journey of 60–70 hours must spend not less than three months on its way to Venus; and light or electromagnetic signals sent out by human hand will reach it in 140 seconds. This is, of course, only at the

TABLE VIII-1

Kinematic Properties of the Terrestrial Planets

	Earth	Venus	Mars	Mercury	Pluto
Mean distance from the Sun (in Astronomical Units)	1	0·7233	1·5237	0·3871	39·52
Light transit time (in minutes)	8·32	6·02	12·67	3·22	328
Orbital period	365^d·256	224^d·701	686^d·980	87^d·969	249^y·17
Orbital eccentricity	0·0167	0·0068	0·0933	0·2056	0·249
Orbital inclination to the ecliptic	0	3°23′·6	1°51′·0	7°0′·2	17°6′
Duration of sidereal day	23^{h}56^{m}4^s	(−)243^d·1	24^{h}37^{m}23^s	58^d·6	6^d·39
Inclination of the Planet's Equator to its orbital plane	23°·5	2°·2	25°·2	$\pm$0	?

Table VIII-2

Physical Properties of the Terrestrial Planets

	Earth	Venus	Mars	Mercury	Pluto	Moon
Mass	1	0·8149	0·1076	0·053	0·18	0·0123
Radius (in km)	6371·0	6056	3394	2440	3500	1738
Mean Density (in g/cm^3)	5·52	5·23	3·94	5·5	6	3·34
Atmospheric Pressure (in bars)	1·013	>100	0·0065	—	?	—
Principal atmospheric constituents	N_2, O_2	CO_2, N_2	CO_2, N_2 or Ne?	—	H_2?	—

time of closest approach; for when Venus happens to be on the other side of the Sun (in so-called superior conjunction) its distance from us increases to 258 million kms.

The apparent diameter of the planet—as seen from the Earth—was found to range from 64″ to only 10″ between the inferior and superior conjunction, which at the respective distances corresponds to a globe of a radius little less than 6,100 kms; and its shape does not deviate significantly from a sphere. Accordingly, the surface of Venus is equal to 90·6% of that of the Earth; and its volume, 0·862 of the terrestrial one. On the other hand, from orbital perturbations which Venus exerts on the Earth (and, more recently, on a fly-by spacecraft), its mass was found to be 81·5% of that of the Earth, or $4·87 \times 10^{27}$ grams. As a result, the mean density of the Cytherean globe is equal to 0·945 of that of the Earth, or 5·23 g/cm³; and its gravitational acceleration on the surface, 0·900 of the terrestrial one, or 882 cm/sec². A man who weighs 160 pounds on the Earth would, accordingly, weigh only 144 pounds on Venus. In all these (and some other) respects Venus would appear to be almost a twin to our Earth. Yet appearances are often deceptive, and so they prove in the present case. For there is a wide gulf between other physical properties of these two neighbouring planets—a gulf whose full depth we did not begin to penetrate until the advent of radar and spacecraft astronomy in the past ten years.

Whenever visible from our terrestrial space station, Venus appear brighter than any other object in the sky (other than the Sun or the Moon), ranging from −3·3 to −4·2 in stellar magnitudes. Since Venus revolves around the Sun in an orbit interior to the terrestrial one, it is bound to exhibit phases in solar illumination much as the Moon does. As it moves from superior to inferior conjunction, an increase in apparent diameter (due to increasing proximity) will at first more than make up for a diminution of the illuminated portion of its disc; and the planet grows brighter. As, however, its crescent begins to narrow, the area of the illuminated portion of the disc commences eventually to diminish in spite of increasing proximity; and with it, the apparent brightness. As a result of the combination of these effects, Venus reaches its maximum brightness, not when it is nearest to us, but about 36 days before or after inferior conjunction—at an elongation of 39° from the Sun (i.e., less than the maximum elongation of 47°.5) when Venus appears through the telescope like the Moon when it is about five days old (two days before the 'first quarter'). At such times, Venus is bright enough to cast shadows in its light, and can be seen with the naked eye in full daylight.

This brightness shows that the surface of the planet scatters incident sunlight pretty effectively—approximately 59% of it (in comparison with a mere 7% scattered by our Moon)—from which we conclude that the visible surface of Venus (i.e., the layer responsible for scatter) must be much smoother than that of the Moon. Moreover, the colour of Venus is only slightly yellower than that of illuminating sunlight; therefore, the scattering process must be almost independent of frequency. In other words, the Cytherean disc appears to be rather monotonously white, as might be expected of a continuous *cloud layer* completely covering the planet. That this is probably the case was also suggested by the fact that—unlike the Moon, or Mars—Venus does not exhibit any permanent surface markings; the usual appearance of the planet shows a uniformly bright disc, shading off smoothly towards the terminator without any trace of recognizable detail.

If, however, the surface of Venus is perpetually covered by clouds, this presupposes that the planet is surrounded by an extensive *atmosphere;* and other telescopic observations indicating this have been on hand for a long time. Near the time of inferior conjunction, the horns of the Cytherean crescent are often seen to extend noticeably beyond the sunrise terminator; and when the planet is very close to the Sun in the sky, the cusps of the crescent have been observed to coalesce in a complete aureola surrounding the whole disc. This phenomenon is due to diffuse reflection of sunlight in the planetary atmosphere (the same process which produces our twilight), and from its intensity we can estimate the total amount of gas necessary to produce it: it is equivalent to a layer of about 1 km of gas at our atmospheric air pressure. This is the amount of gas above the top of the visible cloud layer; for what is below, this method cannot show.

What does this atmosphere above the clouds consist of? As usual, we have to turn to a spectroscope for the answer. In 1932 the American astronomers Adams and Dunham of Mount Wilson Observatory detected in the red part of the Cytherean spectrum molecular absorption bands, subsequently identified with those of carbon dioxide, and their intensity indicated that the amount of

CO_2 above the clouds must be equivalent to a layer not less than 400 metres thick at standard (atmospheric) pressure—which is about 250 times the quantity of CO_2 present in the Earth's entire atmosphere.

What is the temperature of the visible surface (i.e., on the top of the cloud layer) of our sister planet? As is well known, the absolute temperature of any cosmic body can be deduced from the measured intensity of its thermal emission; and for planets surrounding our Sun most of this emission can be expected in the infrared. When the first reliable measurements of the infrared emissions from Venus through our 'atmospheric window' between 8 and 12 microns were made by Pettit and Nicholson in 1955, it transpired that the mean temperature of Venus appears to be about $-35°C$, day or night.

How to explain this curious phenomenon? The correct clue was probably found by Strong, who pointed out that these measured temperatures are virtually identical with that below which saturated water vapour cannot cool without spontaneous crystallization. Therefore, the clouds on Venus are probably high cirrus clouds like those in our own atmosphere—frozen ice crystals—and their failure to cool off at night is probably due to liberation of the latent heat of water vapour as the latter condenses to form clouds. An identification of ice crystals in the Venus cloud layer by their optical 'halo' effect has recently put this beyond reasonable doubt.

How high are these clouds floating above the solid surface of the planet? This question obviously cannot be answered by observations in the visible or infrared light; for the cloud cover appears to be totally opaque at all times. In order to penetrate it, light of much longer wavelengths (which is not absorbed by water vapour or ice crystals) must be employed for our communications. This will, in general, call for wavelengths in excess of one millimetre, constituting the radio spectrum of the planet Venus. Its exploration commenced only in the past ten years, with results which could hardly have been more dramatic. For whereas, in the near infrared, the intensity of the Cytherean thermal emission corresponded to a mean temperature of $-35°C$, that at wavelengths of 8–9 mm proved to correspond to temperatures of $+80°C$; and in the centimetre range, it corresponded to values close to $+400°C$!

This latter temperature refers undoubtedly to the solid surface of the planet at the base of the atmosphere; for at centimetre wavelengths the atmosphere of Venus (like our own) becomes effectively transparent. If, however, it is due to the storage of sunlight by a 'greenhouse' effect which traps solar heat through absorption by its gaseous constituents, the amount of gas involved in this process must evidently be enormous. In point of fact, calculations of Cytherean model atmospheres have disclosed that, in order to account for a ground temperature of 400°C, an atmosphere consisting predominantly of carbon dioxide would have to attain a ground pressure in excess of 100 terrestrial atmospheres; and that the top of the cloud layer should be some 45–50 kms above solid ground. Both these expectations were borne out by subsequent spacecraft and radar work.

Thus it is not until altitudes which, on the Earth, would take us well above the ozone layer, that anyone emerging from the Cytherean atmosphere could get a glimpse of the starry sky. Far below the deceptive calm of these rarefied heights, clouds impenetrable to optical frequencies conceal an inferno of shadowless semi-twilight, filled with compressed carbon dioxide which attains on the ground a temperature of some 400°C and a pressure in excess of 100 atmospheres. Such a medium would act as an ideal sterilizer for any living matter, and provide suitable surroundings for softening-up the most obdurate sinners. And yet even this inferno has already been penetrated—not by any Dante—but by inanimate Hermes-messengers in the form of radar signals, and later by actual hardware in the form of spacecraft (Mariner, Venera).

The first terrestrial messenger to Venus in material form was the Russian probe Venera 1, launched in February 1961. Although it failed to reach its goal, it proved to be a harbinger of greater things to come and paved the way for the U.S. fly-by Mariners 2 and 5 (which paid close calls on our sister planet on 14 December 1962 and 19 October 1965), as well as the fly-by Venera 2 of 27 February 1966 and Veneras 3, 4 and 6 which actually entered the Cytherean atmosphere repeatedly on 1 March 1966, 18 October 1967 and 17 May 1969 and penetrated to an increasing depth, until Venera 7 effected on 15 December 1970 the first soft landing on the surface itself.

The scientific results of these flights, telemetered to us on Earth across a space gap of many millions of kilometres, were far-reaching. The composition of the Cytherean atmosphere was found to consist of some 95% of carbon dioxide, 2% of nitrogen and 1% of water vapour, the bulk of the rest being (probably) neon and argon; but free oxygen seems conspicuous by its absence (its amount, if any, is less than 0·01%). Moreover, magnetometers carried aboard several of these spacecraft failed to detect any planetary magnetic field of more than 0·01 gauss in strength; and the upper limit to a possible magnetic dipole of Venus was estimated to be no more than 0·002 that of the Earth.

In a real sense, however, space exploration of Venus commenced even before the approach of the first spacecraft; on 10 March 1961, in fact, when the first human contact with Venus was established by means of *radar*. On that day, a radio pulse beamed at Venus from the Jet Propulsion Laboratory of California Institute of Technology produced a detectable echo after more than $4\frac{1}{2}$ minutes of double-transit time; and since that date innumerable echoes have been produced and measured at different institutions in the United States as well as in Russia.

Their contributions to the exploration of Venus have been extensive, and some have been entirely unique. By a determination of the time-lapse between the outgoing signal and its returning echo, the distance separating us from Venus can be calculated with a precision far surpassing that of any other previously used method; and this has led to a determination of its orbital elements so precise as to inaugurate an entirely new epoch in celestial mechanics. For instance, the semi-major axis of the Cytherean orbit—0·723329860 of that of the Earth—is now known within an error of two parts in 10^9; and the length of the 'astronomical unit' (i.e., the semi-major axis of the terrestrial orbit around the Sun) was deduced to be 149,597,892 kms, with an error of only ±5 kms. These values are more than 2,000 times as precise as the best previous 'astronomical' determinations of them by celestial triangulation.

But perhaps the greatest single contribution of radar astronomy to the study of Venus has been the recent discovery and measurement of its axial rotation. This white celestial Goddess of Love protects herself from inquisitive terrestrial onlookers by surrounding her entire face with an impenetrable 'veil of chastity'—in the form of a cloud layer, obscuring any surface markings whose motion could indicate the length of a Cytherean day; and spectroscopic measurements of radial velocities with different positions of the slit on the planet's disc have suggested long ago that the axial rotation of Venus—if any—must be very slow. On the other hand, the profiles of radar echoes at cm-wavelengths—our only means of permanent contact with the planet's surface so far—should clearly be influenced by planetary spin.

On the one hand, different parts of the surface return signals with a different time-lag; the 'radar depth' of the Cytherean globe —i.e., the time needed for such signals to traverse a distance equal to the diameter of the planet—amounts to more than 0·02 second, and the radius of 6056 kms of the solid globe of the planet has been deduced from its measurements. On the other hand, the reflection of radar pulses from a spinning globe will also produce detectable shifts in frequency of the observed echo profiles, due to a different velocity of the individual surface elements along the line of sight. If the anatomy of such echoes is dissected according to the time-lag and frequency-shift observed at different positions of the planet in its orbit, it should be possible to deduce from this 'range-Doppler' tracking the period of planetary rotation, as well as the position of its axis in space.

Observations of Venus, conducted over several years at the Jet Propulsion Laboratory in California have disclosed that the planet rotates in a *retrograde* direction (i.e., one opposite to its orbital motion) in a sidereal period of 243·1 terrestrial days; about an axis inclined by 87°.8 to the orbital plane of the planet—as if a forward-rotating globe had tipped over almost upside down! We have already encountered another case of retrograde rotation in Uranus (see Chapter IV) among major planets; but in the inner precincts of the solar system it is truly unique. An even more noteworthy point is the fact that a period of 243·16 days—virtually identical with that deduced from the radar data—would enable Venus to always show us the same face at each inferior conjunction.

Let us explain more closely what we mean. The time interval between successive conjunctions of Venus with the Earth (i.e., a period of the so-called 'synodic orbit') is equal to 584 days—much longer than the 'sidereal orbit' of 224·7 days because the Earth, being farther from the Sun, keeps chasing Venus in space with an inferior orbital velocity; so that 1 year and 7 months will elapse on the average before Venus, escaping us in front, will catch up with us from behind. On the other hand, its 'sidereal day' of 243 such days of our own calendar is defined as a time interval of two successive meridian transits of the same star observed from the planet's surface; while its 'solar day' is an interval between two successive passages of the Sun through the meridian.

On the Earth, because our planet rotates fast and revolves slowly, a difference between the mean solar and sidereal day amounts to only 3 minutes and 56·6 seconds (and this difference is almost negligible for the outer planets); the solar day being the longer of the two because the Earth rotates in the same direction as it revolves. However, on Venus, which rotates slowly in the retrograde sense but revolves fast, the solar day is bound to be much shorter than the sidereal one; and its duration (corresponding to a sum of the angular velocities of the sidereal rotation and revolution of the planet) is equal to only 116·8 days—i.e., exactly one-fifth of the period of the Cytherean synodic orbit.

And more surprises are in store for us when we inquire about a time-interval between the successive transits of the Earth through the Cytherean meridian. This time-interval (corresponding to a sum of the angular velocities of sidereal rotation of Venus and of the Earth's revolution around the Sun) is equal to 146 days— exactly one-quarter of the Cytherean synodic year! This coincidence implies that, between successive conjunctions with the Earth, Venus manages to rotate four times with respect to us, but five times with respect to the Sun. To an observer on Venus, the Sun rises in the west (because of retrograde rotation of our sister planet), reaches the meridian one month later, and eventually sets in the east—repeating this sequence every 117 terrestrial days, with no significant change of seasons (since the axis of rotation is almost perpendicular to the orbital plane). Thus the Earth gets in opposition with Venus every fifth solar day—when an observer on our sister planet would see the same face of 'full' Earth looking down at him exactly at the time of his midnight—a brilliant, dazzling celestial object of $-5·6$ apparent visual magnitude, much brighter than Venus can ever appear to us. This remarkable resonance strongly suggests a secular influence of 'tidal coupling' between the two neighbouring sister planets; but its more detailed mechanism is as yet largely obscure.

A synthesis of the images of Venus illuminated by radar flashes, based on the 'range-Doppler' tracking, is currently making another unique contribution to the study of our sister planet—in the form of the 'radar maps' of its surface, providing a first glimpse of what its solid surface looks like underneath the clouds. They disclose that the surface of Venus is not as rough as that of the Moon (it reflects signals like dry, sandy desert ground on the Earth, but definitely a more compact ground than we sensed by similar techniques to cover the Moon), but it is by no means smooth. In fact, several regions of Cytherean geography appear on its globe as mountainous; though whether these are jumbled rock-strewn fields of rocks or real mountain chains we cannot as yet say; but this much we know for sure: underneath its veil, the face of the celestial Goddess of Love reveals to an inquisitive radar eye wrinkles suggestive of advancing age.

And with this disclosure we come to the end of the story of Venus as far as it can be written up to this time. The reader will notice that most of what we know about it has been found out only in the past ten years, by the methods of radio and space astronomy. An application of these methods of research since 1961 has already deprived our nearest planetary neighbour of many secrets previously hidden by its perpetual veil of clouds; and man-made spacecraft have already effected parachute descents through its atmosphere almost down to the ground. Yet it is unlikely that man will ever land there as he has already done on the Moon, and may soon do on Mars; for the Cytherean surface environment is about as inviting as the abyssal depths of our terrestrial oceans. We could not do anything there that cannot be accomplished better by instrumented spacecraft.

VIII–2 Mars

Our outer celestial neighbour in the planetary world is *Mars*—a planet bearing (because of its colour) the name of the ancient god of war—whom Hephaistos, smoking from the terrestrial volcanoes, and suspecting under the Latinized name his old rival Ares in disguise, keeps at a safe distance from golden Aphrodite. The distance is indeed adequate for the purpose; for Mars revolves around the Sun in 687 days at a mean distance of 1·524 astronomical units in an orbit of marked eccentricity which never brings it any closer to the Earth than 55·5 million kms. And even this happens only seldom—about once every 16 years—when both Mars and the Earth happen to be in opposition with the Sun at a time when Mars passes through its perihelion (the point of its elliptical orbit that brings it nearest to the Sun) while the Earth is simultaneously in aphelion. At all other times the distance between them is greater, much greater, than that separating us from Venus. A spacecraft sent out to pay a call on this planetary neighbour must spend, on the average, about seven months en route (in contrast to a three-month trip to Venus) before it may reach the proximity of its target; but this is largely due to the fact that, in doing so, it sails largely 'upstream' (i.e., against the direction of solar attraction), while en route to Venus (or Mercury) the opposite is the case.

As Mars is an outer planet—revolving in an orbit which embraces that of the Earth—its apparent disc, seen from the Earth, will not depart from 'full' phase by more than 47°—i.e., Mars can appear distinctly gibbous to us, but never as a crescent. Its distance from us in space varies between 55·5 and 378 million kilometres; but even at the closest approach the planet does not become brighter than $-2·8$ apparent visual magnitude. This fact suggests that Mars is not a very large planet, and is borne out by measurements of the size of its apparent disc (attaining only 25".1 at the time of a perihelion opposition).

And neither are the physical attributes of Mars at all conspicuous in the planetary world. Its globe of 6,788 kms equatorial diameter renders it slightly more than half the size of our planet; and it contains only $10·76\%$ of the terrestrial mass; so that the mean density of Mars proves to be $3·94$ g/cm^3, and gravitational acceleration on the surface, 362 cm/sec^2. A man weighing 160 pounds on the Earth would, therefore, weigh only 59 lbs on Mars. Yet in spite of the smaller size and greater distance of this planet, our knowledge of the Martian world is well ahead of our acquaintance with Venus, because—unlike Venus—the Martian surface is exposed to direct view by telescopic observation; and even at the distance separating it from us it has disclosed the existence of many permanent markings which have exercised our curiosity and imagination for decades—if not centuries—in the past.

The first such markings to be detected on the apparent disc of Mars, in the early part of the seventeenth century, were whitish spots near the limb, tentatively identified with the 'polar caps' of the planet (see Plate 16) by analogy with similar features on Earth. This tentative identification derived strength from the fact that two such caps were eventually detected on the disc, in positions opposite to each other, and responding by variations in size to alternating seasons of the Martian year. Moreover, when the localities at which the white caps were observed were found to coincide with the poles of axial rotation of the planet—whose positions were established by the systematic motions of other markings on the Martian disc in the course of the (Martian) day—the identification of these spots with the polar caps of our own planet became complete. But, as we shall see, this analogy was stretched too far when it came to surmising their composition.

Extensive observations carried out throughout the eighteenth century established that Mars rotates with respect to the stars once every 24 hours, 37 minutes and 22·6679 seconds about an axis which is inclined to the orbital plane of the planet by $64°.8$ (for the Earth, the corresponding figure is $66°.55$); and the sense of rotation is direct. A sidereal day on Mars is, therefore, longer than our own by only a little more than 41 minutes of our time. Moreover—as on the Earth—the centrifugal force due to this rotation has flattened the Martian globe on the poles to a small but measurable extent. In point of fact, although Mars rotates somewhat more slowly than our Earth, its oblateness proves to be greater. The reason is the greater homogeneity of the Martian globe. While the density of the Earth increases from less than 3 g/cm^3 on the surface to about 17 g/cm^3 near its centre, for Mars the increase in density toward the centre must be much smaller, and the density should scarcely exceed $4·5$–$5·0$ g/cm^3 in the central regions of the planet (corresponding to a central pressure of only $2·8 \times 10^{11}$ dynes/cm^2).

Does Mars possess an atmosphere above its surface? There have long been indications that this is the case. The simplest was the fact that the apparent disc of the planet does not appear at a distance to be uniformly bright, but is progressively darkened towards the limb—especially when observed in blue or violet light. Such a phenomenon can only be explained by the presence of an atmosphere surrounding the planet, whose absorption dims surface regions illuminated by low Sun. In addition, obscuration phenomena were occasionally observed on the Martian disc which seemed to impose a transient veil of reduced visibility in certain regions of the planetary surface; and this suggested the effects of clouds. Such hypothetical cloud cover was, however, always severely localized and only impeded—rather than prohibited—the visibility of the surface through their veil. This whole phenomenon suggested once more the presence of an atmosphere surrounding the Martian globe, but a tenuous one—a far cry from the massive atmospheric envelope surrounding the planet Venus, or even our Earth.

How dense is the Martian atmosphere, and what does it consist of? The first clue to its composition was discovered in 1947, when absorption bands of carbon dioxide were identified in the Martian spectrum by Kuiper and his associates. The actual structure and composition of the Martian atmosphere did not, however, fully come to light until the advent of spacecraft in the last decade—since 1965 three of them have managed to pay close calls on our sister planet. The first eye-opener was the historic flight of U.S. Mariner 4 which, at the time of its closest approach, overflew the Martian surface at an altitude of only 9,840 kms after a journey of 220 million kilometres—marksmanship which may be compared with rolling a strike in a bowling lane 400 miles long! Moreover, Mariners 6 and 7—which followed in the footsteps of their predecessors with equal success four years later—approached the Martian surface within no more than 2,000 kms during their respective fly-bys on 31 July and 5 August of 1969. It is largely thanks to the contributions of these spacecraft (supplemented by radar work from the Earth) that we can present to our reader as complete and authentic a picture of the Martian environment as we shall outline in this section.

A determination of the pressure and density profile of the Martian atmosphere, from the refraction of the spacecraft's radio signals as they underwent occultation by the Martian limb during their fly-bys, disclosed the following facts. The total air pressure above the Martian ground amounts to only 6–7 millibars (i.e., about one-hundredth of a terrestrial atmosphere—encountered on Earth about 30 kms up), drops to one millibar at about 25 kms, and to one-tenth of a millibar at 50 kms. At least 80% of its mass is carbon dioxide (and possibly close to 100% if nitrogen or neon—as yet unidentified—prove to be absent). The water-vapour content appears to be less than 0·05% by mass; and that of free oxygen, still smaller.

At the average distance of Mars from the Sun, the light of the latter is less than half as bright as it appears to us; but its intensity is sufficient to endow Mars with an ionosphere. According to the measurements of Mariner occultations, the maximum density of free electrons is encountered at an altitude of approximately 120 kms above the Martian surface (in contrast to a 300 km altitude on the Earth), and amounts to only about 10^5 electrons per ccm (about one-tenth of the maximum density of our ionosphere).

Another feat performed by the Mariners was their measurement of the Martian temperatures—both on the ground and aloft. That temperatures on Martian ground are much lower than on the Earth was already known before, from the measurements of thermal radiation emitted by the planet; and the Mariner results confirmed that, in the tropical belt of the Martian globe, the daytime temperature on the surface varies between $-20°$ and $+30°$ centigrade. At a height of only 20 kms above the surface the mean temperature drops, however, to $-70°C$; and to less than $-150°C$ at 50 kms up. Another 50 or 70 kms up—in the ionosphere—the temperature may exceed $200°C$; but even this is much less than the temperatures in excess of $1,000°C$ encountered in the densest parts of the corresponding terrestrial layer. During noontime in the Martian tropics the ground temperature can, however, attain the comfortable range of $20°$-$30°C$ (compare this with a lunar temperature of $120°$—$130°C$ at the same time); but it drops far below freezing well before sunset.

The night-time temperatures on Mars are impossible to measure from the Earth, because the Martian night hemisphere is largely hidden from our view; and those of the polar regions are difficult to measure even in daytime because of foreshortening. Mariner 6 and 7 did this for us in 1969, and arrived at a most interesting result. On the rim of the north polar cap the ground temperature proved to be only about $-120°C$ with an uncertainty of $\pm 10°C$ reflecting the errors of measurement. If we compare this value with a temperature of $-125°C$ at which carbon dioxide solidifies at a pressure of 6–7 millibars, the message of the measurement immediately becomes clear: that the Martian polar caps are not icefields of frozen water such as we find in the polar regions of our Earth, but rather frozen layers of 'dry ice'—or solidified carbon dioxide. This fits in with what we know now of the composition of the Martian atmosphere, with its preponderance of CO_2 and virtual absence of water, and one of the age-long problems of the Martian environment has thus definitely been solved.

With the approach of winter, the arctic air temperatures on Mars apparently become low enough for carbon dioxide to freeze out of the atmosphere and cover the ground with snowshowers of dry ice, which melt again (partly in the north, more completely in the south) with the advent of spring. The snow cover even at the height of the winter appears, however, to be quite thin—only inches or yards in depth—with no indication of permanent glaciers; a far cry from the massive ice-caps covering the polar regions of our own planet. As, moreover, dry ice of CO_2 never melts but sublimates directly into the air, no liquid ever flows from the Martian polar regions to the tropical belt; and no need exists for any 'canals' to drain it off.

One of the most important parts of the Mariner missions has been to record for us views of the Martian landscape as seen from a close proximity to its surface, and to televise these views across a distance which electromagnetic waves took many minutes to traverse before they could deliver their message to us. Pictures reconstructed from the signals of Mariner 4 in 1965 covered only a little more than one per cent of the entire Martian surface; but Mariners 6 and 7 in 1969 recorded almost all of the remainder, and the best of some 200 photographs secured by these spacecraft have attained a resolution of close to half a kilometre on the Martian ground—about as high as that attainable on the lunar surface with our largest telescopes from the Earth.

What did these photographs (see again Plate 16) reveal? A stark, arid landscape, highly mountainous in most places, and profusely dotted with pockmarks identical in size, shape and other general characteristics with the 'craters' so familiar to us from the Moon. Some are (as on the Moon) hundreds of kilometres in size; their walls are 3–4 kms deep; and many also possess 'central mountains' with which we are familiar from lunar topography.

Their origin—or at least the origin of most of such formations—is in no doubt: they represent impact craters of the type we have already discussed in connection with our Moon. The surface of Mars (likewise unprotected by any atmosphere of appreciable density) represents just another cumulative scoreboard, in the solar system, of hits by meteors and meteorites, asteroids or comets; and because the Martian orbit just skirts the inner border of the ring of asteroids, it may in the past have suffered many more hits by them than our Moon which is tucked in more snugly in the inner precincts of the solar system.

The heavily pockmarked face of Mars—like that of the Moon—bears witness to its great age, and to a well-nigh complete absence of any erosion processes that could have levelled off its stony surface relief after long intervals of time. We know now that the Martian air is very thin, and its surface bone-dry. The stony sculpture of its surface testifies, moreover, that it has been the same way from time immemorial.

Indeed, the Martian surface appears to be very rough—much more so than that of Venus. Radar rangings of the planet's profile have disclosed level differences amounting to ten kilometres in altitude—the dark regions of the planetary disc (see Plate 16) being lowlands of considerably greater surface roughness than the more elevated brighter areas. But of the Martian 'canals', which have exercised the human imagination so much in the past hundred years, the spacecraft found nothing. An illusion of their existence must have been due to a combination of actual surface roughness and the shadows cast by its relief, below the limit of optical resolution by the telescopes used on the ground; and their disappearance under the more searching glance of the spacecraft should caution over-optimistic observers in future from fishing for information too close to the limit of performance of their instruments.

And not only are there no canals on Mars; the spacecraft also failed to discover there any mountain chains which could—as on the Earth—be due to a folding of the crust. Indeed, the Martian crust—with its altitude differences of 10 km and absence of folded mountains—gives every impression of a rigidity far greater than that possessed by the terrestrial crust; and this rigidity is probably the consequence of a relatively low temperature prevalent in the interior. Since Mars is but one half of the Earth in size and contains only a little more than 10% of its mass, it could not have developed and stored nearly as much internal heat as our own planet. All external manifestations of its surface known to us so far appear to be consistent with this view.

And more: we are practically certain that, unlike our Earth, the planet Mars contains in its interior no metallic core of any size. We conclude this not only from the absence of any pronounced concentration of density in its interior (which would be consistent with the observed polar flattening of the planetary globe), but also from the fact that—unlike the Earth, but like Venus—Mars does not possess any measurable magnetic field. Magnetometers aboard the Mariners failed to detect a magnetic moment of Mars which exceeded one or two ten-thousandths of that of the Earth; and for a planet rotating almost as fast as our Earth, so complete an absence of a magnetic field signifies that a metallic 'dynamo' is not a part of the equipment stored in the Martian interior. Thus, Mars, like Venus, is not surrounded by any 'van Allen belts' of charged particles like that possessed by our Earth; though it does possess an ionosphere.

Under all these circumstances, could a planet like Mars ever have given rise to, or could it harbour, life? Whatever hopes we may have entertained in this respect before the advent of spacecraft, the results of their first three space missions in 1965 and 1969 were sufficient to shatter these hopes beyond resurrection. The Martian environment appears to be almost as inhospitable—if not hostile—to life as that on our Moon; and should we, against all our present expectations find any traces of living matter on its surface, it would be of interest to micro-biologists rather than to humanists. The hope of finding life on the planet Mars has evaporated together with the canals into thin air. It is now almost certain that we are alone in the solar system; and in the Universe—who knows?

VIII-3: Mercury and Pluto

Of these two remaining planets belonging to the terrestrial group in the solar system not much can be said; for our acquaintance with them is so far rather limited. This is due largely to external circumstances rather than to any lack of interest. Mercury—the innermost planet of the solar family—never elongates far enough from the Sun in the sky to make it an easy object of observation; while Pluto—the outermost sentinel of our system—is so far away from us and so faint that it requires a really large telescope merely to spot it.

Both these planets revolve around the Sun in elliptical orbits which are markedly eccentric (for Mercury, the eccentricity is $0 \cdot 206$;

while for Pluto it is 0·249); and inclined much more to the ecliptic (7°.0 for Mercury and 17°.1 for Pluto) than all the other planets. They differ widely in size, however; for whereas the mean distance of Mercury from the Sun amounts to only 57·9 million kms—a distance which light traverses in a mere 3·22 minutes—the mean distance to Pluto is 5,910 million kms, or 328 light-minutes (i.e., it is more than 100 times as far). Their orbital periods differ accordingly; for while Mercury needs slightly less than 88 days to travel once around the Sun, one orbit of Pluto takes a little more than 249 years.

What these two planets have in common is a relatively small size and mass. On account of its proximity to us in space, Mercury has been contacted by radar from the Earth; and according to its message the diameter of the planet is equal to 4,879±1 km, while its mass has proved to amount to only 5·3% of that of the Earth. A combination of these data leads to a mean density of 5·5 g/cm³ for Mercury—about the same as for our Earth, but unexpectedly high for a planet of so small a mass. And the same appears to be true of Pluto as well. Its absolute diameter—still uncertain because of the difficulty inherent in measurements of its very small angular diameter—should be between 6,000–7,000 kms; and since its mass appears to be close to 18% of that of the Earth, its mean density is unlikely to be less than that of Mercury—possibly higher.

Radar observations (of the same kind as described on pp. 215–16 in connection with Venus) have recently disclosed that Mercury rotates about an axis almost perpendicular to its orbital plane, and in the same direction as it revolves, in a (sidereal) period of 58·6 days. A sidereal day of 58·6 days of terrestrial time on Mercury corresponds, however, to a solar day of 176 days of our own; and this latter period is just three times the length of the sidereal day of 58^{d}6, and two-thirds of Mercury's sidereal year. Thus—contrary to previous belief—Mercury does not always show the Sun the same face. To an observer on its surface the Sun—a huge fiery disc whose apparent diameter would be two to three times as large as we see on the Earth—would rise in the east and set in the west every 176 terrestrial days. At the time of each perihelion passage, the Sun would appear to pause in the sky, and actually reverse the direction of its motion for about two weeks. This should cause rather excessive heating at the sub-solar point at that time, giving rise to two super-tropical regions, situated on the planet's equator opposite to each other; and seasonal effects (due to the negligible inclination of the planet's equator to its orbital plane) would probably be—as on Venus—non-existent. Pluto also seems to rotate about an axis (of unknown orientation) in a much shorter period of 6 days, 9 hours and 17 minutes. We know this from the measured periodic changes of its brightness (due to meridian transits of spots of different reflectivity, even though their size is below the resolution limit of our telescopes).

The radar reflectivity of the surface of Mercury appears to be almost identical with that of our Moon. We surmise, therefore, that the physical structure of the Mercurian surface—which, like that of the Moon, is unprotected by any atmosphere—will be similar to that of the Moon; and possess a similar kind of regolith. If our telescopes possessed the requisite resolving power, we would probably see the surface of Mercury to be pockmarked with impact craters like the surface of our own Moon, or of Mars. Being nearer the Sun, the hemisphere should experience noon temperatures as high as 400°C; while its nights may become as cold as on the Moon (since they last much longer). Experimental verification of these extremes is, however, difficult on account of the close proximity of this planet to the Sun, which means that all measurements must be made in twilight hours. As to Pluto, nothing whatever is known about the structure of its surface so far, except that it is not uniformly bright (as witnessed by its periodic changes in brightness, no doubt caused by axial rotation). At a mean distance of 39·5 astronomical units, absorption of diluted sunlight (which, on Pluto, would be so dim that stars could be seen day and night) could not warm up the surface to more than $-220°C$ in daytime; but how close the actual temperature comes to this limit remains to be seen.

CHAPTER IX

Comets and Meteors

OUR SURVEY of the principal constituents of the solar system is still incomplete in one respect: for we have not yet brought to the stage a class of celestial objects which constitute a significant and enigmatic part of its structure: namely, the comets.

Comets have enjoyed for a long time a rather unsavoury reputation as harbingers of evil tidings for people and nations who probably deserved no better; and whose fear of cometary apparitions may have reflected the qualms of their own guilty consciences. In more modern times—when ancient superstitions began to give way to the inquiring scientific spirit—cometary reputations have hardly improved; and their ancient role as precursors of calamities gave way to dark suspicions of celestial poisoners—if not of our waters, then of our atmosphere. We shall try to demonstrate in this chapter that these latter suspicions are as unfounded as all other astrological superstitions of ancient and medieval times. Comets were traditionally distrusted for reasons with which modern astronomers are partly inclined to sympathize: their unpredictable behaviour in the sky, like strangers coming seemingly from nowhere, staging unexpected appearances and exits in a manner quite contrary to the doctrines of heavenly immutability.

The complaints of the unpredictable celestial behaviour of the cometary population are indeed well founded. Consider, for instance, the motions of the comets in the sky. We mentioned earlier that all the major constituents of our solar system conform to a certain basic set of 'traffic rules' constraining their motions. They revolve around the Sun in the same direction, in orbits which are approximately circular, and situated in very nearly the same plane. The comets represent the only class of bodies in the solar system which defy all three rules in a most disrespectful manner: their orbits are, in general, highly eccentric—so much so that they often skirt the parabolic limit—and their planes are inclined virtually at random to the 'invariable plane' of the solar system, so that many of them (whose poles are 'tipped over' upside down) are revolving in a retrograde direction. Halley's comet—whose periodic visitation about every 75 years has become a permanent feature of human history in the past 2,000 years—belongs to this class (see Plate 17).

Motion along such orbits can take comets from distances far beyond the orbit of Pluto to nearer to the Sun than Mercury. While at a great distance from the Sun (beyond the orbit of Jupiter) a comet—if seen at all, and detected by its motion on stellar background—would be of star-like appearance, in no way indicative of its true nature. At distances between those of Mars and Jupiter, the image of a comet would, however, begin to grow fuzzy like a small diffuse nebula, tending to get elongated in a direction mostly away from the Sun—an elongation which would eventually give rise to a cometary tail.

Very few comets are visible to the naked eye, or develop proper tails, at more than one astronomical unit away from the Sun; but the nearer they approach our central luminary, the brighter they become and the more magnificent the tail which they can spread out over the sky. Comets with conspicuous tails have been scarce in this century; and probably few readers still living have seen one with their own eyes. The preceding century saw, however, several comets spread their tails over a major part of the sky; and Cheseaux's comet of 1744—that peacock of the cometary tribe—possessed no less than six tails at the same time, spread out like a fan in the sky to the admiration of countless onlookers.

The great variation in brightness which a comet experiences in its orbit at varying distances from the Sun strongly suggests that the origin of its light is nothing else but sunlight in disguise. At great distances—in the 'cold storage' of the outer parts of the solar system—a comet is reduced to a solid *core* which merely reflects sunlight like a minor planet. With increasing proximity to the Sun, however, this core slowly begins to evaporate and surround itself with a gaseous *coma* which begins to shine with a light of its own excited by sunlight, and is dragged along by the core through space (cf. Plate 17). However, with increasing proximity to the Sun the gas liberated by evaporation can no longer be contained in the coma and begins to escape in a direction generally (though neither exactly, nor always) away from the Sun. This escaping jet of gas—generally called the *tail*—represents, therefore, a net loss of cometary material which the feeble attraction of the nucleus is powerless to prevent. The luminosity of such tails—their main title to celestial fame—is wholly excited by sunlight; and their development as well as dispersal is at the mercy of the forces—gravitational as well as electromagnetic—prevailing in interplanetary space.

The anatomy of a comet can, therefore, be broadly divided into a core, its coma, and the tail. But—in spite of external appearances—it is the inconspicuous cometary core which really matters in the long run. Its dimensions are insignificant, barely a few kilometres across; for whenever a comet transits across the Sun, it vanishes completely out of sight down to its core, with no trace of a 'black dot' seen against the solar disc. Its mass must likewise be minute by astronomical standards; for even the closest approach of a comet fails to disturb in the least the appointed motion of any other celestial body in the solar system. We surmise that the masses of cometary heads do not, on the average, exceed some 10^{17} or 10^{18} grams. An exceptional comet may, perhaps, be more massive; but an average formation of this kind would not exceed a trillion tons.

A mass of this order of magnitude may seem large in comparison with our common terrestrial standards; but it represents only one-billionth of that of the Earth as a whole, or one ten-millionth of that of the Moon. Since, moreover, the size of the cometary cores should not exceed a few kilometres, their mean densities will not exceed about one gram per cubic centimetre.

So low a mean density of the core indicates that the bulk of its mass is not formed by solid rocks, but by 'frozen ice' of more volatile substances which, with increasing proximity to the Sun, should begin to sublimate into interplanetary space. The cometary comas and tails represent, in fact, by-products of such a process. The volume of cometary tails is certainly enormous; but the mean density of gases escaping through them is only about 10–100 times higher than that of the surrounding interplanetary substrate.

What does cometary matter consist of? As long as it remains confined to the solid state of the core, we have no way of probing its composition at a distance. However, as soon as its material evaporates to form the coma and the tail, the gas becomes luminous by solar photo-excitation; and its principal constituents can be determined by spectral analysis. Needless to say, the degree of photo-excitation varies with the distance from the Sun. The only molecular bands apparent in the spectra of the comets outside the orbit of Mars are those due to the neutral molecules of CH, CN or of C_2. Inside the Martian orbit ionized diatomic molecules (of carbon monoxide, nitrogen or hydroxyl) begin to make their appearance, together with tri-atomic molecules like CH_2 or NH_2. At distances smaller than one astronomical unit from the Sun, even metallic lines (sodium, iron, nickel) begin to show up in the spectrum as the cometary tails reach their full bloom. All these (and other) elements must be present in the cometary cores, from which they are released by melting and evaporation. However, what kind of molecules—possibly much more complex—they were part of in the solid state we do not know; all that the spectroscopic analysis can disclose is the composition of gases dissociated by sunlight.

Therefore, as the comet begins to approach the Sun through the inner precincts of the solar system and starts developing a tail, it is bound to lose mass irretrievably to the interplanetary substrate. How long can a comet afford to sustain such a loss and avoid complete disintegration? The answer is hardly surprising: cosmically speaking a very short time. A more exact verdict depends essentially on the degree of proximity within which a comet may actually approach the Sun. Its disintegration obviously proceeds faster, the longer it stays near the Sun. But an assessment of the amount of mass lost in the course of each orbital cycle discloses that the average lifetime of a comet that approaches the Sun within less than the distance of the Earth is limited to centuries—or, at most, millenia.

This time represents so small a fraction of the total age of our solar system that one must ask with some concern: whence do the comets come from, and from where are they replenished if we are to see any around us at all at the present time? The bulk of cometary matter is highly volatile, and chemically akin to the composition of interstellar matter (see Chapter III–1) or of the major planets (Chapter IV) rather than to the planetary bodies of more moderate mass. Moreover, if they are being melted down by the scorching heat of the Sun in their dozens each century, where do they come from, and what tempts them to burn their wings in the solar glare like moths circling a lamp?

That there are more comets in the sky than fish in all the waters of the Earth was opined by Johannes Kepler at the beginning of the seventeenth century; but in what kind of reserve pool could these cosmic fish survive $4\frac{1}{2}$ billion years without becoming extinct at an earlier evolutionary stage of the solar system? It is obvious that such a pool can be located only towards the periphery of our system, sufficiently far away from its central luminary, where the prevailing climate approaches that of interstellar space. Outside the orbit of Pluto, the temperature of solid material floating in space drops below $-200°C$; and cometary ice kept in storage so cold can afford an almost endless lifetime.

Whether the comets too constitute the left-overs from the days of the formation of the solar system, or whether they were acquired subsequently by the Sun from adjacent regions of interstellar space, we do not yet know; both possibilities must still be kept in mind. But what force can lure them out, now and then, from the relative safety of their cold storage on to the treacherous stage of the inner precincts of the solar system? The most probable answer is: the attraction of the major planets—mainly of Jupiter and Saturn. It is these planetary giants which—if the configuration is favourable—manage to persuade comets approaching them from outer space to take a sightseeing trip deeper into the solar system; and for comets which succumb to this gravitational temptation such a course is tantamount to a death-warrant, to be implemented after they have gone around the Sun—midget-like—a few dozen times.

Once cometary orbits have been reduced to ellipses which happen to graze the Sun within a short distance, only one event can rescue these comets from impending doom. If on their outward journey away from the Sun they manage to approach a major planet, its gravitational pull enables them to put on speed and escape back into the relative safety of the 'cold storage' in the outer parts of the solar system. Each century more than one comet disappears from the list of our cosmic visitors for ever, and we have seen several of them disintegrate virtually in front of our eyes; and others have become pale shadows of their former glamorous selves by gradual dissipation of their mass into space.

Taking into account the method of acquisition of the comets as well as the rate of their loss from our neighbourhood, we conclude that the total supply of cometary cores still available in the 'cold storage' which our Sun drags along with it through space must be of the order of 10^{10} to 10^{11}—an enormous number; no doubt very large in comparison with the number of fish still surviving in the polluted waters of the Earth. Since, however, each such core weighs, on the average, only 10^{17}–10^{18} grams, the total mass of cometary material available in the solar system is likely to amount to the mass of only one planet like the Earth—or, at most, Uranus or Neptune.

The main part of this mass consists probably of frozen hydrocarbons and other compounds of the light elements like carbon, nitrogen, and oxygen. However, cometary material does not consist only of loosely-packed 'ices' of this kind; but rather of 'dirty ice' containing also solid particles—silicates, even metals—which comets sweep up on their journey through space and accrete in snowball fashion. As their snowballs continue to melt and disintegrate in the scorching rays of the Sun, solid particles contained in them commence to split away again—like refuse thrown off by careless travellers; and this debris will continue to trail the motion of the respective comet until it eventually clutters up most of its path.

Such 'stragglers' may, in turn, be intercepted by the Earth whenever the latter intersects (or comes close to) a cometary orbit, and manifest themselves as 'meteors' during the last seconds of their cosmic existence as atmospheric resistance heats up their mass to vaporization. Most of the meteors you can spot as they flash across the night sky are no larger than pin-heads of cosmic matter (solid grains of ice crystals), which vaporize mostly in rarefied atmosphere at altitudes between 80–120 km and can become visible to the eye only because they enter our atmosphere with relative velocities of many kilometres per second—and possess, therefore, an amount of kinetic energy whose conversion into heat by atmospheric friction can produce luminous effects visible at a great distance. It is estimated that our Earth sweeps up thousands of tons of such meteoritic material from space each year.

Most meteors which attract our attention in the sky at night spend themselves completely in a second or two at altitudes of many kilometres above the ground, and in doing so become no brighter than most stars in the sky. Now and then, however, you may be fortunate to witness a much more spectacular phenomenon: a large meteor—appearing suddenly in the dark sky—illuminates the entire landscape with dazzling light and for several seconds changes night into day. Such meteors represent kilograms—rather than milligrams—of cosmic matter which may penetrate much deeper into the denser layers of our atmosphere; and some of them do actually hit the ground.

A few times in a century, meteorites penetrate the atmosphere with a residual mass amounting to hundreds or even thousands of kilograms, and impact on the terrestrial surface amidst spectacular effects which attract world-wide attention. The last such fall occurred in the Sichote Alin Mountains of eastern Siberia in February 1947, when a whole swarm of metallic meteorites collided with the Earth. Against impacts of bodies of this size our atmosphere ceases to provide much—if any—protection. Smaller meteorites may still be decelerated by it enough to survive on impact in solid state; but a very large body pays little attention to our air and impacts on the ground with a relative velocity which may approach 72 km/sec.

In such cases, a sudden conversion of kinetic energy into heat on impact is more than sufficient to vaporize the entire mass of the intruder which explodes like a bubble of hot gas; and the resulting 'impact crater' may thus be very largely devoid of any trace of the actual material of the cosmic intruder. We have discussed such phenomena in Chapter VII–2, in connection with the history of the lunar surface. On the Earth, erosive processes due to the combined action of air and water limit the lifetime of such 'astroblemes' to less than one million years. Several dozens of them have, however, been discovered by geologists in different parts of the world as proof that the days of the bombardment of planetary surfaces by cosmic projectiles of a calibre heavy enough to produce impact formations ranging from several hundreds to a few thousand metres in size are not yet over even now.

When particles of meteoritic matter are recovered from such falls and find their way to our laboratories, their analysis can furnish not only their composition, but also their ages. The 'exposure ages' of such meteorites—measuring the time during which such particles split up from larger bodies and travelled through space as individual stragglers—turn out to range from a few million to a few hundred million years. However, the ages which elapsed since their matter last solidified come in most cases remarkably close to 4·6 billion years—i.e., the same age as was established for the oldest rocks of the lunar surface.

This coincidence strengthens our conviction that the latter age represents a very important date in the history of the solar system—probably identical with the time of its origin. Moreover, a relatively small dispersion in age of the individual rocks and meteorites around 4·6 billion years suggests that the formative age of the solar system lasted no longer than a few dozen million years. Its more specific details are still a matter of controversy among contemporary students of the subject; but the influx of new data through modern methods of space astronomy entitles us to hope that this great problem—which has exercised the human mind for many centuries—may at last yield to a rational explanation within our lifetime.

CHAPTER X

The Solar System—Its Origin and Grand Design

THE AIM of this chapter will be to cast a retrospective glance at all that we have learned about our planetary family and other constituent members of the solar system, and to sketch a more general outline of its design. Why is the solar system arranged as we find it today, and what kind of processes may have led it to acquire its present structure?

Let us first sketch a *model* of this system on a scale which should bring home to the reader its essential characteristics. If we were to identify the Sun in such a model as a balloon one metre in diameter, Jupiter would be represented by a globe of the size of a grapefruit, one-tenth as large as the Sun, revolving around it at a distance of a little more than half a kilometre (or, more exactly, 559 metres away); and Saturn, of the proportional size of an orange, could be found at a little less than twice that distance. The mean distance of the Earth (resembling in size a cherry) from the Sun would, on this model, be just about 107·5 metres; and our Moon (akin to a cherry stone) would revolve around it at a distance of about one foot.

The light rays from the Sun—the fastest messengers in the Universe— would reach the Earth in 8·32 minutes (just under 500 seconds); Jupiter in 43·27 minutes (just under three-quarters of an hour); while Pluto—the outermost sentinel of our system—receives sunlight which has been en route, on the average, for 328 minutes or just under $5\frac{1}{2}$ hours. At the distance of Pluto, the Sun would appear to the naked eye as a star-like object of about the same angular diameter as the planet Venus shows to us at the time of its closest approach, and would illuminate the bleak Plutonian landscape not much better than our terrestrial nights at the time of full-moon. These comparisons should underline the vast dimensions of our planetary system, and the relative smallness of all bodies constituting it. Its principal ingredient is empty space; and

The Solar System—Its Origin and Grand Design

if the Sun were to expand to the dimensions of the orbit of Pluto, its mean density would be reduced to only 2×10^{-12} g/cm^3.

Next let us consider briefly the principal *kinematic characteristics* of the solar system, which are faithfully conserved (or change extremely slowly) over long intervals of time. We have seen already in preceding chapters that the motions of most material constituents of the solar system conform to a certain basic set of 'traffic rules' which can be summed up as follows: the orbits of such bodies deviate only slightly from circles, and are inclined but little to the 'invariable plane' of the system (though considerably to the solar equator); and the bodies revolving in these orbits do so in the same direction. The larger the mass of the respective body, the more closely these rules seem to be followed; large planets observe them more meticulously than smaller terrestrial ones (such as Mercury or Pluto) or than even smaller asteroids; and only the comets show flagrant disrespect for them all. Cometary orbits frequently exhibit eccentricities bordering on the parabolic; and the inclinations of their orbits range so widely that many of them revolve, in effect, in a direction opposite to those of planetary motions.

It is easy to see what may have led to the establishment of such cosmic traffic rules in our solar system: namely, self-preservation. A motorist driving on motorways would not get very far if, in a dare-devil mood or a fit of absentmindedness, he entered such roads at the exit rather than the entrance, and thus found himself moving against the traffic rather than with it; a collision with an oncoming lorry would soon shatter his vehicle to pieces. Similarly, a reckless driver who habitually tries to drive faster than others and cuts across their paths too often, would likewise not survive such stunts for very long. In the solar system, the same kind of cosmic justice is being dispensed by the 'laws of motion' of celestial bodies, and has been for a very long time. As a consequence, planetary bodies not mindful of the rules may no longer be with us, and have paid the price of being shattered to pieces, or ejected from the system—which we still see happening to the comets. The solar system as we see it today may, therefore, not represent its true initial state, but may rather be a torso—all that remains of its original state some 4·6 aeons ago. If the initial conditions with which the planets originated were chaotic, many of its original constituents could have been lost to the solar system by the dynamical action of their neighbours before this system assumed its present well-ordered form.

These considerations should explain why most remaining charter members of the solar system revolve around the Sun as they do in nearly circular orbits and in the same direction. That they also do so in almost the same plane goes back to a cumulative effect of secular 'perturbations' of planetary motions by Jupiter and Saturn—the two most massive planetary bodies of our system—which through their gravitational attraction have, since time immemorial, gently but relentlessly urged all other less massive bodies to join them in travel in the same plane. This phenomenon constitutes, perhaps, another example of 'cosmic democracy', and testifies to the efficiency with which 'big shots' can push little fellows around in the planetary world as well. And what is true among major planets continues to hold good, by and large, in the families of their satellites—of which Jupiter possesses 12, Saturn 9, Uranus 5 and Neptune 2. They too revolve around their central planet largely in the plane of their equators, in direct orbits deviating but little from circles—and conform to these rules the more closely, the greater their mass. The reasons why they do so may have been the same as for the planets themselves; and this suggests that the processes by which the solar and planetary systems originated may have been largely the same, differing only in scale.

The second dynamical property which most members of the solar system (again apart from the comets!) share in common is *axial rotation*—so that (at least for the planets) their equatorial planes are only mildly inclined to that of their orbits. For Jupiter this inclination amounts to only $3°$; and for the Earth, Mars, and Neptune it remains moderate $23°-29°$). However, for Uranus it is $98°$ (so that the planet rotates in a direction opposite to that of its motion around the Sun); and for Venus, this inclination amounts to $177°$—implying that the celestial north pole is within $3°$ of the planetary south pole! The periods of their axial rotation (i.e., the lengths of the planetary solar day) are short for the major planets, and very long for Mercury and Venus. Moreover, certain intriguing resonances between the rotation and revolution of the inner terrestrial planets have been indicated by recent observations; but their real cause is still largely obscure.

Axial rotation and orbital revolution endow each planet with a certain amount of *angular momentum* (equal, basically, to a

The Solar System—Its Origin and Grand Design

product of the mass times the angular velocity of its motion) which remains conserved even through long planetary lives; and which—together with the mass itself—represents one of the two fundamental dynamical attributes of each body. When we evaluate the magnitudes of planetary angular momenta arising from their axial rotation and orbital motion we find that, whereas the overwhelming bulk of the mass of the solar system rests in the Sun (all planets added together do not constitute more than 0.13% of the whole), an almost equally overwhelming preponderance (98%) of the total momentum of the solar system is stored in the orbital momenta of the major planets. Moreover, this preponderance of the orbital momenta over rotational momenta among planetary bodies is similar to the situation already encountered among double stars (cf. Chapter III–3); but in total variance to the state of affairs prevalent among the families of satellites of the major planets, for there the bulk of the total momentum of the system is confined in the axial rotation of the central body.

Turning now to the *chemical composition* of the different classes of objects in the solar system, we find that the major planets—Jupiter, Saturn, and (to a lesser extent) Uranus, with Neptune, are essentially of the solar composition—i.e., containing three-quarters of hydrogen and the rest largely of helium—with some admixture of elements of the carbon-nitrogen group for Uranus and Neptune. The masses of these planets range between 318 terrestrial masses ($\oplus$) for Jupiter and 14.7 $\oplus$ for Uranus. When we come, however, to the Earth itself and to the rest of the terrestrial planets in the mass-range of 1.00–0.01 $\oplus$, we meet something quite different: the principal chemical constituents of their interiors appear to be oxygen, silicon, and iron; and the mean densities of their globes range between 5 ± 1 g/cm^3—in comparison with 1.0 ± 0.5 g/cm^3 for the major planets. The asteroids by their composition belong (probably) to the terrestrial group. On the other hand, the comets with their hydrocarbons and other constituents are much more akin to the major planets.

A contrast between the two groups of planetary bodies—of 'solar' and 'silicate' composition—is striking; and is among the most fundamental aspects of the problem of the origin and evolution of the solar system. An approach to this problem is, perhaps, indicated by the location of the respective types of bodies in our system as a whole. While formations of quasi-solar composition occur in the outer parts of the solar system (and this includes the comets), silicate bodies are concentrated in its inner precincts where the energy density of solar radiation is greater. Is the difference due, therefore, to the evaporation of lighter elements from inner planets caused by the heat of the Sun?

Suppose, for the sake of argument, that the composition of all planets of the solar system was initially the same and similar to that which we find today in the solar atmosphere. The latter should constitute an unadulterated sample of this primordial matter accessible to quantitative (spectroscopic) analysis: unadulterated because the large mass of the Sun, and the gravitational acceleration to which it gives rise, should prevent any selective escape of the elements even at a relatively high prevalent temperature; and because (unlike in the interior) this temperature is still far too low to cause nuclear transformations on any appreciable scale. Suppose, therefore, that we take a sample of gases now found in the solar atmosphere, and allow for the escape of its lighter elements by relaxing the gravitational field. How large a mass do we need to siphon off the Sun for this purpose so that its residue would make up a planet of the mass and composition of our Earth?

The answer turns out to be between 250 and 300 present terrestrial masses; and a similar proportion for Venus and Mars. In other words, the requisite mass of the primordial Earth turns out to be almost equal to the present mass of Jupiter; and the difference between them may be reduced to the fact that while Jupiter has managed to retain its initial composition up to the present, the Earth lost its more volatile elements on account of its greater proximity to the Sun, and has been left with its iron-silicate residue. We do not yet know for certain whether this has actually been the case (the chief question is whether the difference in cosmic climate at distances of 1 or 5 astronomical units is sufficient to account by itself for the removal or retention of volatile elements); but that it was remains a distinct possibility; and if so, a difference between the 'major' and 'terrestrial' planets in mass as well as composition may in this way find its natural explanation.

But even within the group of the terrestrial planets intriguing differences are encountered in their masses and the composition of their atmospheres (and, possibly, crusts). Because of their small mass, neither the Moon nor Mercury can retain any detectable

The Solar System—Its Origin and Grand Design 241

atmosphere; but Venus, Earth and Mars have done so, to a different extent which cannot be accounted for by the differences in mass, gravitational attraction, or temperature of these planets. The relevant differences in chemical composition have already been mentioned before and summarized in Table VIII–2. The outstanding feature of these data is the great difference in the total amount of gas surrounding Venus, Earth and Mars. Whereas the air pressure on the Cytherean surface appears to be not less than one hundred terrestrial atmospheres, that on Mars is barely one-hundredth of an atmosphere—with our Earth situated in between. Most of the air around Venus is carbon dioxide—some 10^5 g/cm^2 in contrast with only about 1 g/cm^2 of the same gas in the terrestrial atmosphere. Much of the terrestrial CO_2 is now locked in solid-state carbonates (limestones, etc.) present in the crust of our planet. Geochemists estimate that a total decomposition of these carbonates could generate a CO_2 envelope around the Earth of 70 atmospheres air pressure; so that the total supply of CO_2— both gaseous and fossil—on Venus and the Earth need not necessarily be very different.

But with water it is another story. The average amount of water vapour in our air gives rise to a partial pressure of about $0 \cdot 001$ of an atmosphere. However, if all ocean water were to evaporate, the air pressure on the Earth would be increased 400-fold. On the other hand, in the Cytherean atmosphere water occurs in an amount 10,000 times smaller than carbon dioxide; and this is, moreover, its total supply since—at a temperature of 400° centigrade—no part of the surface of Venus can be covered with liquid water. The large amount of water on the Earth may explain why most of the terrestrial carbon dioxide has been locked up in solid carbonates; but why is Venus—as well as Mars—so excessively dry? And is the relatively large amount of gaseous CO_2 on Venus, or Mars, primordial, or was it liberated by gradual degassing of the interior? We do not as yet know.

We encounter a similar discrepancy in connection with atmospheric oxygen. On the Earth, it amounts to not less than 20% of our air. Moreover, geochemists tell us that at least 40,000 times as much of it is stored in different oxides of the terrestrial crust; and much of this could also have been extracted in the past from the atmosphere. We do not know, of course, how much of such 'fossil' oxygen can be contained in the crustal layers of our sister planets Venus or Mars; the well-known reddish colour of Mars may be indicative of the presence of iron oxides on its exposed surface. In their atmospheres free oxygen now appears, however, to be excessively scarce—much more so than water vapour itself.

Now oxygen is so reactive a gas that it cannot remain in contact with almost any kind of solid surface in a free state for an astronomically (or geologically) long time; sooner or later all of it is bound to be locked up in solid compounds. Geophysicists (as well as biologists) are in substantial agreement that our atmosphere can possess and maintain its 20% of free oxygen only because the supply lost through oxidation is constantly being replenished by the photosynthesis of green plants. In other words, the free oxygen we breathe is probably all of organic origin; and since the amount of it on Venus or Mars appears to be negligible, this can be taken as almost sufficient proof of the fact that no life on an appreciable scale can exist there at the present time—not a surprising conclusion, perhaps; but nevertheless true.

If we turn back our thoughts once more to the general features of the solar system and to its grand design as a whole, what could have been its *origin*? While we are still far from being able to reconstruct the details of such a process, certain general features have already emerged from the age-old quest which are unlikely to mislead us; and these we wish now to recapitulate.

First, we are virtually certain today that—contrary to the views held from the days of Kant and Laplace almost up to the middle of this century—the formation of our planetary system represented an act that occurred simultaneously with the formation of the Sun, and was not consecutive to it. An independent dating of these two acts, by methods which we described in earlier parts of our book, led to so close a coincidence of the ages of the Sun and the Earth or the Moon (or of the oldest meteorites) that their agreement cannot be accidental.

Besides, nothing whatever could have induced the Sun, once formed, to give birth to a planetary system. It is true that the greater part of the angular momentum of the solar system as a whole resides in the orbital momenta of its major planets, and not in the axial rotation of its central star. If, however, we were to transfer all planetary orbital momenta on to the Sun—and everything is possible on paper—its axial rotation would speed up from 26 days to about 12 hours. So fast a rotation should render the

Sun very appreciably oblate; but this oblateness would still be far from the limit at which the Sun would become equatorially unstable. Besides, the solar equator is inclined by 17° to the invariable plane of the planetary system; so that even if the Sun ever shed any amount of mass off its equator to form the planets, it would have done so in the wrong direction!

A tidal disruption of the existing Sun in the course of a close approach by another star—a process proposed by Jeans and Jeffreys in the first half of the twentieth century—seems likewise to be out of the question. The density of stars in space is known to be so low that a close encounter of any two of them at a distance that would lead to tidal disruption could occur, at most, only a few times in the Galaxy during its entire life-span. If so, planetary systems should be excessively rare in the Universe; and yet we know now (cf. Chapter II) that at least 1% (and probably more) of the stars in our immediate neighbourhood possess companions whose mass is of planetary, rather than stellar, order of magnitude. Therefore, planetary systems would seem to be reasonably common in the realm of the stars which we know best; and if so, their origin cannot have anything to do with events as rare as close stellar encounters.

Besides, it is virtually certain that no material now constituting the planets could have come out—by whatever process—directly from the interior of the Sun. Such gas would have been so hot as to dissipate thermally in a few hours without any possibility of condensing into planetary globes. No; the formation of the planets must have been the result of some process that went on in parallel with the formation of the Sun itself—i.e., through the collapse of a primordial cloud of material which may have contained not only solid particles and neutral gas, but also plasma; and in the presence of a magnetic field such a collapse may have represented, not only mechanical or hydrodynamical, but hydromagnetic problems. Moreover, the total mass which went into the formation of the planetary companions of the Sun at that stage may well have been of the order of $0\cdot01$ $\odot$, of which about $0\cdot001$ $\odot$ is still left around today. While our present major planets may have retained the bulk of their original mass throughout their entire past, terrestrial planets may represent only residues of masses they may have once possessed before the loss of their more volatile elements.

If spherical symmetry could be retained throughout this process, the result would have been the creation of a single star. We know, however, that in many instances the stars do originate in pairs; and if the collapse occurs towards a *plane* rather than a single centre (perhaps as a result of an excess of angular momentum), the intermediary stage would be a disc which may well have eventually condensed into a planetary system. The exact mechanism of the terminal stages of such a process may as yet be debatable; but if planetary systems exist, Nature must know how to accomplish this task even if she has not seen fit to confide in us fully as yet. But one aspect of the problem seems clear; namely, that the parent substrate from which the planets of the solar system—including our Earth—originated must have been 'cold', or only moderately warm. It could, at some time, have been heated up to a temperature of a few thousand degrees, but not tens of thousands; for otherwise this material would not have assembled into individual globes of planetary masses and composition.

If we now regard our solar system as having been born at the same time as the Sun, and from a material similar to that which now constitutes the bulk of the Sun's mass, we can do so with—perhaps—one reservation; and that concerns the (as yet doubtful) origin of the *comets*. Did these too originate as a part of the same creative process, or are they interstellar—the products of interstellar space—which we only pick up on our orbital journey around the galactic centre? It is clear from their great abundance as well as their relatively rapid perishability that a source must exist from which cometary supply is being constantly replenished if we are to have any of them around us at all. Whether this source is to be sought in a 'cometary cloud' at a distant periphery of our system which we drag along with us through space, or whether we accrete them directly from interstellar space, is still uncertain.

None of the comets (or, for that matter, meteors) that we have a chance to observe from the Earth come to us directly from interstellar space (i.e., approach us along a hyperbolic path). Reserves drawn from an interstellar supply may, however, have undergone a prior extensive process of 'domestication' in the outer parts of the solar system before some of them accidentally penetrate into its inner precincts to become known to us and be given a proper name. Their aboriginal birthplace and domicile are, however, as yet shrouded in a mystery even deeper than that which still surrounds the circumstances of the origin of other—more legitimate—members of our system.

This, then, is the picture of our local 'village' in the Universe; a village in which we hold cosmic domicile, and where the Earth is our home. The time has now come to bid goodbye to this cosmic home and turn to inspect our heavenly kingdom in its wider aspects. To do so will take us much farther afield than we have so far ventured to go in our thoughts—to places which are, not light-minutes or hours, but light-centuries and millenia away from our terrestrial abode; and on the way we shall come across exotic corners and weird creatures which our grandfathers would not have recognized as the celestial bodies they knew in our stellar neighbourhood. Great distances in space—like great depths of time—hold secrets in store which beckon from afar, like an enchanted land that we shall attempt to enter and penetrate—knowing that once we have tasted their forbidden fruit, we may never want to return home to the Earth.

PART THREE

The Universe at Large

In the first part of this book we introduced our readers to the fundamental building blocks of our Universe, the stars. We outlined the way in which the stars are born, lead lives in which a steady course alternates with extravagant stunts, and eventually retire into obscurity. In the second part, we took under a magnifying glass the immediate neighbourhood of one particular star—our Sun—not because the Sun is a very conspicuous object as stars go, but because it happens to provide the setting for our celestial home.

In this third and concluding part of our book we wish to return in our thoughts to the realm of the stars, but no longer to consider their individual fortunes. Instead, we shall outline the ways in which Nature makes use of these fundamental units for the construction of larger structures in our Universe. What kind of associations do the stars form around us, and how are they organized? What are the typical properties of the systems in which the stars associate in space? Do such systems follow certain general patterns, and how are they distributed in the Universe?

The aim of the chapters which follow will be to give answers to these questions that will interest the more general reader. In Chapter XI it will be shown that all the individual stars we see in the sky—with the naked eye or through the telescope—constitute a stellar system of the Milky Way—a 'galaxy' of some 10^{12} stars—a veritable island in the Universe in which our stellar neighbourhood represents only a very small hamlet. In Chapter XII we shall establish that other island-universes—akin to our own Milky Way system—exist everywhere around us in space. Some are larger, many more are smaller than our own; and they are separated by abyssal depths of space which appear to be devoid of matter.

Nimble-footed photons of light—the only travellers which can traverse these depths after journeys lasting millions of years—bring on their wings strange tales of faraway galaxies, and clusters of galaxies, which fill the space up to the limits of the now observable Universe. Its outer landmarks appear to be so far that their light was already on the way before our Earth was formed, and before the Sun contracted to the Main Sequence; and the story it brings describes an expansion of the Universe with velocities which attain a large fraction of the speed of light at distances to which we can penetrate with our telescopes.

What kind of structure of the Universe is suggested by the observations now at our disposal? Is the Universe infinite or finite in space and time—and if it is finite, can we extrapolate its present state backwards to reach its beginnings? Such answers as can be given will be found in Chapter XIII; while in the concluding Chapter XIV we shall assess the possibility that intelligent life may exist outside the confines of our solar system, and consider the chances of our ever getting in touch with it.

CHAPTER XI

The Community of the Stars and Our Galaxy

IN CHAPTER III we outlined the life-story of a star from its cradle to the grave; but in following up this story we were concerned mainly with the stars as individuals—or, at most (in Chapter II–3) as partners in close pairs. However, in section 1 of Chapter III we stressed that stars—or, at least, most of them—are born in groups. Interstellar clouds whose collapse produces the stars contain enough mass to give rise to a large number of stellar 'units'— ranging from a few dozen to several hundred individual formations of this type. These groups are formed—cosmically speaking— almost instantaneously; and the age differences between individual members may not exceed more than a few million years.

What will happen, however, with such groups in the future? This depends on the degree of compactness of each new-born group—i.e., on the strength of the gravitational bonds holding the group together—as well as on the severity of gas turbulence in the parent cloud which has endowed its individual stars with differential velocities tending to disperse the group. Two cases may, therefore, arise: namely, the total kinetic energy of the differential motions of the group members may be either larger, or smaller, than the total potential energy which represents the binding force. In the former case, the group will disperse soon after that period of star formation (in a period depending on the extent of disparity between the initial kinetic and potential energy), and merge with the surrounding star field so thoroughly as to make it difficult to identify its initial members after 10–20 million years. Such dispersing groups we call stellar 'associations'; and the astronomical detectives delving into the history of the stars around us have identified about a dozen of such fleeting associations formed in the recent past—certainly since the Tertiary period of our geological timescale (Plate 18).

On the other hand, associations of stars in groups whose self-attraction exceeds the dispersive tendency of peculiar motions are much more lasting. Some stars may now and then escape them, but only those which get abnormally accelerated by close encounters among group members—in qualitatively the same way as comets are ejected (cf. p. 232) from the solar system. This process works slowly, however; and such groups of positive total energy can stay together for hundreds of millions of years. We call them 'open clusters'—with populations ranging from hundreds to thousands of individual stars—and thousands of these have been spotted in the sky. One of the best-known such clusters in the sky are the Pleiades, whose brightest members are visible to the naked eye (cf. Plate 3); though the total number of individual stars in that cluster exceeds twelve hundred.

How far away are such clusters, or the stars between them which telescopes have uncovered for us in almost limitless numbers? Up to a distance of about 50 parsecs the location of the stars in space can be triangulated; but beyond 100 parsecs stellar parallaxes become too small to be measured trigonometrically with any significance. In order to penetrate deeper, methods must be used other than those based on angular measurements; and our principal tools for these measurements will be photometric. For suppose that we can estimate the absolute brightness M of a star—or any other celestial object—from such features as can be disclosed by its spectra; and then measure its apparent brightness m. If, moreover, the intensity of the light source diminishes with inverse square of the distance (i.e., if the space between the stars is perfectly transparent), the equation on page 51 Chapter II–1 would enable us to evaluate the parallax π; and its reciprocal is then equal to the distance of the respective object in parsecs.

The gist of such a method is our ability to estimate the absolute brightness of such objects from observable characteristics which do not depend on the distance; and one such characteristic may be the star's spectrum. In Chapter II–2 we pointed out that the spectrum of a Main Sequence star is a safe indicator of its absolute brightness (within the limits of uncertainty of the width of this sequence in the HR-diagram); and for other stars similar criteria have been developed in the course of time. The parallaxes of such stars computed by the equation on p. 51 from the measured apparent brightness m and the spectroscopically estimated absolute brightness M are generally referred to as 'spectroscopic parallaxes'; and these permit us to push the limits of our exploration in space to several thousand parsecs—and even more for especially bright objects.

But it is not the normal stars—shining with constant light—that have proved to be our best tools for deeper penetration into space. Much more powerful tools for this have been provided by Nature in the form of certain types of 'variable' stars, some of which we described briefly in Chapter III–2. Most such variable stars—Novae, long-period or even eclipsing variables—carry some kind of an absolute brightness tag which can serve as a clue to their distance; but it was not until variable stars akin to δ Cephei ('cepheids', as they are called) were utilized that this method of 'photometric parallaxes' has really come into its own.

The amplitudes of light variation of the cepheid variables are moderate, and seldom exceed $1\frac{1}{2}$ magnitudes between maximum and minimum. But the characteristic form of their light changes makes it easy to distinguish them from other types of variable stars; and their light varies with clock-like regularity in periods which range from several hours to a few weeks. Most important, the periods of light variation of cepheid variables have turned out to be closely correlated with the absolute brightness of such stars—in the sense that the longer the period of light variation of a cepheid, the greater its intrinsic luminosity. The period of cepheid variability can be ascertained from photometric observations with relative ease; and to each there corresponds a certain absolute brightness. But if this is so, the measured apparent brightness of such stars should become a direct indicator of its distance.

The power of this particular method for the determination of 'photometric parallaxes' is greatly increased by the fact that cepheid variables of periods longer than 10 days belong among the absolutely brightest stars known in the Universe; and as such they represent 'standard candles'—or, rather, immense cosmic beacons—distinguishable across vast expanses of space. To estimate reliably in this manner the distance of a more normal star is a much more difficult task. In fact, if we look at the stars at night with the naked eye or through a telescope, it may be as difficult to estimate their distance by their brightness as it is to guess at the distance of shore lights from a ship. During the night, many lights may be visible at sea along the horizon; but our estimate of their distance may be out by a hundred million times if we take for a ship the light of a setting planet—let alone a star! But perhaps we spot on the horizon a light which flashes and disappears at regular intervals of time. Such a sequence of luminous 'dots-and-dashes' will tell us, of course, that we are watching a lighthouse; and knowing its candle-power we can estimate its distance—provided that there is no fog!

And what is true at sea, should be true in the sky. The stars we see at night may appear to be of different brightness because some are nearer to us than others, or because of differences in their intrinsic luminosity. But if we spot in the Milky Way a star whose light varies like δ Cephei in a period of 5 days, 8 hours and 37 minutes, we know that this particular star must be intrinsically 1,600 times brighter than our Sun; and it would be 15,000 times as bright if its period were one month. Such is the candle-power of these cosmic beacons in space!

The 'period-luminosity relation' of cepheid variables has proved to be one of the most important tools for exploration of more remote parts of the Universe; and the first major advance scored with its aid was in enabling us to gradually reconstruct the grand structure of the systems of stars we see everywhere around us. If we look at the starry sky at night at almost any time of the year, the main feature to catch our attention will be the feebly shimmering bright belt of the Milky Way, which during the summer months passes through the zenith and girdles the entire sky from north to south. The ancient Greek philosopher Democritos conjectured that the Milky Way represented a large agglomeration of distant stars, too close together to be resolved with the naked eye; with the discovery of the telescope vastly more of its individual stars have come into view. Towards the end of the eighteenth century, the famous 'star gauges' undertaken by William Herschel with his large reflectors disclosed that the stellar system in which we live represents a disc-shaped agglomeration of millions of stars, which is apparently quite thin in the direction perpendicular to the plane of our galaxy; but in its plane it extends to depths which were not properly fathomed till the first part of this century.

Until 1915, the system of the Milky Way—or our Galaxy, as it should be called—was still regarded as no more than a mere conglomeration of millions of stars in the form of a strongly flattened disc; with stars concentrated in the plane of the Galaxy and towards its centre. Our Sun with its planets was thought to be located in the central part of this system, thus occupying—for the last time in the history of astronomy—some kind of a privileged position. However, it has also been known for a long time that the belt of the Milky Way in the sky is accompanied by more than one hundred dense, compact groups of stars, aptly named 'globular clusters'. A photograph of one of the best-known formations of this type, easily visible (though not to the naked eye) from the northern hemisphere, is shown on Plate 19.

Such globular clusters consist, not of hundreds or thousands, but of hundreds of thousands or even millions of individual stars; and although their condensation peters out smoothly into space, most of their stars are confined to spheres of not more than 10–20 parsecs across. The star density in the central parts of such clusters is of the order of several thousand stars per cubic parsec (i.e., at least 10,000 times as high as it is in the space around us); and if we were living on a planet located in such a region, our sky would be studded with unimaginable numbers of bright stars. At a distance, these look less impressive—there are no really bright blue stars around them; and in their absolute magnitudes they do not quite measure up to the jewels in the sky around us. However, a search for variable stars in globular clusters led to the discovery—in most of them, but not all—of short-period cepheids in numbers running into hundreds, a fact which earned them the epithet of 'cluster-type variables'. Between 1915–1918, Harlow Shapley used these variable stars to disclose the distance of the clusters with which they are associated.

It had been known for a long time that the distribution of these globular clusters along the belt of the Milky Way was highly asymmetric—almost all of them are situated in one part of the sky, centred on the Milky Way clouds in the southern constellation of Sagittarius. Their distances from us as determined from the apparent brightness of their cluster-type variables turned out to range from thousands to tens of thousands of parsecs. And when Shapley constructed a model of the system of globular clusters, he found its centre to lie in the constellation of Sagittarius, at a distance from us which we now know to be approximately 8,500 parsecs (28,000 light years). This point Shapley identified boldly with the centre of the entire Milky Way system—consisting as it does of a flat disc of stars surrounded by a 'halo' of globular

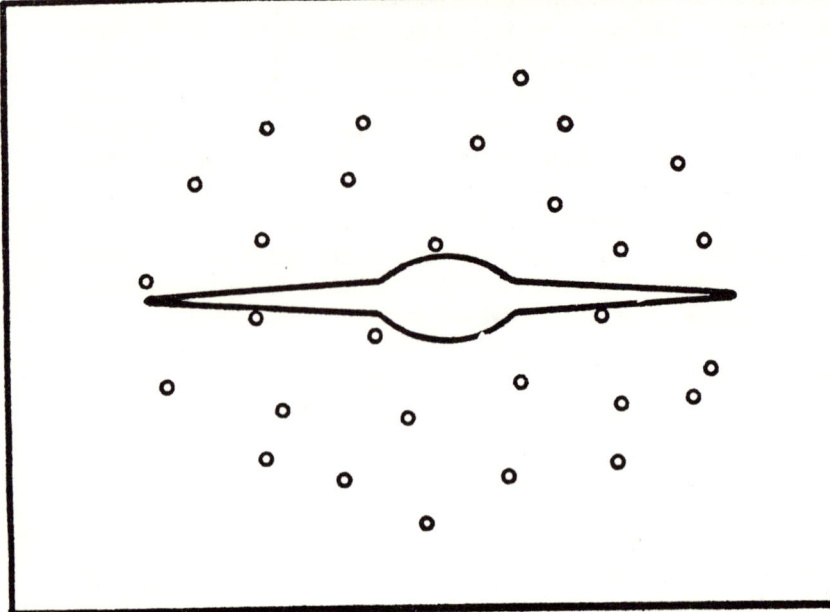

Figure 6 The Milky Way, and its associated system of Globular Clusters (schematic).

clusters, a schematic view of which is shown on the accompanying Figure 6.

This realization deprived us of the last vestige of any claim to a privileged position in the Universe; and our Sun became only one of myriads of other stars constituting our Galaxy.

In the direction perpendicular to the plane of our Galaxy, the extension of our stellar system is very limited—its star field peters out into nothing only one to two hundred parsecs away from the Sun; but the disc of the Galaxy extends more than 30–35 thousand parsecs (or 30–35 kiloparsecs—kpc for short) across—thus giving our Galaxy the shape of a very flat disc. This disc bulges somewhat near the centre, and remains remarkably flat within 8,000 parsecs from the centre; though in its outer parts our Galaxy bends upwards on one side, and downwards on the opposite side of the centre. These deviations from the mean galactic plane run up to about 500 parsecs at distances of 15 kpc from the centre, and probably still more at greater distances.

The Community of the Stars and Our Galaxy

The origin of this curious bending of our Galaxy remains unexplained, but the cause of its lenticular shape is not in doubt: the rapid rotation of the galactic disc about its short axis, generating centrifugal force which prevents gravitational contraction of the whole disc towards its centre. It has long been clear on dynamical grounds that the Galaxy as it is cannot represent a stationary system of stars moving at random, but that its flattened form must be due to axial rotation. However, the way in which such a rotation would leave specific imprints in the proper motions and radial velocities of the stars in our neighbourhood was not investigated till Lindblad and Oort examined it in 1926–27; with the result that the centre of rotational motion was located in almost exactly the same position as Shapley had deduced earlier from globular star clusters.

The Galaxy was, moreover, found to rotate, not like a rigid wheel, but with an angular velocity increasing towards its centre. At the distance of the Sun, one revolution around the centre—the so-called 'cosmic year'—lasts about 200 million years of our terrestrial time. Therefore, when our Sun with its planetary system last occupied the same relative position in its galactic orbit, our Earth was in the Triassic period of the Mesozoic age—the time when the great reptiles were emerging from the swamps to take over solid ground only recently liberated from the Permian ice-age. And in another cosmic year—who knows?

A determination of the spatial velocity of our revolution (about 270 km/sec) around the galactic centre permitted us, moreover, to estimate the total mass of our Galaxy—in much the same way as we inferred the mass of the Sun (cf. Chapter I-1) from the annual motion of the Earth around it. This mass of the Galaxy turned out to be close to 10^{11} $\odot$; but since we have reason to believe that most stars in the Galaxy possess a mass rather smaller than that of the Sun, its total number of individual stars may be close to a trillion (10^{12}).

How are these myriads of stars distributed within the Galaxy? Before we can deduce the fundamental features of our Galaxy from the observations, we have to consider another question which may fundamentally affect the answer. How far can we see through the Galaxy with our telescopes? Is the space between its stars really transparent, or is it hazy—especially in the plane of the Galaxy; and if so, to what extent?

That the space between the stars is far from empty we have already learned in Chapter III–1, in connection with our story of the origin of the stars from interstellar substrate of gas and dust. We stressed that such gas or dust does not become visible to us unless a sufficiently bright star is on hand to excite the gas to shine, or illuminate the dust. Far away from individual stars interstellar gas is fairly inconspicuous; and can reveal its presence through absorption at discrete frequencies (producing the telltale 'stationary lines' described in Chapter III–1 and seen on Plate 7) rather than by giving rise to any general haze, continuous absorption or scattering.

With dust however, it is a different story; for solid particles in space can not only weaken the starlight passing through the dust clouds much more effectively than gas, but can also make starlight appear redder than the original source, and partly polarized. It is, therefore, primarily an agglomeration of dust clouds in space that may impose an upper limit of cosmic visibility in our Galaxy. How widespread are they, and where are they to be found?

A casual look at the Milky Way which girdles our sky during summer nights will disclose that its background appears to be distinctly patchy; and a great dark rift runs through it from the constellation of the Swan in the zenith down to the great clouds of Sagittarius near the horizon—a feature which extends far below the horizon, and to parts of which astronomers refer by the scarcely complimentary term of a 'coalsack'. In such parts of the Milky Way we find regions where stars are obscured by dark clouds, which condense locally into 'dark nebulae' of the kind already seen on Plate 5, but more often look like the dark clouds shown on Plate 4.

The dark region in the centre of the field of Plate 4 is no 'hole in the sky'—as was once believed by astronomers in the age of our innocence—but signifies the presence of an obscuring complex which both dims and reddens the light of the background stars shining through it. In its foreground, stars are uniformly distributed all over the field; and from the apparent magnitude of stars which become scarce in the dark complex we can infer its distance; while from the apparent brightness (and extent of reddening) of the background stars we can fathom its optical depth and, hence, the density of dust in the cloud. In regions where obscuring dust is present in less concentrated form, the outline of the dark regions may be less definite; but the characteristic reddening of the light of background stars shining through will tell the story and fix both the distance and density of the obscuring veil.

A systematic search for the effects of interstellar obscuration in the past decades has revealed that, in directions inclined more than 20° of 'galactic latitude', the transparency of space is virtually complete; and what we see through these 'polar caps' of our Galaxy will be detailed in the next chapter. In the plane of the Galaxy the situation is, however, very different—in particular, in the direction of the galactic centre. There the interstellar space becomes very hazy (see Plate 6); and observations in visible or photographic light do not permit us to penetrate deeper than some 2–3 thousand parsecs—much less than half the distance separating us from the centre of our system.

Careful studies of the distribution of stars in space—taking account of its limited transparency—disclosed that, at high galactic latitudes, our Galaxy virtually ends only a few hundred parsecs away from its plane; but within this plane the distribution of stars in space is far from uniform. In fact, the stars around us appear to be largely concentrated in three distinct 'arms'. One—the nearest—is represented by the main stream of the Milky Way from Orion to Cygnus (the 'Orion Arm'); and our Sun with its neighbourhood appears to be located on its inner rim, only about 10 parsecs away from the galactic plane. About 2,000 parsecs outward we encounter another such stream (the 'Perseus Arm'), to which the double cluster χ and h Persei belongs (see Plate 18).

Finally, well inside the Orion arm, at a distance of 1,500–2,500 parsecs from us towards the galactic centre, we come across the 'Scorpio-Sagittarius Arm', consisting of some of the most impressive clouds of the Milky Way of our southern sky (see Plate 6) interposed between us and the galactic centre, and concealing the latter from view. The interstellar absorption of light in this direction is particularly heavy; it has been estimated that less than 0·01% of visible light can penetrate the interstellar haze between us and the centre of our Galaxy. Even in a transparent space the light of individual objects 8,500 parsecs away would be greatly weakened by distance; and the heavy haze diminishing the apparent visible brightness by ten thousand times gives us no chance to get even a glimpse of the galactic nucleus from our cosmic station in the outskirts of the 'Orion arm' of our Galaxy.

At some distance away from the galactic plane, observations in red light disclosed the existence of a faint glare emanating from the galactic centre; but its nucleus is hidden from our view by obscuring haze much too dense to allow us a glimpse of it from the Earth.

This is, of course, true only of the stars observed in light which we can see or photograph. However, our Galaxy does not consist of stars alone. Its disc also contains a sizeable proportion of gas—mainly hydrogen; and the spectrum of interstellar atomic hydrogen in its ground state contains a 21-cm line of its radio-domain. At its frequency of 1420 Mc/sec, interstellar medium is very largely transparent, and radiation of this line can reach us from any part of the Galaxy—including the galactic centre. A mapping of the Galaxy, undertaken in the past twenty years on a large scale in Australia, Holland, and the United States, has disclosed a structure quite similar to that deduced from the distribution of stars observed at more conventional wavelengths. In particular, interstellar hydrogen seems, like the stars, to be largely concentrated in the galactic plane in numerous 'arms' of the Galaxy, including those which we have been able to identify optically; but the density of gas seems to be diminishing, rather than increasing like the stars, towards the galactic centre. However, bright individual radio sources have been identified in the nucleus of the Galaxy; and one of them—Sagittarius A—is regarded as marking the position of the galactic centre itself.

What kind of model of the Galaxy transpires from investigations of all known aspects of its structure? It can, in brief, be divided into two parts: a *disc* with its discrete arms and central nucleus; and surrounding it a *halo* of globular clusters with a galactic 'corona' of tenuous gas in between. The halo appears to be essentially spherical in shape, but it contains only about 5–7% of the mass of the entire Galaxy; the bulk of the mass is stored in the disc, and—in particular—in its central nucleus. In the disc itself the bulk of the mass consists of the stars; interstellar gas seems to constitute (at least, in our neighbourhood) only about 20% of the total; and the dust, much less (the gas-to-dust mass ratio being of the order of 100).

The disc of the Galaxy is highly flattened by rapid rotation, but whether or not its halo of globular clusters shares this rotation is still not clear. In addition, the disc seems to possess a general magnetic field of the strength of a few micro-gauss (much stronger in individual gas clouds). The origin of this field is as yet unknown; but its presence (attested by the 'Faraday rotation' of the plane of polarization in extra-galactic radio sources) is not in doubt.

What types of stars do we find in different parts of the Galaxy? As long as we do not stray too far away from our celestial home, the bright stars around us are very much of the same kind as our Sun. Most of them are smaller and less luminous than the central star of the solar system, but others are very much brighter—so bright, in fact, that they could only have been 'born yesterday'. Their velocities relative to us are moderate and their chemical composition is broadly similar to that of the Sun.

On the other hand, when sufficiently large telescopes were turned to study the stars constituting globular clusters, it was as though we entered a different world. Their stars were generally dimmer, and the brightest among them were found to be red, not blue. In point of fact, the upper part of the Main Sequence seemed to be completely missing from their HR-diagrams (see Figure 7)—which indicates that all more massive stars have had the time to evolve away from it to the domain of red giants.

And the most revealing feature of all: the spectra of these stars have shown evidence of a conspicuous scarcity of metals and other heavier elements relative to hydrogen and helium—suggesting that, at the time such stars were formed, heavy elements were substantially scarcer in the Universe than they are at the present time. In some extreme cases—like that represented by the stars of the well-known globular cluster Messier 3 (see Plate 19)—metals appear to be a hundred times less abundant than they are in the Sun.

How to account for such a striking disparity? The only conclusion we can reach is that the halo stars are very much *older* than those constituting the disc of the Galaxy—let alone its arms. They have in recent years been described as *Population II stars*—in contrast to *Population I stars* concentrated in the disc which fill our skies with their splendour. Population II stars must have been formed in the early times of the existence of our Galaxy—more than ten billion years ago—before the Galaxy collapsed into a disc. This disc provided, in time, the place of birth to new generations of stars whose formation from interstellar gas and

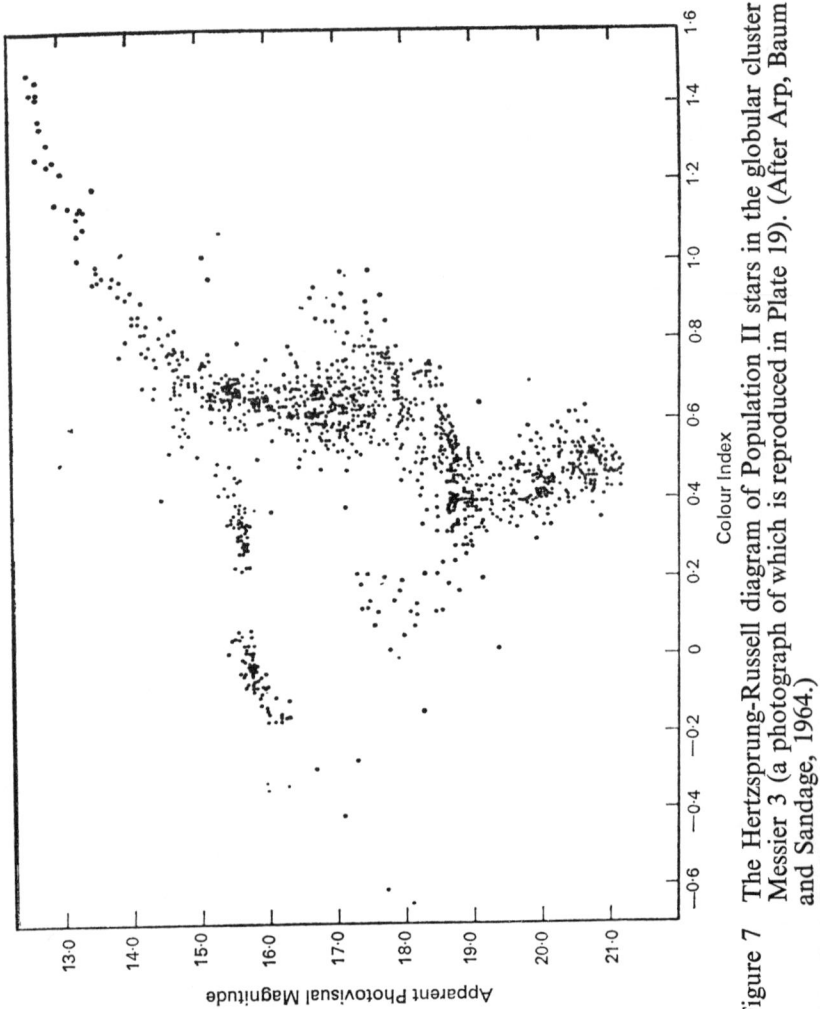

Figure 7 The Hertzsprung-Russell diagram of Population II stars in the globular cluster Messier 3 (a photograph of which is reproduced in Plate 19). (After Arp, Baum and Sandage, 1964.)

dust in the arms of our Galaxy has continued up to the present time.

Stars formed at different stages of evolution of our galactic system can—at least in principle—be distinguished by their chemical composition, because the composition of their parent interstellar substrate is changing, and is gradually being enriched by heavier elements. Where does our Sun fit into this general picture? Its age of close to $4 \cdot 6$ billion years makes it intermediate between the stars of extreme populations I and II; and it belongs to a generation of 'disc stars' which are as much younger than old Population II stars as they are older than the stars being born in the arms of our Galaxy at present.

Since the time of its formation, the Sun with its planetary system has, therefore, gone at least 20 times around the centre of the Galaxy, and seen much of its past long gone beyond recall. In the meantime, a multitude of stars originating in the halo, at a time even more remote from the present, became fugitives from globular clusters, gradually infiltrated the disc of the Galaxy, and intermingled with its local population—substantially younger in age—to such an extent that today it is such stars that form the bulk of the 'galactic cake', to which the bright young stars of Population I have added only the 'frosting'. Galactic stars of these two populations can, however, also be distinguished by their kinematic properties; for while the young Population I stars move about rather lazily through space like bumble-bees, old Population II stars travel like little dragonflies with velocities ten times as high.

And this ends our brief account of the structure of our Galaxy and its diverse population, representing successive generations of stars born from its primordial matter. How did the Galaxy come into being, and how did it evolve to its present form in the course of time? These are questions which we must eventually attempt to answer. But before we do so it is natural to ask: are there other galaxies around in space akin to our own; and what can we learn from their study at a distance? To this question we shall address ourselves in the next chapter.

CHAPTER XII

The Realm of External Galaxies

IN AN outline of the main properties of our Galaxy in the preceding chapter we mentioned that heavy absorption of light in the galactic plane prevents us from seeing very far into space in this direction —save through a number of galactic 'windows' of greater transparency which are few and far between. However, with increasing galactic latitude the interstellar haze rapidly clears up and a grand view of the Universe opens up before our astonished eyes. The aim of the present chapter will be to outline the main features of this view, and to explain its significance.

The first inkling of this wider world outside our Galaxy dawned upon our uncomprehending ancestors some time in the fifteenth century of our era, when the Portuguese navigators, stargazing from the quarterdecks of their frigates sent out to explore a sea route to the Indies, discovered near the south pole of the sky two little clouds—barely a few degrees in diameter (see Plate 20)— which they found useful in fixing the position of the pole. Variously designated by the early navigators, they appear to have first been described by Antonio Pigafetta, the historian of Magellan's first round-the-world tour of 1518–1520, and ever since have been associated in astronomical literature with the name of Magellan.

The next extragalactic celestial object was not discovered till shortly after the discovery of the telescope by Simon Mayer (Marius), who in 1612 noticed a faint cloud in the constellation of Andromeda—the famous Andromeda nebula (Plate 21), twin sister of our Galaxy, the third and last extra-galactic object visible to the unaided eye. The number of known telescopic objects of this type grew slowly at first, but by the end of the eighteenth century the reflectors of William Herschel at last began to disclose them in the sky by the hundred; and with the advent of astronomical photography a century later their numbers began to grow into tens and hundreds of thousands.

At first, their significance in the sky was enigmatic; but William

Herschel conjectured that they were unresolved systems of distant stars; and among these—with striking prescience—he placed the Andromeda nebula. On calculating how far away they must be to escape resolution by his telescopes, Herschel concluded that they must lie far beyond the boundaries of our Milky Way. And this led him to propose his celebrated theory of 'island-universes'—systems of stars of which our Galaxy was but one.

This suspicion was strengthened in the nineteenth century when such nebulae were found to exhibit spectra akin to those of the stars, in contrast to the bright-line spectra of other nebulae (see Chapter III-1) consisting of tenuous gas. Moreover, the 72-inch telescope of Lord Rosse—the largest astronomical instrument built in the nineteenth century—disclosed that nebulae akin to the one in Andromeda did not appear amorphous, but exhibited indications of spiral structure. And the advent of photography confirmed this to be true for many other objects of this class.

What was the size of such objects, however, and where were they located? Did they belong to our galactic system, or were they external to it? The answer hung in the balance until the completion of the 100-inch telescope at Mount Wilson. One of the first feats of this new giant eye with which astronomers commenced to watch the sky in 1917 was the resolution of the arms of the spiral nebulae in Andromeda (Plate 21) and Triangulum (Plate 22) into individual stars—a feat which had previously defied William Herschel and Lord Rosse. And more than that; for what came into view among the multitude of stars into which these nebulae were being decomposed were not only ordinary stars shining with constant light, but also certain types of variable stars, of known luminosity, which could serve as 'standard candles' for a determination of the distance (Plate 23).

In particular, Curtis and Duncan first discovered in the Andromeda nebula a number of flare stars known as 'Novae' (cf. Chapter III-2)—stars which, at a certain stage of their evolutionary careers, undergo spasmodic outbursts of light which make them attain a known and fairly constant maximum absolute magnitude. Moreover, in 1924 E. P. Hubble—soon to become the leading investigator of external galaxies in the first half of this century—also discovered in them cepheid variables; and the apparent magnitude of these celestial 'standard candles' in the Andromeda or Triangulum nebulae established their extragalactic location beyond a shadow of doubt. The foremost student of galaxies in the post-Hubble era was Walter Baade, and the primary tool of exploration since 1948 has been the 200-inch telescope at Palomar mountain. In 1952 Baade corrected the calibration of the period-luminosity relation for cepheid variables, and the actual distance of the Andromeda nebula from us proved to be about 700,000 parsecs (2·3 million light years) if space between us were completely transparent; but as there seems to be some absorption along the line of sight inside our Galaxy, the probable distance of the Andromeda nebula from us is not much more than 570,000 parsecs (1·7 million light years).

At this distance—which is about 15 times the dimensions of our own Galaxy—the Andromeda nebula turns out to be about the same size as our galactic system (approximately 35,000 parsecs across); and its absolute luminosity is brighter than -20th magnitude (or 10^{10} times as bright as our Sun). Its mass (as deduced from the measured radial velocities of different parts of its disc) proved to be close to 3×10^{11} $\odot$—about three times as large as that of our own galactic system. The Andromeda nebula should, therefore, be regarded as the 'elder sister' of our Galaxy, and the more massive as well as (probably) the more luminous of the two.

The structure of this impressive stellar system, as revealed by long-exposure photographs taken with some of the world's largest telescopes (see Plates 21 and 23), discloses many features strikingly similar to those described in Chapter XI for our own Galaxy. In particular, the nucleus of the Andromeda nebula (which in our Galaxy is concealed from our view by interstellar absorption of visible light) is almost resolved into stars on a photograph shown on Plate 23; while Plate 24 shows the spiral structure of the outlying arms interspersed with dark lanes of obscuring dust. As in our own Galaxy, these spiral arms are rich in bright blue Population I stars; while Population II stars abound in the central parts of this galaxy. Moreover—like our Milky Way—Andromeda nebula is attended by an extensive halo of globular clusters, in addition to two more substantial systems (NGC 205 and 221), shown on Plate 21, which can be regarded as giant globular clusters (or small 'spherical galaxies'), of mass $4-8 \times 10^9$ $\odot$, consisting exclusively of Population II stars.

The giant Andromeda galaxy is not the only spiral nebula

near us in space. Another system of the same type was discovered in the constellation of Triangulum (see Plate 22)—at about the same distance from us in space, but somewhat smaller and less massive ($1 \cdot 2 \times 10^{10}$ ☉) than our own Galaxy or that in Andromeda. Like the latter, its outer parts exhibit a distinct spiral structure; and there is ample evidence of gas and dust in spiral arms abounding in young stars of Population I. A close comparison of similar features of our Milky Way system with the two neighbouring galaxies in Andromeda and Triangulum leads us to conjecture that our own galactic system—if seen from outside—would represent a spiral nebula, with arms trailing behind (i.e., winding up) in the course of its rotation. The Sagittarius, Orion and Perseus arms which we identified (cf. Chapter XI) in the structure of the disc of our Galaxy are probably nearby parts of such a spiral structure—though the picture of the Galaxy emerging from studies of the distribution of interstellar gas, based on observed Doppler shifts of the 21-cm line of atomic hydrogen, appears to be too complicated for any oversimplified interpretation of its meaning.

The spiral nebulae in Andromeda and Triangulum at a distance of some 600 kiloparsecs from us are not the nearest galaxies to us in space. Our nearest galactic neighbours are the two Magellanic Clouds in the southern sky (Plate 20), whose distance was disclosed by their cepheids to be only 52–60 kiloparsecs. These small galaxies are, therefore, no more distant from us than are the spheroidal galaxies NGC 205 and 221 from the Andromeda nebula on Plate 21. The masses of the Magellanic Clouds are between 2 and 6×10^9 ☉—closely comparable with the elliptical companions of Andromeda. Unlike the latter, however, the Magellanic Clouds represent small and rather irregular spirals; with plenty of gas and dust left in between their stars.

An intensive exploration of the sky with wide-angle optical systems in the past fifty years has led to the discovery in our neighbourhood of nine other 'dwarf' galaxies of masses of the order of 10^8 to 10^9 suns—the nearest of which are in the southern constellations Fornax and Sculptor, 100–200 kiloparsecs away—so that altogether 16 galaxies are now known to us within the distance of one million parsecs. These form what we call the 'Local Group' of galaxies, of total mass close to 5×10^{11} ☉; and the number of individual stars contained in them will be well in excess of 10^{12}.

What lies beyond the confines of our Local Group? Ten major galaxies have been located in space at distances of up to 11 million parsecs or 11 megaparsecs (Mpsc for short), some of which are shown on Plates 25–27. The galaxy in the constellation of Canes Venatici which bears the catalogue number NGC 5154 (see Plate 25) is a beautiful example of a typical spiral nebula seen from a direction normal to its plane. It is at a distance of some two million parsecs—just outside the limits of our Local Group; and the spiral nebula NGC 3031 in Ursa Maior at three million parsecs is not much further; a glance at its photograph reproduced on Plate 26 shows that the Universe is not static.

At a somewhat greater distance, but still within 10–11 Mpsc, we find the spiral nebula NGC 4565 in Coma Berenices, shown edge on (Plate 27), and disclosing the amount of obscuring dust agglomerated on its rim; while Plate 28 shows us a pair of galaxies NGC 4647—9 in the constellation of Virgo at a distance of 11 Mpsc. One of these (the brighter) is a giant elliptical galaxy surrounded by a large system of globular clusters; while the other is an irregular spiral.

In this part of the sky we find ourselves in a region of space thickly populated by galaxies—in fact, within a region of about 12° across the sky we find some 2,500 external galaxies forming what is called the 'Virgo Cluster'. Its brightest galaxies attain the 9th apparent magnitude and are no longer visible to the naked eye; but they occupy a volume in space so large that our local group may, in fact, constitute but one of the 'suburbs' of this cluster. Moreover, systematic surveys of the sky have disclosed the existence in space of other such clusters of galaxies at greater distances from us. Thus in the constellation of Coma Berenices, we find about 1,000 galaxies spread over an area of 6° (a part of which is reproduced on Plate 28) at a distance of 70 megaparsecs. Another group of some 2,900 of them in the constellation of Hercules (Plate 29) is over 100 megaparsecs away; one in Corona, 200 Mpscs; and another one in Hydra, some 600 Mpscs—or about a thousand times as far from us as the spiral nebulae in Andromeda or Triangulum. The Hydra cluster (see Plate 30) covers an area of less than half of the apparent diameter of the Sun or the Moon in the sky. The brightest members of this cluster are only of the 19th apparent magnitude; and their distance, close to two billion light years.

The Realm of External Galaxies

How can we determine such stupendous distances in space? Within our Local Group of galaxies, which can be resolved in part at least into stars, this can be done by the methods already discussed in the last chapter. Beyond a few million parsecs the resolution of our telescopes is, however, no longer good enough to enable us to identify in them any individual stellar objects (except for Supernovae); but the role of the cosmic 'standard candles' can be taken over by the galaxies as a whole.

For from our survey of galaxies within the nearest 10 million parsecs we learned that the maximum absolute brightness of a galaxy is between -20 to -21 absolute magnitude; and our own galaxy, the Andromeda nebula, or the elliptical galaxy NGC 4647 in the Virgo cluster, are within this range. If the same remains true in all other more distant clusters of galaxies—and if space between them is completely transparent—the measured apparent magnitude to the brightest galaxies in distant clusters offers by itself a clue to their distance; and their values for different clusters mentioned earlier in this chapter have been deduced in this manner. There are also other ways in which we can estimate the distance of such galaxies independently of their apparent brightness—based on the 'red shifts' of lines observed in their spectra; and to this subject we shall return in the next chapter. But before we do, let us consider some further aspects of the galaxies as we see them in the sky or can count and measure them on our photographs.

Apart from the individual clusters of galaxies detected in great depths of space by the best telescopes now at our disposal, how many galaxies do we discern in the whole sky, and how rapidly do their numbers increase with diminishing brightness? Do they fill space without end, or are they distributed in some way indicative of the structure of the Universe as a whole?

In order to understand the evidence provided by our telescopes, let us assume that an endless space is filled with galaxies—individual, or in clusters—animated by random motions with respect to each other. If, furthermore, the average number of galaxies per unit volume (i.e., the spatial 'density' of galaxies) is n, their total number (N) inside a sphere of given radius should be related with the limiting stellar magnitude m by $\log N = 0.6m +$ constant, where both quantities m and N can be established from observations all over the sky, or any part of it.

The constant $0 \cdot 6$ gives the slope of the straight line connecting $\log N$ with m if galaxies of equal brightness were uniformly distributed through space, and if the intensity of their light would diminish with inverse square of their distance. If their intrinsic luminosities are not equal, but their dispersion remains the same in different parts of space, the argument becomes somewhat more complicated, but the result still remains the same. The slope of a plot of $\log N$ versus m less than $0 \cdot 6$ would indicate that there are more galaxies in the foreground than at greater distances; while if the slope were steeper the opposite should be the case.

The observed distribution of apparent luminosities of distant galaxies—observed in both the optical and radio domain of their emission—discloses, however, a slope of the log N–m relation to be *steeper* than that indicated by the above equation. If this discrepancy represents a real effect (of which there is still some doubt), it means that galaxies—in particular, radio-galaxies (cf. p. 282)—are more crowded in distant parts of the Universe than they appear to be nearer home. The most distant sources available for our statistics are such that their radiation takes billions of years to reach us; and our result could mean that, in so remote a past, galaxies were more closely packed in space than they are now.

The situation is complicated by the fact that the light of faraway galaxies may not diminish strictly with the inverse square of their distance. In the next chapter on the structure of the Universe we shall point out that other phenomena known to us from the observations indicate that the apparent brightness of faraway objects diminishes faster than with the inverse square of the distance; and the actual value of the coefficient of m bears a definite relation to the model of the Universe of which our Galaxy is a part.

These and other related problems will be considered in the next chapter in their cosmological context. For the present we wish to stress that galaxies do *not*, on the whole, appear to be distributed in the Universe at random. The distribution of galaxies on long-exposure plates taken with large telescopes discloses that all galaxies in space tend to be bunched up in discrete clusters—with vast expanses of no-man's land in between. In other words, there seems to exist virtually no general 'background field' of galaxies, of which their clusters would be local condensations. The existence of such clusters, consisting of hundreds to thousands of associated galaxies, seems to represent a basic design feature which the Great Architect of the Universe must have had in mind in giving concrete expression to his thought; though why this should be so lies beyond the limits of our comprehension.

But let us defer to the next chapter further discussion of the cosmological implications of the observed distribution of galaxies in the sky, and consider briefly another question. What is the origin of the galaxies in the Universe, and how do they evolve in the course of time?

Let us suppose—and we shall come to this back in section XIII-2—that in the remote past, far beyond the age of any object we have so far had occasion to mention, our Universe consisted at first of a thin gas in turbulent motion, in which eddies were forming and dissolving essentially at random. Such motions were bound to produce transient condensations of matter denser in some places than in others. At a certain stage, gravitational force due to self-attraction of matter in such condensations apparently became sufficient to overcome the random velocities of turbulent gas motion with which all matter was primordially endowed. Such aggregations could then have detached themselves from the primordial substrate to form the first distinguishable features of our Universe possessing their own identity—which we can well describe as 'proto-galaxies'. The masses of proto-galaxies were of the order of magnitude of 10^{43}–10^{45} grams—each containing enough material to form 10^{10}–10^{12} stars.

The aboriginal form of such galaxies did not depart much from spherical symmetry; and this was apparently true still at the time when the first crop of stars was seeded in the proto-galactic substrate—to form Population II stars constituting galactic 'halos'. A predominance, in such halos, of globular clusters leads us to conjecture that Population II stars were even less prone to be born otherwise than in large groups—not hundreds, but tens or hundreds of thousands at the same time. Moreover, as the medium from which they were formed may still have retained a large degree of its original turbulence, the random space velocities of objects born from it were still large—of the order of 100 km/sec and more—and (as it is very difficult for a star to get rid of its kinetic energy) have remained their distinguishing hallmarks ever since.

We do not know with any assurance when this process occurred, or how long it lasted. The earliest Population II stars of our Galaxy, now constituting some of its globular clusters, are certainly more than 10^{10} years old and probably older—it is very difficult to assign an upper limit to their age solely from their observed characteristics. It appears probable, however, that—not less than 5 billion years ago—the gas still remaining in the galactic halo collapsed by rapid rotation to form its highly flattened disc, essentially as we see it today. This act, far from producing an obstacle, may have stimulated the formation of the stars at that time, to give rise to a new 'disc-population' of stars; and there are reasons for believing that our Sun happens to be one of them.

The disc of our Galaxy—and, probably, of others at the same stage—did not yet possess the spiral structure that many galaxies have acquired in the course of time. There are strong reasons for concluding that spiral arms represent unstable configurations which form and dissolve in the course of time—few may survive more than a few dozen rotations of the galaxy to which they belong; but while they last, interstellar gas and dust becomes concentrated in their structure. As, moreover, this gas and dust constitutes the remaining nutritious substance from which new stars can grow, stars are being formed at this stage mainly—if not only—in the transient spiral arms, a fact amply borne out by observational evidence in our own Galaxy, as well as in other nearby galaxies (in Andromeda or Triangulum) which we have been able to resolve into stars. A trend indicating such an evolution is documented on a collection of photographs of different spiral nebulae reproduced on Plate 31.

If the cosmic age of a galaxy is manifested by its ability to bear stars, it could be measured by the amount of gas and other material still constituting interstellar substrate. According to this criterion, the Magellanic Clouds (especially the Smaller Cloud) should be cosmically younger than our own Galaxy; for a greater fraction (about one-third for the Smaller Magellanic Cloud) of its total mass still consists of hydrogen gas. On the other hand, the elliptical galaxies—like the companions to Andromeda nebula (NGC 205 and 221), or one in Virgo—show no evidence that hydrogen (or any other) gas is present in their interstellar space; nor is the symmetry of their image marred by any dark lanes indicative of interstellar dust. The space between the stars in such systems appears to be free from any kind of interstellar matter from which new stars could still be formed; and in this sense, elliptical galaxies represent probably the evolutionary end product of their line, after the discs of spiral galaxies have lost most of their angular momenta, and their ageing population has shrunk towards the centre.

But once we leave the confines of individual galaxies, is there, perchance, some tenuous matter still remaining in intergalactic space from which ageing galaxies could draw matter needed for rejuvenation? At present there appears to be no direct evidence against the view that intergalactic space around us is anything but empty. This does not rule out the presence of occasional intergalactic stragglers or 'tramps'—especially in the form of globular clusters, whose gravitational allegiance to specific members of our Local Group of galaxies is rather equivocal. However, the fathomless depths of the space between galaxies appear to be virtually free from any gas; and if the masses of all stars and galaxies were uniformly interspersed throughout the space, the mean density of such a substrate would be only of the order of 10^{-30} g/cm—corresponding to one atom of hydrogen for each cubic metre of space. Since, however, most of the matter in the Universe now appears to be condensed in the stars, the actual density of intergalactic substrate—if any—is bound to be very much less.

But let us, in closing, return to the globular clusters which constitute an important part of galactic haloes and can, in many ways, be regarded as miniature elliptical galaxies in which no gas or dust has been left to form new stars. Their population—well advanced in age—has no future other than a general decline. The globular clusters surrounding our Galaxy shine feebly in the sky like pale ghosts of the distant past, which from the days of their youth remember the Galaxy long before the latter assumed its present spiral form; and from the height of the wisdom of old age they look down upon the exuberant young stars of Population I still flourishing in its spiral arms—knowing full well the ephemeral nature of their fleeting attractiveness. But all processes in Nature —on a cosmic or a human scale—slow down with the advent of old age; and globular clusters may still be here without perceptible change after the greater part of the galactic disc shrinks in size to join the present nucleus of our Milky Way and forms a super-elliptical galaxy, as seen on Plate 28 in the Virgo cluster. But a long time will elapse before this comes true—none of us is going to see it on the Earth!

CHAPTER XIII

The Structure and Evolution of Our Universe

IN THE two preceding chapters we introduced the main types of stellar systems which fill the space as far as our telescopes can discern, and described the principal features of their morphology. We found that—just as the stars constitute the fundamental building-blocks of the galaxies—the latter constitute the typical formations for a study of the large-scale structure of the Universe in which we live. How large is this ultimate structure, and what binds it together into a single system? Is this system stable or unstable; and if unstable, in which direction is it evolving and on what time-scale? What is the past age our Universe has attained and what may the future hold in store for it? These are the ultimate questions which our ancestors have asked themselves since the dawn of human science, and attempted to answer as well as they could.

In the present chapter we shall follow in the footsteps of our predecessors and carry our inquiry further than it was possible for them to do; and while we cannot yet hold out the promise of any ultimate answers, we shall attempt to summarize what we have learned about the probable nature of the problem in the course of a quest which will take us to depths of space beyond the wildest imagination of our ancestors. Although we are still far from our ultimate goal, we have already travelled some distance towards it; and we invite the reader to share with us the gains and experiences which we have made on this journey so far.

XIII–1: The Size of the Universe

Since the dawn of human civilization man has always believed that the Universe in which he lives could be encompassed by his understanding; and written records of the effort to do so go back several thousand years. Thus the first book of the Bible contains a story of the creation of the world, which reflects the prevalent views in the second millenium before the commencement of our era; while the Homeric poems and sacred scripts of other nations contain other—perhaps less systematic—versions of the same story attesting to man's efforts to understand the world around him.

The Universe of the ancients was a little parochial corner of space dominated by the Earth at its centre, and surrounded by a sphere of fixed stars at a distance which was not inordinately large in comparison with known terrestrial dimensions. Aristarchos of Samos was the only genius of antiquity (3rd century B.C.) who got a glimpse of a much larger world, in which the Sun stood still and all the planets—including the Earth—circled around it. And when—after a lapse of eighteen centuries—the same idea was revived by Copernicus and Kepler, the Universe in which these masters were content to live was not essentially different from the snug little corner of the ancients. For Galileo Galilei, who ushered in the era of telescopic astronomy at the commencement of the seventeenth century, the distance to the stars amounted to only 13 million times the terrestrial radius (i.e., only a little more than the actual size of the solar system); and Johannes Kepler was unwilling to place it much beyond twice that distance.

In Kepler's own time, Giordano Bruno proclaimed that the fixed stars were nothing but distant suns, distributed in infinite numbers through infinite space. To Kepler this was, however, sheer blasphemy; and an idea so repugnant that when Bruno was burned at the stake in 1600 by the Church authorities as a heretic, the usually mild and placid Kepler wrote to a friend that Bruno got only what he deserved.

The actual dimensions of the solar system were not established, to a realistic approximation, until the French academicians of the 1680s; and although the actual distance to the nearest stars did not yield to triangulation till 150 years later, the self-made reflectors of William Herschel by the end of the eighteenth century 'broke the barriers of the heavens' and opened up to inquisitive human eyes the first inkling of the realm of the galaxies. Our own Milky Way system began to assume a form somewhat reminiscent of the other galaxies we saw beyond the confines of our own 'island' in the Universe; and if such neighbouring islands defied resolution into individual stars in Herschel's powerful telescopes, they must obviously be separated from us by distances many times as large as the dimensions of the Milky Way system itself.

Does this realm of the galaxies extend without end, and is the total number of their stars finite or infinite? Is, moreover, the Universe infinite in time, or does it present state disclose traces of evolutionary processes which might imply the beginning and the end of such processes on a finite time-scale; and if so, how far from the beginning or end do we find ourselves at the present time? Attempts to answer such questions, placing no reliance on revelation other than that forthcoming through astronomical telescopes, have gradually come to constitute a separate branch of science called 'cosmology'—a discipline concerned with a study of the large-scale structure of the Universe on the basis of observational data accumulated by astronomers, and with their interpretation—in the light of the pertinent laboratory experiments—in terms of mathematical theories which can integrate all available knowledge into a unified picture.

Thus, in cosmology—as indeed in any other branch of human science—facts and theory are bound to be inextricably connected, and cannot be separated except at the cost of crippling amputation. Theories which are not anchored in facts would constitute as sound a cosmology as a literal interpretation of the Book of Genesis. On the other hand, facts alone would be lifeless unless they were synthesized by our desire to discern in them a reflection of an orderly system of a Universe governed by universal laws of nature.

The prime purveyor of the data which can raise cosmology to the rank of a scientific discipline remains, however, the astronomer. A philosopher, or mathematician, can conjure up visions of different plans of the Universe—like Hamlet, they can be enclosed in a nutshell and consider themselves kings of infinite space. But only the astronomer can tell such self-styled majesties whether the particular thought they have in mind may, or may not, correspond to the Universe in which we live.

Imaginative theorizing in cosmology has a long history, from the authors of the first Book of Genesis to Immanuel Kant, and after, and is far from extinct in our own time; only its garb has changed with the fashions. In its present form, verbal semantics have been largely displaced by mathematics as a vehicle for ideas which can be equally speculative. Such speculations possess definite value in subjects (like cosmology) which call for an exploration of all imaginable possibilities. But they can also degenerate into a dangerous addiction if carried out without due regard to observational checks.

The astronomer contemplates our Universe as an entity revealed to him by the instruments of observation at his disposal—and these can range from the naked eye to the largest optical or radio telescopes. In carrying out his work he must, moreover, also pay attention to the location of his observing station in space. Most astronomical work so far has been carried out from the surface of one planet. We happen to live near a star—our Sun—but from the cosmological point of view this fact represents only a minor nuisance; and to obtain a less restricted view of the Universe we must look at it at night. Even so, the starry sky over our heads may not be quite typical, for we live in a galaxy; and because of that our sky is brighter than it would be for an observer in intergalactic space, though not as bright as if we were inside a globular cluster.

But let us content ourselves, out of necessity, with our galactic night sky. From no direction in it do the stars provide more light than one standard candle about 100 metres away. We are so used to this subdued light that we do not find the darkness of the night sky remarkable. But the first person who did so was H. W. M. Olbers—a German astronomer living between 1758–1840—who in 1826 first considered the following seemingly paradoxical question: if the Universe is infinite in space and time, why does not the entire sky radiate as brightly as a stellar surface, in a blaze of light with no dark patches in between?

In order to explain the gravity of such an inquiry, let us invoke a two-dimensional analogy of an observer in the midst of a large forest. No matter how sparsely planted the forest may be, provided it is sufficiently large the horizon of our observer would be completely blotted out of view by a superposition of tree-trunks at different distances. In the same way—provided only that space is filled with stars or galaxies to an infinite distance—the entire sky should be studded with stars, leaving not a single point of it uncovered. Why isn't it?

In raising this question Olbers assumed—reasonably, he thought—that the transparency of space was perfect, and that starlight travels through it along straight lines. If so, then wherever we look our line of sight should eventually intercept the surface of a star whose disc would be only diminished in apparent size by distance; but its surface brightness per unit area should remain the same. Therefore, the sky at night should really be as bright as in the daytime, and much brighter than our present day sky—as bright, in fact, as the apparent disc of the Sun or even brighter if the majority of stars covering the sky at various distances are hotter than our Sun.

A single glance at our sky at night or during daytime is, of course, sufficient to verify that this is not the case. In fact, one of the most marked features of the Universe around us is the extraordinary scarcity of radiation. We are quite used to the fact that the sky is very dark everywhere in the Universe (except, perhaps, in the immediate proximity of a star), and know that the average energy density of radiation in the observed parts of space constitutes but a minute fraction of the energy density of matter.* In the realm of cosmic physics, we consider the state of lowest energy (the 'ground' state) of any atom to represent its natural state—to which most atoms return readily after every excitation by getting rid of their surplus energy by radiation which space will swallow up without return. The heating of a star by radiation received from other stars is utterly negligible in comparison with that generated by its own internal energy sources.

All these facts are symptoms of an extreme thermodynamic disequilibrium of our Universe; and a consideration of their significance for its general structure and evolution commenced with the Olbers paradox of 1826. Olbers, and his descendants for almost a century, were very puzzled by what could have gone wrong with expectations based on such plausible assumptions. They conjectured that it was the assumed transparency of space which was at fault; and that the light of more distant stars is dimmed by dust in interstellar space. Although we know now (*cf.* Chapter III–1) that space between the stars does contain a certain amount of dust—at least within spiral galaxies—such dust would, in time, be heated by absorption of starlight to a finite temperature, and emit as much light (although of a different colour) as it absorbs; hence, it would exert no shielding effect. In order to explain away the Olbers

---

*For example, each gram of matter is—according to Einstein's identity $E = mc^2$—equivalent to 9×10^{20}: ergs of energy; but even the Sun manages to squeeze out of each gram of its mass an average trickle of only 2 ergs per second; and very few stars in space can do substantially better.

paradox, something else must have gone amiss with the reasoning on which it was based; but what it was did not come to light until almost a century later.

In the meantime, decades and generations have come and gone in which astronomers were mostly concerned with an exploration of the Universe at closer quarters—work which paved the way for the far-flung celestial exploits of the twentieth century, but lacked some of the glamour with which astronomers have succeeded in investing their subject in more recent times. Olbers and his contemporaries in the early decades of the nineteenth century lived in the wake of the first period of exploration of galaxies through the reflectors of William Herschel. Its efflorescence came to an end, however, in the declining years of that great astronomer; and was followed for almost a century by the 'era of the refractor', which astronomers largely used for investigation of the motions of the nearby stars.

By the beginning of our century a new turn was given to the study of the Universe by a renaissance of the astronomical reflectors—instruments which alone were capable of gathering enough light from the distant galaxies to bring into focus eerie visions of worlds whose distance from us vastly exceeded the size of the Universe known to our grandfathers only 60–70 years ago. Let us now outline another aspect of it, which gives us a clue to the dynamical aspects of the Universe—and through them to its past as well as the future.

The beginning of this story goes back to the commencement of spectroscopic studies of the motions of external galaxies in the line of sight—the only component of motion which can be measured with the optical means at our disposal; for apparent transverse motions at such distances are bound to be negligible. Low-dispersion spectra of several spiral nebulae were taken by Huggins and others during the nineteenth century; but the first investigator to measure the spectral line shifts—which could disclose the motions of such stellar systems towards us, or away from us in the line of sight—was V. M. Slipher at the Lowell Observatory in Arizona.

Between 1912 and 1914 Slipher succeeded in measuring the shifts of spectral lines of 13 external galaxies accessible to his 24-inch reflector. He found, to his surprise, that not only were the measured shifts about ten times as large as for most stars in the sky around us, but—in the case of every single nebula investigated by him—their spectral lines were shifted to the red; and if we interpret such shifts as Doppler shifts due to relative motion (*cf.* Chapter II), they would indicate a systematic *recession* of these galaxies from us, with velocities of the order of 100 km/sec. Between 1916–1917, F. G. Pease at Mount Wilson Observatory found much the same to be true for many other objects of this class.

As soon as these facts became known, astronomers began to analyze the measured radial velocities for the relative motion of our own Galaxy among the rest. It was the German astronomer Carl Wirtz who first pointed out (in 1924) that if the red shifts measured in the spectra of extragalactic nebulae are Doppler shifts indicative of radial motions, these nebulae recede from us at a rate which increases with their distance. This bold suggestion was not, however, readily accepted by contemporary astronomers; and the matter hung in suspense for five years—until E. P. Hubble confirmed in 1929 that Wirtz's suggestion was indeed well-founded.

By 1929 Hubble knew no more radial velocities of the spiral nebulae than Wirtz had known five years before. However, two new factors enabled Hubble to advance the quest. The first was a determination, in 1926–27, of the rotation of our own Galaxy (cf. Chapter XI), which disclosed that our Sun with the rest of its system revolves around the centre of our Galaxy with a velocity close to 270 km/sec. A knowledge of this velocity enabled Hubble to reduce the observed 'heliocentric' red shifts to values that would be measured by an observer situated at the centre of our Galaxy—in much the same way as radial velocities of the stars observed from the revolving terrestrial platform are reduced to their heliocentric values. Secondly, on the basis of his own photometric work with the Mt. Wilson 100-inch reflector Hubble possessed much better estimates of the distances of the extra-galactic nebulae with known red shifts.

When he set out to plot the magnitude of such shifts (cf. Plate 32) against improved distance, he obtained essentially a straight line—making the red shift proportional to the distance of the source. This relation—which has since become generally known as Hubble's Law—has been extended by Hubble, Humason, and their successors (Sandage, Schmidt, Baum) at Mt. Wilson and Palomar observatories to ever-increasing distances of space. Thus the cluster of

galaxies in the constellation of Virgo—the nearest cluster to us in the Universe—was found to have the spectral lines of its prominent members red-shifted by 0·4% of the speed of light indicating a distance of 34 million light years. The same method localized a cluster of galaxies in Hercules (Plate 29) at some 300 million light years; and that in Hydra (Plate 30) at a distance in excess of 1·8 billion light years. For objects still farther and too faint for their light to be decomposed into a spectrum, an indication of the magnitude of the red shift can be obtained from the general reddening of light which can be measured more readily by photoelectric techniques.*
The most remote galaxies whose red shifts have been measured so far would—by Hubble's Law—be situated more than two billion light years away; and their red shifts would correspond to velocities of recession approaching one-third of that of light!

But even these stupendous velocities did not prove to be the last word—thanks to the discovery, in the last decade, of a new class of enigmatic objects in the sky now commonly known as 'quasars'. In order to give a brief account of this exciting subject, we must return to the time—only a quarter of a century ago—when astronomers began to survey the sky with radio-telescopes collecting microwave radiation of the electromagnetic spectrum. As the first outlines of the 'radio' maps of the sky began to emerge from such accumulated records, they bore at first little or no resemblance to the sky as we have been accustomed to seeing it from time immemorial. Like the sky visible to our eyes, however, the microwave records of it began to disclose the existence of an increasing number of discrete sources ('radio-stars') standing out of the background noise. But the locations of these 'stars' failed to coincide with the conspicuous objects of the visible sky—as though the two had nothing in common.

Gradually, however, a persistent quest for identification of the radio-sources with optical objects began to bear fruit. Thus the so-called Cassiopeia A—the strongest radio-source of the sky—proved identical with the remnant of a Supernova (see Chapter III–2) which flared up in that part of the sky around the year 1700 in a region of the Milky Way so heavily obscured (absorbing

---

*Doppler shifts in the stars should affect equally the light of all wavelengths of the line spectra as well as their continuous background. Displacements of spectral lines from their normal positions are merely measurable with greater accuracy than the general reddening of the continuous spectrum.

light, but not radio waves) that it completely escaped detection by astronomers of that time, and other historical Supernovae—such as the Chinese object of 1054 A.D., or Tycho's star of 1572—were all found to be associated with known discrete radio sources. On the other hand, Cygnus A—the second strongest known radio-source in the constellation of the Swan—was identified with a pair of external galaxies in collision at a distance of some 500 million light years.

By 1960, prolonged efforts by many investigators led to the identification of about 300 discrete radio sources with specific optical objects. More than half of these proved to be colliding galaxies or other extended objects—galactic or extragalactic; but the rest failed to exhibit detectable angular diameters, and earned such objects the title of quasi-stellar radio sources (abbreviated to 'quasars'). In some cases, such quasars were identified with certain optical objects—faint bluish stars—but none was distinguished by any particular appearance.

The real history of quasars did not commence till 1963, when Maarten Schmidt at Mt. Wilson and Palomar Observatories obtained the spectrum of the brightest of these quasars—identical with object No. 273 of the 3rd Cambridge Catalogue of Radio Sources (or, for short, 3C273)—and found its lines to be red-shifted to such an extent that—should this shift be 'cosmologic' (i.e., should Hubble's Law remain applicable)—this quasar should be the most distant cosmic object known up to that time. Moreover, since 1963, red shifts have been measured for about 40 additional quasars; and their amounts proved to be so large as to render 3C273 one of the nearest; for its velocity of recession would correspond to 'only' 16% of that of light, and Hubble's Law would place it at a distance of some $1\frac{1}{2}$ billion light years. At this distance, the quasar would have to radiate more than a hundred times as much as an entire giant galaxy to appear to us as a star of 12·7 magnitude. Another quasar—3C9, likewise observed by Schmidt—shows a much larger red shift of its spectrum which, interpreted as a Doppler shift, would correspond to a velocity of recession of almost 80% of that of light; and if this shift is wholly cosmological, the distance of 3C9 should be of the order of 8 billion light years, and its light reaching us now would have been almost half-way here by the time our Earth was formed!

The greatest red shift which has so far been measured is that for a quasi-stellar object known as 4C534 in the constellation of Canis Minor, for which the American observers Lynds and Wills at the Kitt Peak Observatory recently established a value of the ratio of the shift to the wavelength to be 2·9 for the emission line $L\alpha$ of hydrogen. The normal wavelength of this line is equal to 1216 Å —in the far ultraviolet part of the spectrum, which does not penetrate through our atmosphere. In the spectrum of 4C534 this line appears, however, at the wavelength 4714 Å in the green; and, in addition, several ultraviolet lines of ionized carbon, nitrogen, and silicon which normally occur between 1240 and 1909 Å have been shifted to the yellow part of the visible spectrum. Such red shifts are, therefore, by no means microscopic phenomena, but completely alter the entire character of the spectrum. If, moreover, we regard them as Doppler shifts due to cosmological recession, they would correspond to stupendous velocities close to 260,000 km/sec (i.e., 87% of that of light); and an extrapolation of Hubble's Law would place them at a distance in excess of 30 billion light years!

We have reason to doubt that Hubble's law continues to be literally applicable to such extreme cases; and the observed red shifts of the quasars may not be wholly due to cosmological recession. First, in several quasars for which $\delta\lambda/\lambda$ is greater than 2, absorption lines in their spectra exhibit shifts which are smaller than those of the emission lines—a fact which is not consistent with a uniform recession of the object as a whole. Secondly, if such objects were to remain visible at the hypothetical distances assigned to them by Hubble's Law, their intrinsic brightness would have to be so tremendous that no conceivable physical mechanism (other than an outright annihilation of matter with anti-matter) could maintain them for any length of time. And, as we shall explain in the subsequent section, objects seen now at such distances would have to be older than the Universe; and this leads to contradictions which we shall attempt to resolve later on in this chapter.

For the time being, let us note that more than 150 quasars have been detected in the sky; and from the fact that their apparent distribution in the sky pays no regard to the existence of the Milky Way we conclude that quasars are extragalactic objects. They all radiate strongly in the ultraviolet, but need not emit detectable radio noise; in fact, the majority of them (the 'quiesars', discovered by Sandage in 1965) do not. Moreover, the light of some quasars fluctuates on a time-scale of days or weeks—a fact from which we surmise that their dimensions do not exceed light days. If so, however, quasars may well constitute super-dense compact galaxies; and if so, their unusually large red shifts may be partly due to a difficulty which photons of their light may experience in departing from an intense gravitational field of the parent body.

For according to the general theory of relativity, a strong gravitational field retards the flow of time and diminishes the frequency with which atomic vibrations are emitted—thus giving rise to a 'gravitational' red shift. The existence of such a phenomenon has now been experimentally verified sufficiently for us to place confidence in the theoretical prediction; and there is no reason why quasars should be immune to it if their configurations are sufficiently compact. Since such a hypothesis is not at variance with the observations, we surmise that their observed red shifts are the result of 'cosmological' as well as 'gravitational' effects working in the same direction; but as long as we cannot separate them, the distances of the quasars—and their absolute luminosities—remain undetermined.

At 'cosmological' distances, the luminosity of the quasars should exceed 10^{46} ergs/sec, or about 100 times the luminosity of a large galaxy—even more in extreme cases like 4C534. It is very difficult to see what physical process could account for an emission of this order over astronomically long periods of time. However, if these objects are actually nearer, this difficulty would be proportionally diminished; and at present there are hopes that this may indeed prove to be the case.

XIII–2: The Expansion of the Universe and its Age

Let us, however, abandon the quasars wherever they may be, and return to the more normal galaxies for which Hubble, Humason and their successors have established red shifts of lines in their spectra, increasing with the distance as indicated by diminishing brightness of the respective object. If we interpret these red shifts as Doppler shifts due to radial recession, we are led to conclude that the Universe around us is not stationary, but *expanding*—at a rate (indicated by the slope of the straight line representing Hubble's Law) which is now taken to be between 50–120 km/sec per megaparsec ('Hubble's constant').

The Structure and Evolution of Our Universe

The significance of this phenomenon is profound; for its literal interpretation would imply that the Universe of the galaxies occupied only a very small fraction of its present volume some 12–15 billion years ago—the time at which the expansion started, and which is generally referred to as the 'age of the Universe'. Moreover, its present 'horizon'—i.e., a distance at which the velocity of expansion would approach that of light (and beyond which light would, accordingly, cease to reach us) would not be more than 10–20 billion light years away! Whether or not this space is 'open' or 'closed' should (within the framework of the general theory of relativity) depend essentially on the amount of mass enclosed within its volume; and a mean density of 10^{-30}–10^{-29} g/cm^3 estimated in Chapter XII from available data on the galaxies should bring it very close to the limit at which our Universe could actually be *finite*—both in space and time.

This new Universe, which we are beginning to perceive dimly through the mist of observational errors besetting its exploration in depth, would therefore seem to differ only in size and age—rather than in kind—from the snug little Universe of the ancients, supported by biblical traditions through the times of Galileo and Kepler. Their estimates of the size of the Universe we have already quoted earlier in this chapter; and in 1658 a distinguished biblical scholar—Archbishop Ussher of Armagh—even fixed the time of its creation to a day in 4004 B.C. (Sunday, October 23rd at 9 a.m.)—a date accepted by Isaac Newton, the sage of his age, more than half a century later with only slightly less certainty.* Throughout the 18th and 19th centuries it was the geologists—studying phenomena closer at hand on the Earth—who pressed for an extension of this time-scale; while the astronomers in the post-Herschelian era began to form visions of space without end. Were they mistaken in their expectations?

For natural philosophers of the seventeenth century, from Kepler to Newton, the guideline in their cosmological view of a Universe finite in space and time was still the biblical tradition; while Newtonian mechanics provided a possibility of interpreting the celestial discoveries of William Herschel and his successors in

---

*In his *Chronology of the Antient Kingdoms Amended* (London, 1728) Newton stated that 'I do not pretend to be exact to a year: there may be errors of five or ten years, and sometimes twenty, but not much above.'

terms of a Universe with no visible boundaries in space and time—a view prevalent among scientists of the nineteenth century, and popularized by such successful writers of that age as Camille Flammarion. However, logical difficulties arose—exemplified by the 'Olbers paradox'—which the concept of an infinite Universe could not resolve; and with the advent of the twentieth century the stage was set for a re-examination of its basic premises.

The latter were rooted in the Newtonian mechanics which reigned supreme over human minds for two hundred years—until, with the commencement of the twentieth century, it began to develop symptoms of old age, manifested by the inability to account for a growing array of observed phenomena which—though small—could not be accommodated within its framework. And between 1910 and 1920—at the same time as Slipher and Pease detected the dispersive tendency of external galaxies—Albert Einstein created his famous general theory of relativity which superseded Newtonian mechanics in its cosmological aspects; and at the same time enabled us logically to connect the metric of space and time with the amount and distribution of matter which it contains.

Unlike the 'special relativity', concerned with uniform and rectilinear motions—which was amply attested by experiment and soon became a well-established part of modern physics—the merits of the more general theory concerned with curvilinear motions long remained in balance. Only recently have several of its predictions been satisfactorily tested by astronomical observations (in particular, by those of extra-terrestrial 'clocks' provided by the 'pulsars' of Chapter III-2). At present there seems, therefore, little room for doubt that the general theory of relativity—now at the mature age of over fifty years—does represent a significant advance over classical mechanics in our understanding of the connection between mass, time and the metric properties of space; and the question arises as to its bearing on the fundamental issues of cosmology.

The cosmological contents of general relativity are contained in its famous system of 'field equations' relating the metric of space with its mass. Locally (on a small scale) such equations coincide with those of classical mechanics, but are more general in content; for the inverse-square law of universal attraction does not have to be accepted as an axiom (as it was in Newtonian mechanics), but becomes a local consequence of more general principles expressing the effects of mass on the geometry of the surrounding space. The equations expressing such principles are not solvable in general terms by any method known to contemporary mathematics; but particular solutions can be constructed—though so far only under severe restrictions dictated by mathematical rather than physical necessity.

Einstein himself, de Sitter, and others were the first to construct possible theoretical models of the structure of our Universe which are consistent with the general theory of relativity. None of these is of more than historical interest today; for it was soon proved (by Friedmann in 1922, Lemaître in 1927, and Eddington in 1930) that the Einstein–de Sitter models were static, and unstable with respect to motion; any disturbance of their static state would set them expanding (or contracting) in a manner depending on the structure of the equations. We shall have more to say on these expanding models later on in this section; for the present we wish to stress some features of these model-universes which were acquired with the advent of the theory of relativity, and have remained with us ever since.

First, the space defined by the field equations of general relativity is not Euclidean, but *curved* and possesses many interesting properties. It can be finite in size but possess no boundary (and no centre); and if you proceed straight ahead in any direction, you are liable to come back to the place from which you started. There is nothing mysterious in such a space; and the world we live in— the surface of our Earth—represents its two-dimensional analogy. A two-dimensional curved space like the Earth's surface is no harder to think of than the flat space of a table top. And occasions arise when we think more naturally in terms of the curved two-dimensional Earth's surface than of the three-dimensional space of which it is a part. When we describe the distance between London and New York to be 3,000 miles, we think of the shortest arc on the globe between these points, and not of going along a hole bored through the interior.

When we pass from two-dimensional to three-dimensional curved space imagination deserts us; but its mathematical description can be generated without difficulty; and some properties of such a space are of vital interest to cosmology. In particular, light rays no longer propagate along straight lines; and if the space is expanding*—in the sense that a distance between two points increases with time—the intensity of light will fall off more rapidly than with the inverse square of the distance between them.

This fact alone is sufficient to dispose of the 'Olbers paradox' noted in the first section of this chapter. The existence of the Olbers paradox is, therefore, an indication that the intensity of light in our Universe must diminish more rapidly than with the inverse square of the distance—i.e., faster than is necessary to offset the growth in the number of stars or galaxies in a cone subtended by a constant sight angle which (for random spatial distribution of the objects) increases with the square of the distance. In other words, the necessity of escaping from the dilemma of the Olbers paradox requires that we live in an expanding Universe (and not contracting—in which case the dilemma would be aggravated); but the mode of expansion still remains open.

The first—and, in many ways, the simplest—relativistic model of an expanding Universe was discovered by Friedmann in 1922. This model is based on Einstein's 'orthodox' field equations, and starts from the initial state of a point size of infinite density, expanding secularly thereafter. Such a Universe is finite in space as well as in the duration of its past, but its evolution starts from an initial singularity which may or may not possess a physical meaning.

In order to escape its limited age, Eddington (following Einstein) introduced in 1930 a 'cosmological term' in the field equations—representing an arbitrary force of repulsion that grows with the distance—to relegate the origin of the Universe to an infinite past; while Lemaître proposed in 1927 an even more arbitrary model, in which the 'cosmological term' was deployed to render the age of the Universe finite, but its velocity of expansion non-uniform.

Friedmann's model with its singularity at the origin is now currently referred to in more profane terms as the 'big-bang' Universe; while the particular features of Lemaître's model have earned his Universe the epithet of a 'primaeval egg'. Which one of

---

*An expansion of this kind affecting all distances would result in an apparent recession of celestial objects as seen from any point of space. Therefore, if a recession of external galaxies mentioned earlier in this chapter is due to this cause, this phenomenon has nothing to do with the symmetry of the Universe as a whole, or with our position in it.

these—or of any other that can be based on the field equations of general relativity—may actually correspond to the Universe in which we live can only be decided by comparing their respective consequences with the observations. General relativity itself does not furnish any unique answer; it requires only that the models contending for recognition be consistent with it; and we are still far from a position in which we could make a census of all possible alternatives. All we can do today is to look over the credentials of such candidates as have presented themselves, and confront them with the principal features of the Universe around us.

Did this Universe really commence its existence with a 'big bang', or did it evolve from the state of a 'primaeval egg' to the structure we see around us today in a finite time? If the present rate of recession of the extragalactic nebulae around us—as embodied in Hubble's Law—can be extrapolated linearly in the past, it would follow that the Universe would indeed have dwindled to a very small fraction of its present size only some 12–15 billion years ago. At that time—which is not more than some three times the established age of our Moon or of meteorites within the solar system—the structure of the Universe and its composition would have been drastically different from what it is today. The creation and subsequent evolution of not only all stars and galaxies, but also of all chemical elements constituting them would have to be accomplished within this time.

While this is not perhaps impossible, astronomers in the past forty years have chafed under the stringent restrictions on the available time-scale imposed by Hubble's constant specifying the rate of expansion of the Universe to be between 50–120 km/sec per megaparsec. It is, of course, possible to extend our elbow room on the cosmological time-scale by introducing a suitably large 'cosmological constant' into the field equations of general relativity to render the expansion of the Universe non-uniform in time; and, in so doing, abandon Friedmann's model for that of Lemaître or Eddington. Those who find it philosophically repugnant to tamper with the relativistic field equations by the introduction of terms of an essentially ad-hoc nature are, however, driven to compress too many feats of creation into too short a time at the very beginning of evolution. Their difficulty may differ only in degree, but not in kind, from that experienced in the early part of the eighteenth century by Isaac Newton, who set out to compress within 1,656 years the creation of the Universe and its subsequent evolution to Adam and Eve and history up to the time of the Deluge and Noah's Ark. Is the Friedmann model of the Universe going to prove a safer guide to ancient chronology than did the biblical Book of Genesis at the hands of Archbishop Ussher or Isaac Newton?

In one respect the possibility of an initial 'big bang' offers greater physical interest: namely, it can account more satisfactorily than other hypotheses for the origin of the chemical elements in the abundances observed at the present time. Any quest for an understanding of the nature and history of our Universe can hardly do better than to begin by an examination of what this Universe is made of. As we know from laboratory analysis of such parts of it as come into our hands—or by spectroscopic analysis at a distance with the aid of our telescopes—it consists of an orderly system of elements increasing in complexity from hydrogen to uranium. These elements had to be created from pre-existent and more 'elementary' particles by physical processes taking place in different parts of our Universe and at different times in its evolution. Since, moreover, such processes are largely irreversible, the extent to which they have progressed so far should be reflected in the observed composition of its constituent bodies; and the relative abundances of the elements attained so far should furnish a clue as to the age and past history of our Universe.

In earlier parts of this book we stressed that the cosmic matter now constituting our Universe—whether in the form of stars or interstellar matter—consists predominantly of hydrogen, the lightest and simplest element of all, followed by helium and other heavier elements in proportions diminishing so rapidly with increasing atomic weights that species with atomic weights over (say) 20 can almost be regarded as impurities. It is probably correct to say that more than 99% of the total mass of our Universe now consists of hydrogen and helium; but the fraction of helium contained in this mixture (about 20%) appears to be disturbingly large.

We know, of course, that helium is being produced on a large scale in the Universe by the burning of hydrogen in the interiors of Main Sequence (and, to a lesser extent, other) stars; but if all the helium now present in interstellar space and elsewhere had been produced by equilibrium thermonuclear processes in stellar interiors, it would have been necessary for cosmic matter—both compact and dispersed—to be re-cycled through stellar interiors, not once, but several times; and a cosmic time-scale of the order of 10^{10} years would not have offered enough time for this process to get very far.

It was with this difficulty in mind that Eddington retained the 'cosmological term' in the gravitational field equations, to gain enough time for the creation of all chemical elements through the combined efforts of several generations of stellar thermonuclear plants. On the other hand, in a Universe only 10^{10} years old, most of the stars we see in the sky—and, in particular, all Population II stars—would still belong to the first generation; and not enough of these would have had time to blow up and disperse the heavy elements that may have been synthesized in their interiors into the interstellar substrate.

However, the protagonists of the 'big bang' theory of the Universe can argue that, at the time of the big bang, the hydrogen of the Universe was compressed to a state so dense that extensive nucleogenesis could have taken place for a short time throughout its entire mass—with the result that the first crop of helium and other heavier elements could have been seeded in the primordial mass of the Universe before the first stars and galaxies were formed in it at all. Detailed studies of the energy density required for this purpose, and of the time-scale on which this process could have been operative, are under intensive study at the present time; but whatever the details turn out to be, that this could have happened cannot be ruled out by any theory or observations.

Moreover, several other facts have emerged in recent years which give at least a qualified support to this picture. Thus it has been known for a long time that the space velocities of the old (Population II) stars are very high in comparison with those of the stars born in more recent time. Since the kinematic properties of the stars are largely preserved over long intervals of time, this indicates that the material from which these old stars were born was much more agitated—and possessed a much greater degree of turbulence—than the substrate that gave rise to stars of more recent vintage.

Moreover, in recent years astronomers and physicists detected the existence of another very curious phenomenon: the fact that the whole sky seems to emit a very faint glow equally intense in all directions. The intensity of this glow is very low, its colour very red; for it has so far been possible to observe it only in the microwave domain at frequencies ranging from 1 mm to about 20 cm. At longer wavelengths, the intensity of this radiation becomes insensible; while at wavelengths shorter than one millimetre it becomes completely gobbled up by atmospheric absorption. From so small a fragment of the spectrum it is impossible as yet to arrive at firm conclusions about the origin of this radiation emanating isotropically from the whole sky; but if it is thermal, the observed distribution of its intensity would point to a temperature of approximately 3 degrees on the absolute scale.

It is still too early to be sure that this apparently isotropic field of radiation is of thermal origin; but if so, it may indeed represent a red-shifted remnant of an earlier, hotter, and denser phase of our expanding Universe—in brief, a relict glow of the primaeval 'fireball' in which our Universe may have come into being. If you were troubled, in the days of youthful innocence, by the biblical statement that God made light several days before he created the Sun or the Moon or the stars, and wondered where that light came from, you may note with satisfaction that modern cosmology seems to have come back to the same concept in a roundabout way. But as regards the origin of the 'primaeval fireball', the biblical theory still remains almost as good as any other that can be conjured up by human imagination.

And this is as far as our science can take us at the present time. In pursuing the vistas opening up on the horizon of our age-long quest to understand the structure of the Universe in which we live, we have arrived at the confines of our present knowledge. It is not much more than half a century since this subject began to claim the close attention of astronomers; much has already been discovered; and there is scarcely a limit to what may be known to us a century or more hence. But if we look around now to take stock of our present knowledge supported by observations, what can we say in brief answer to the basic questions?

First—if we define the Universe as an expanse of space in which communications between any two points are possible by means of light rays—it appears that a Universe of mean density close to 10^{-30} g/sec and expanding at a rate indicated by the present values of Hubble's constant is *not* infinite in space and time, and possesses a finite past. In saying so we must stress, however, that the actual duration of this past is still subject to considerable uncertainty; for the observed red shifts in the spectra of very distant cosmic sources need not be wholly due to Doppler shifts of recession.

The only observed phenomena supporting the notion of an expanding Universe are the darkness of the night sky and the extragalactic red shifts. Galaxies show, in fact, no other indications of being in relative motion; their apparent positions do not change, nor do they exhibit any appreciable change of angular diameters in the course of time. Moreover, the interpretation of the red shifts as being due to the Doppler effect requires a constancy of the ratio $\delta\lambda/\lambda$ for all lines of the spectrum—including the radio part of the spectrum in which wavelengths are measured in centimetres rather than microns. This appears to be the case in the spectra of galaxies up to the distance of some 200 light years (for which $\delta\lambda/\lambda$ is less than $0\cdot02$)—which are, however, still (cosmologically speaking) on our doorstep. Whether or not this continues to be so in greater depths of space has not so far been verified by observations (because of the scarcity of distinguishable lines); but differences in shifts between absorption and emission lines in the quasar spectra should sound a note of caution.

We have, in fact, reason to doubt that the enormous red shifts observed in the spectra of quasars are wholly (or even largely) cosmological. For example, if this were true of 4C534 mentioned on p. 283, its light reaching us now would have been en route for a period several times the 'age of the Universe' as deduced from the present value of Hubble's constant; and if the latter varies with time, a relation between red shift and distance becomes less clear.*

It is also possible that large red shifts observed in the spectra of distant cosmic sources are only partly connected with the expansion of space, and may be partly due to other causes. For quasars—which may represent extreme cases of compact galaxies—a 'gravi-

---

*Possible variability of Hubble's constant in time can, in principle, be studied on the basis of the red shifts of objects at distances of several hundred to a few thousand million light years—for in observing such objects we are looking that far into the past of our Universe. But no conclusive results have so far emerged from such studies—largely because of the difficulty of establishing independent criteria for the distance of objects near the limits of telescopic detectability.

tational' red shift may be a contributing cause, but not necessarily the only one. For less compact objects—like ordinary galaxies—we have so far no obvious reason to doubt the Doppler nature of their red shifts, or the validity of Hubble's Law as an indicator of distance. However, it is also true that in the great depths of space this constitutes only a simple assumption lacking as yet any independent confirmation. Within our solar system, or in double stars of our Galaxy, the Doppler nature of spectral shifts caused by motion is amply attested by independent evidence. But at cosmic distances amounting to hundreds of millions of light years this is not yet the case.

Is it, moreover, certain that photons of light reaching us from distant parts of the Universe after a travel-time of hundreds, or thousands of millions of years will do so with their original energy (*i.e.*, wavelength) unchanged—or do they, perchance, lose some of it en route? We know remarkably little of what light does while it travels through empty space. Our experiments and observations tell us mostly what happens when light impinges on matter and interacts with it after transit times which are triflingly short in comparison with the aeons of light years separating us from distant galaxies. Will photons emitted by distant galaxies retain their exact identity before we may collect them in our telescopes, and test their energy contents hundreds or thousands of millions of years after they embarked on their journey through empty space?

Theoretical physics offers no support for a hypothesis that a slow decay in the energy of photons may produce cosmological red shifts of a different kind, which would superimpose on those due to recession. The absence of theoretical guidance in matters transcending so widely the range of our experimental facilities need not, perhaps, signify too much; for physics—like astronomy—is also in a constant state of flux; and its recent history in particular should teach us to keep an open mind.

But if the red shifts observed in the spectra of extragalactic nebulae are due partly to causes other than recession, the age of the Universe would be within the rather uncomfortably short time-span of 12–15 billion years; or if we increase its age—*à la* Eddington—by the introduction of a suitable 'cosmological constant', we can make the past of the Universe as long as we please. There are, however, other indications—unconnected with the red shifts—that this age is not only finite, but probably not more than 20–30 billion years long. The reason is the fact that we still live today in an essentially hydrogen Universe, which could no longer be the case if the bulk of its mass were re-cycled through stellar interiors more than a few times.

For example, we have already mentioned that old Population II stars of certain globular clusters exhibit in their spectra indications of a marked deficiency of metals and other heavy elements in relation to hydrogen; in some of these (as in the well-known globular cluster Messier 3) metals seem to be present in abundances ranging between one and ten per cent of those obtaining in the Sun and other stars of its generation. If, however, metals were still as deficient as that in the cosmic matter from which this cluster of stars was formed, the date of its origin must have been much closer to the stage at which the Universe still consisted mainly of hydrogen, than it was at the time when our Sun and other stars akin to it were born. But if so, and if the globular star clusters belonged to the nth generation of stars formed in our Universe while our Sun belongs to the $(n+1)$st one, then obviously n cannot be a very large number; for otherwise a difference in composition between stars of two successive generations would tend to become only marginal.

On the other hand, one could argue that if the bulk of the heavy elements now present in our Universe were created during its initial 'big bang' stage, then the stars of old globular clusters should still differ but little in their composition from those born at a later time; for at the time when these clusters were formed the period of nucleogenesis connected with the 'big bang' would have been over. A conspicuous difference in the chemical composition of the globular star clusters and of stars formed later in the spiral arms of our galaxy is, therefore, difficult to explain by any approach initiated so far; and continues to confront us with a real problem.

Moreover, another great problem stares us in the face when we consider the 'big-bang' theory and its implications: namely, what could have been the cause of such a cosmic explosion? A possible clue to the answer may be furnished by another fundamental feature of the Universe which we have so far failed to point out with sufficient emphasis. We have repeatedly stressed in this chapter that, chemically speaking, the predominant constituents of our Universe are hydrogen and helium, followed by other elements of increasing atomic weight in diminishing amounts. But an even more fundamental property of this Universe is the fact that if we convert these elements by ionization into a plasma—and most of the matter in the Universe does consist of such a plasma—a great disparity in mass between particles carrying positive and negative charges is encountered: positive particles are present in cosmic plasma in the form of protons (or α-particles and even heavier atomic nuclei), negative charges occur predominantly in the form of electrons which are 1836 times less massive than the protons.

There is no obvious reason why this should be so; for positive electrons as well as negative protons likewise exist in nature; and a combination of the negative nuclei with positive electrons could give rise to 'anti-matter', the possibility of which is very much under discussion at the present time. But the fact remains that wherever we look around—on the Earth or in outer space as far as our telescopes permit us to penetrate it—we find only ordinary matter of the familiar kind; anti-matter seems conspicuous by its absence.

Not completely, perhaps; for its two essential ingredients—negative protons and positive electrons—do exist, and have in recent decades been produced in our laboratories (usually as a result of an interaction of matter with energetic particles—called 'cosmic rays'—accelerated to high energies in the stars or interstellar space). But they are condemned to lead a very furtive life; and when pried out of their respective niches within larger nuclear structures they disappear in a jiffy—usually, in one-millionth of a second or less—in a flash of light. It is the positive protons and negative electrons which possess a virtual monoply on the kind of plasma which we find in our Universe wherever we look.

Since there is no reason why such an obviously lopsided state of affairs should be necessary a priori, the contemporary physicists Alfvén and Klein regard it as an acquired rather than initial characteristic—acquired in the pre- 'big-bang' stage of our Universe; and the big bang itself could have been a symptom of this acquisition. According to Klein and Alfvén, in the utmost past the matter constituting our Universe existed in the form of a tenuous plasma in which positive and negative particles in each mass-range were equally represented ('ambi-plasma'). As long as this plasma was tenuous enough for the mean free path of the particles constituting it to be of the order of magnitude of the dimensions of the Universe (as the mean free path of the light photons is virtually still today), particles of opposite polarity had little chance to destroy each other.

However, such conditions could not have lasted for ever; for gravitational attraction of the material was bound to build up condensations from any local irregularities brought about by random fluctuations in density of the material in space; and, as a result, the Universe as a whole began to collapse—slowly at first, but with increasing acceleration. Such a process was bound to bring individual plasma particles into closer proximity more often. During such encounters, elementary particles of opposite polarity began to annihilate each other with increasing frequency; and, in so doing, converted their former energy into light.

The 'big-bang' may, indeed, represent a cataclysmic stage of such a process, in which most of the free negative protons and positive electrons perished in a universal holocaust that gave rise to the 'primaeval fireball', of which the relict $3°K$ radiation observed now in the microwave domain of the spectrum may represent a distant glare still seen across the aeons of time; and what emerged from this holocaust was the highly asymmetric plasma (Alfvén and Klein call it 'koino-plasma') constituting the Universe as we see it today. A synthesis of our chemical elements from such a plasma in stellar interiors and other cosmic reactors capable of accomplishing these feats may have been the principal physical process going on during this second act in the history of our Universe, just as a wholesale destruction of the 'ambi-plasma' may have been a climax of the first.

These boldly new views do not provide a logical answer to every question arising in this connection. For instance, they do not explain why certain kinds of particles (such as negative protons, or positive electrons, of the initial ambi-plasma) became so completely the victims of the victorious cohorts of the 'koino-plasma', and failed to survive the holocaust except by hiding in sheltered places. But they enable us to take a major step into the cosmic past—to a highly diffuse state of the Universe when material plasma possessed simpler and more symmetrical properties; and they enable us to relate the relict glare of the primaeval fireball with the amount of mass which should have been converted to light in the holocaust.

But whatever may have occurred in the past, and at whatever time the Universe we see now may have originated, advancing age is bound to deprive it of much of its former glory; and the night sky will look very different to our descendants than it does to us today—for two reasons. First, the continuing expansion of the Universe will tend to disperse the realm of the galaxies, and even the individual galaxies themselves. Their clusters can be compared with dispersing ships at sea; the hailing distance between them gradually increases beyond the horizon of visibility. Moreover, as more and more material of which the Universe consists will get repeatedly re-cycled through the blast furnaces of stellar interiors, and more and more hydrogen (or helium) converted into heavier elements with nuclei of diminishing 'packing fractions', stars of such composition will possess less and less nuclear energy available for production of light.

As the hydrogen-helium Universe in which we live now thus gradually gives way to one consisting predominantly of iron and its neighbours in the periodic table of the elements, more and more of its stars will become reduced to the stage of 'white dwarfs'; while the more substantial objects which once upon a time were the glories of the skies will be resting even more securely as 'black holes' in their gravitational coffins—entirely oblivious of their surroundings. Thus while our Universe may have been launched on its cosmic career in a blaze of light to the sound of a 'big bang', its distant future will see the energy density of its radiation dwindle to zero; with ghostly shadows of former stars and galaxies roaming aimlessly in the twilight of their existence, and eventually drifting out of sight of each other into the cold embrace of closed space in which there is no end to any path on which one may choose to travel.

The cosmic twilight, in which our Universe will be gradually submerged, is still a long time in the future—perhaps 50 to 100 billion years—a time many times as long as all our past. This fact should make us feel young as citizens of the Universe, and eager to see what the future may still hold in store. However, the future—while long—is not inconceivably long; for 100 billion years contains a number of consecutive average human life-spans of 70 years equal to the number of seconds that will elapse in 45 years;

The Structure and Evolution of Our Universe

while the past of the Universe—not less than 12 billion years—is equivalent to some two hundred million human lifetimes (or 4×10^8 generations).

But however much we may enjoy our cosmic youth and look forward to the future, we cannot readily dismiss from our minds thoughts running deeper than anything exposed in this book so far —thoughts which go back to the obvious question: if the Universe in which we live originated in a finite past, and now occupies a space of finite size—as many observed facts described in this chapter seem indeed to indicate—what was there before this Universe was formed, and what may exist beyond its present confines which no ray of light can penetrate?

What other divine messenger could traverse its barriers of space and time faster than light, and whom may the theory of relativity be powerless to confine to its world-lines? These are questions which many people have asked themselves—out of intellectual curiosity or mental anguish—in the past and present; but honesty compels us to admit that science can so far give them no answer. It cannot, however, prove that the Universe which is accessible to our exploration in space and time must necessarily be unique. Other Universes may conceivably co-exist with which we cannot communicate by light or gravitation; but whether or not they do actually exist you should not expect to learn from the astronomer —he does not know, but would like to know it as much as yourself.

CHAPTER XIV

Life in the Universe?

IN THE preceding parts of this book we have outlined the principal features of the inanimate cosmic scenery which at present surrounds us in space. In its second part (Chapter VI) we singled out for closer scrutiny the natural processes capable of giving rise to life and leading to the development of intelligent creatures which can contemplate our cosmic environment with understanding. Are we—the human beings—alone in possession of this ability to give rise to life, or are there other 'pockets' in the Universe where life may have developed to a level even more advanced than on our Earth? The Earth is almost certainly the only planet in our solar system which could have given rise to life on its surface, and support its development. The aim of this concluding chapter will be to extend our inquiry over the rest of the stellar Universe as we know it so far, and to say what we can on the basis of such knowledge as our ancestors and ourselves have accumulated from a study of our environment and from observations of the Universe around us.

First, virtually all biologists are now in substantial agreement that physical systems which can be described as 'living'—i.e., capable of metabolism and self-reproduction—could have originated only in 'temperate' cosmic climates, where their basic ingredients exist not only in solid, but also liquid state. Moreover, we shall probably not err by asserting that of all the liquids which can be formed in a Universe of the observed chemical composition, water (H_2O) is the only one that is likely to occur here, there and elsewhere in sufficient abundance to provide the parent environment for life and nurse its subsequent development in tender age. If so, however, this further limits the range of cosmic climate where life can be conceived and relegates its cradle to that class of astronomical bodies which we call the planets.

How many planets, or planetary systems, are there in the

Universe? We do not know yet the exact process by which stars like our Sun can surround themselves with a planetary system. However, we know from direct observations (*cf.* Chapter II) that a considerable number of stars in our neighbourhood possess companions whose masses are of planetary rather than stellar order of magnitude. When, moreover, we consider the effects of observational selection which hampers their discovery, we surmise with some confidence that at least one star in a hundred (and, possibly, as many as one in ten) may possess companions of planetary size and mass, which can be regarded as potential harbingers of life.

On the other hand, we learned in Chapter XI that our galaxy alone contains some 10^{12} (or more) stars not too different from those we find in our neighbourhood; and our photographic surveys of the sky have recorded some ten million stellar galactic systems in the depths of space that we have so far been able to penetrate with our telescopes. If, moreover, we take account of the fact that the Universe we live in may be at least ten times as large in size as the sample of it which we have already explored, it should consist of not less than 10^{21}–10^{22} individual stars; and of these, about 10^{20} may possess one or more planetary companions. Not all of these may prove suitable cradles of life by any means; in our own solar system only one planet—our Earth—out of nine proved capable of doing so; but as our estimate of the total number of stars in the Universe is probably conservative, we expect that—perhaps—life in our Universe could be nursed in something like 10^{20} individual cradles.

Now 10^{20} seems a very large number. It would represent the age of the Earth expressed in milliseconds; or again the number of molecules in a milligram (i.e., cubic millimetre) of water. But it is certainly large enough to convince us—no matter how difficult it is for Nature to nurse an agglomeration of organic molecules to form a human brain—that we are not alone in the Universe. Among the countless galaxies, each with its billions of stars, there must be a very large number of planets on which life is flourishing concurrently with our own.

It need not be the same kind of life as we know on the Earth. In giving an account of the development of terrestrial life in Chapter VI we stressed the fact that large organic molecules which constitute living matter are built around the atoms of carbon—a relatively light element whose nucleus is surrounded by six orbiting electrons. Its neighbours in the periodic table of the elements—the atoms of boron with five orbital electrons, and nitrogen with seven—do not possess a trace of the same sociability which enables the carbon atoms to gather around them, and hold together, such a numerous company of congenial elements—a company in which hydrogen, nitrogen, oxygen, or the heavier and more sedate phosphorus (necessary for the formation of nucleic acids and proteins which govern the metabolism of living cells) hold an especially prominent place. Everything else—atmospheric oxygen, for instance—is less essential; for our free terrestrial oxygen is no doubt largely a by-product of life itself (created by photosynthesis of green plants); and low organisms (bacteria) are known which subsist on methane or sulphur dioxide, and for which oxygen itself is as lethal as CH_4 or SO_2 would be for us. In fact, wherever we find in the spectrum of any planetary body absorption bands of molecular oxygen, we have the right to suspect that its origin may be organic, and indicate the presence of life of the same general type as on the Earth; for if it were not constantly replenished by some continuous process, it would soon get locked in solid oxides.

The converse of this is, however, not necessarily true, for carbon is not the only gregarious element of the periodic table which can serve as a centre of attraction for the formation of relatively large molecules. The other (among the light elements which are not too scarce in the Universe) is silicon—well known from the silicate compounds constituting a substantial fraction of the Earth's crust. Silicon atoms on the Earth (or on the Moon) did not give rise to any life; but the possibility cannot be ruled out that they may have done so on planets of other stars, where matter may be present in different overall composition, or exposed to physical conditions different from those in our own solar system. If so, it is intriguing to speculate in what respects such silicon-based life would differ from our carbon-based one; but this speculation remains so far purely theoretical, for physical chemistry in its present state of development can still offer little or no guidance as to the actual outcome.

The problem of the possibility of extra-terrestrial life is intimately connected with that of its origin—on the Earth or anywhere else. If it appears that life emerged from the primitive terrestrial environment by a synthesis of organic molecules activated by electrical discharge or ultraviolet light, similar processes are likely to have occurred (*mutatis mutandis*) under the right conditions on other worlds as well. In Chapter VI we took the view that the origin of life on the Earth was not optional, but rather a necessary consequence of the physical conditions then prevalent on our planet; and if so, we have every justification for expecting that life may have developed in, perhaps, a large fraction of the 10^{20} stellar systems which may contain a planet suitable for harbouring it. Unfortunately, statistical arguments of this nature are unlikely to satisfy that blend of scientific curiosity and love of adventure which may motivate the human quest for intelligent beings beyond the confines of the Earth, or of our solar system.

Where and how should we look for life in the Galaxy or beyond? The principal difficulty in the way of a discovery of planetary companions of the stars goes back to the enormous disparity in the apparent brightness of the stellar and planetary images; and a combination of this difference with angular proximity makes such a discovery utterly impossible with any kind of astronomical equipment on the surface of the Earth. In order to illustrate the point, let us recall that from the distance of our nearest stellar neighbour in space—the star α Centauri, a mere 4·29 light years away—our Sun would shine in the sky as a star of magnitude $+0·3$ (about the same as α Centauri appears to us). However, Jupiter—the largest planet of the solar system—would appear to us only as a tiny object of 23rd magnitude, separated from the Sun no more than $3''.9$ at maximum elongation; while our Earth would be still four times fainter (being ten times smaller in size, but five times nearer to the Sun) and only $0''.76$ away from the Sun. Moreover, at greater distances these angular separations would be proportionally diminished; while the apparent brightness would fall off with the inverse square of the distance. It is obvious that the light of such objects can never be detected by any tools available to the astronomers on the surface of the Earth. Space astronomy may offer new avenues of approach in the future; but the observational difficulties will continue to be formidable and the prospects are not hopeful.

This is true of natural light emitted (or reflected) by the celestial bodies. Ordinary light produced by most natural processes represents electromagnetic vibrations in different planes, with different wavelengths and phases. Atomic processes are known to emit light which is pretty nearly monochromatic (i.e., in which all vibrations possess nearly the same wavelength). It is, furthermore, possible by suitable devices to segregate waves vibrating in the same plane, and thus obtain light which we call polarized; but even in such a beam the phases of individual vibrations may be entirely uncorrelated (and thus constitute light which lacks coherence). Sunlight, as well as the artificial light of electric bulbs or flourescent tubes, is not coherent, because the atoms which are responsible for it emit light independently of each other. On the other hand, the electromagnetic waves transmitting our radio or television programmes are coherent, because the electrons which are responsible for them move in concert with each other within the appropriate electrical circuits.

Do any celestial bodies emit such a radiation which could be sent out by the deliberate action of intelligent beings? A systematic watch for coherent messages from the depths of the Universe in the domain of radio-frequencies was initiated in the United States during the last decade under the code name of Project OZMA, and the fact that it has so far proved fruitless should not detract from its potentially high interest; for in a matter as important as a search for intelligent life on other celestial bodies outside our solar system we cannot expect to obtain positive results in a few years. Besides, a drawback of the radio-astronomical approach is the relatively low angular resolution of the underlying observations. Suppose that we do detect a source of coherent radio emission in the sky: the 'field of view' of the radio-telescope employed would probably encompass hundreds of stars at very different distances from us, so that a unique identification of the source would be virtually impossible.

This latter difficulty would be lessened if, instead of radio-waves, coherent messages were beamed at us on substantially shorter wavelengths. Coherent light at optical frequencies, called *laser* (acronym for 'light amplifier with stimulated emission of radiation') was not produced by human hand till during the last ten years or so; and it should offer inestimable advantages for communications across cosmic distances in space. First, unlike coherent radio-emission which is also produced by natural processes (in pulsars, for instance), coherent emission variable at optical frequencies can only be produced by the artificial action of intelligent beings. Therefore, should we find a source of it blinking at us from any celestial body (whose identification in the sky would be relatively easy), we should have a *prima facie* case for the existence of intelligent life outside the confines of the solar system. Moreover, since a beam of coherent light can be made highly parallel—and thus largely immune to the attenuation of its intensity with inverse square of the distance—it could become detectable across vast expanses of space.

If a laser beam of the power of an ordinary pocket flashlight aboard the spacecraft Surveyor 7 on the Moon in January 1968 became easily visible on the Earth at a distance of 380,000 km—how much further one could penetrate with laser flashes packing megawatts of power! It is true that optical laser—like ordinary light—would suffer from a limited transparency of interstellar space. For example, we could not hope to see any such flash originating in (or on the other side of) the nucleus of our galaxy consisting of a huge number of individual stars. If, however, its originators are more intelligent than ourselves and can produce coherent beams of X-rays (possible in principle, but not yet produced on the Earth) of sufficient intensity, they could not only reach a galaxy-wide audience, but would also provide adequate means for pin-pointing its source.

On the production side, optical laser—and, in particular, X-ray laser—constitutes the most efficient way of squeezing out energy from atoms by concerted gymnastics of their electrons without disturbing their nuclei. An even more powerful laser ('gayser') can, in principle, be devised for squeezing out in unison the gamma-rays from radioactive nuclei. This should represent the ultimate in the production of intensive parallel beams of coherent light for interstellar communications across the whole galaxy. Are there, perhaps, such messages being beamed on us while you read these pages? We do not know; for we lack as yet any suitable apparatus or systematic programmes for monitoring them. For this we shall have to await the establishment of observing facilities in space, or on the Moon—hopefully in the not too distant future.

Suppose that such messages are received and identified one day: what should our reaction to them be? The immediate sentiments of adventure which such an event might evoke should be followed by thoughts of a more sobering kind. Evolution represents a very slow process; the evolutionary gap separating the human beings from their closest relatives in the ranks of the primates appears to be about 20 million years; and that between man and insects, perhaps 300 million years. This latter time interval represents only 1½ times the period in which our Sun revolves around the centre of our Galaxy—an interval quite short in comparison with the life-span of most stars. And what is true of a star, should also be true of its planets; for they should be of the same age. Therefore, in a cross-section of planetary life which we may find in our Galaxy at the present time we could encounter life at all stages of its evolution—from hundreds of millions of years behind our level, to hundreds of millions of years ahead of us.

If such is the case what could we hope to gain from an encounter with life which developed indigenously elsewhere, but from which we may be separated by such phase-lags? Life lagging behind us by such intervals of time could not attract our attention at a distance; moreover, even if we went out to find it, it would scarcely be of interest to anyone except microbiologists as inmates of their test tubes. If, on the other hand, we ourselves were to receive a visitation by extra-terrestrial beings intelligent enough to have discovered our existence, the chances are overwhelming that the boot would be on the other foot; and that we might find ourselves in their test tubes or other contraptions set up to investigate us as we do insects or guinea-pigs. Perhaps they would ignore us altogether; but if so, why would they have made the long journey through space to visit us? And if—perhaps the least likely contingency—they were resolved to treat us in a 'humane' manner and do us no harm, what could we learn from them or gain from such an encounter?

It is not, perhaps, realized that a meaningful—let alone fruitful —encounter between different civilizations is possible only if these do not differ too much in their degree of maturity. From the history and literature of bygone days it is obvious how wide a gap separates us from the civilization of the Middle Ages—let alone of ancient times. And—on the contemporary plane—it has been amply demonstrated that an impact of a more advanced civilization upon a less developed one brings peril rather than advantage to the weaker partner. Human history is replete with examples of the brutality of such encounters—not the least being the European colonization of America and of other parts of the world during the 16th–19th centuries.

Moreover, on a more civilized plane, our knowledge has for many centuries been increasing so fast that if, by some kind of a miracle, Aristarchos or Archimedes—great scientists of the Hellenistic civilization—woke up after two thousand years separating their time from the present to join us in our scientific discussions today, only small vestiges of our present knowledge would be intelligible to them. But, in the meantime, our intellectual advance proceeds at so fast a pace that, should we ourselves be able to listen to our scientific descendants a thousand years from now, it is highly doubtful if we could comprehend them at all. To our medieval ancestors who lived but one thousand years ago, we would certainly appear like magicians—to be venerated on their altars (or burned at their stakes); while our descendants equally removed in time from us in the future would probably consider us asinine.

A thousand, or ten thousand, years of evolutionary difference is just nothing on a cosmic scale; and the chances that we could come across another civilization in the Universe at approximately the same level of development—and with which we could effect some kind of intellectual understanding—are, therefore, vanishingly small. The risks entailed in an encounter with another civilization would vastly exceed any possible interest—let alone benefit; and could easily prove fatal. Therefore, should we ever hear that 'space-'phone' ringing in the form of observational evidence which admits no other explanation, for God's sake let us not answer; but rather make ourselves as inconspicuous as we can to avoid attracting attention.

And on this note of uncertainty, we are ready to part company with the reader. The entire contents of this book have not been exactly flattering to our terrestrial ego in so far as our cosmic importance is concerned; and there is little that we, the 'lords of creation', can do to bolster it up. In the centuries past we have seen astronomers dethrone our Earth step by step from a privileged position to a most insignificant place in the Universe; and our sense of cosmic importance as denizens of this place has gone down accordingly—except, perhaps, in one personal respect: no matter how many other stars may possess planets that can harbour life, or how many living creatures may populate any of them, the chances are overwhelming that each of us—you and I—are unique creatures in the whole Universe.

The reason rests in the astounding complexity of life as it has developed on the Earth so far. Our entire biological heritage—which took hundreds of millions of years to assemble—is contained in the set of genes in the chromosomes of parent cells from which we grew up. Suppose (to deliberately simplify the situation) that this treasure-chest consists of ten chromosomes, each containing one thousand genes. The total number of combinations in which these building-blocks could have organized themselves is equal to 10^{1000}—overwhelmingly the largest number we have encountered in this entire book. Compare it with the niggardly number of 10^{22} individual stars which, we estimate, constitute our Universe, weighing some 10^{55} grams; the mass of which should contain some 10^{79} elementary particles.

How small is even this latter number in comparison with 10^{1000} combinations in which our biological heritage could be reorganized! Therefore, the probability that life on another planet that may attend any one of the 10^{22}-odd stars has given—or will give in a finite time—birth to an individual just like you or me, with exactly the same gene structure, by a random process out of a sample of $10^{1000}-1$ alternative possibilities, is overwhelmingly negligible. No matter how many planets may exist in the Universe akin to our own Earth, and how many of these may have harboured—or will harbour—life, we cannot expect to have, or have had, any real *Doppelgänger* elsewhere than in our own imagination. Each one of us has a chance to appear only once on the grand stage of the theatre of our Universe as the individuals we are. Is not this sufficient reason for each of us to make the best use of the time which is vouchsafed to us on our Earth, and sufficient claim to a real distinction of cosmic validity?

The great depths of space—like the great ages of time—still possess secrets which they disclose only with reluctance, knowing that such secrets form a part of their lure. Most of these secrets are still hidden from us by an almost impenetrable veil; but we inwardly feel that their exploration may be connected with the ultimate aim of human existence. By studying the Universe in space and time, we can make our modest personal contribution to a permanent and cumulative fund of human knowledge that can provide a bridge to a better future. When we look back and contemplate the history of the past five thousand years of human endeavour, with its triumphs and pitfalls, when our ancestors carried forward—haltingly at times—the gradual conquest of ignorance by reason and understanding, can we not hear the categorical imperative inside our souls commanding us with an irresistible voice: 'Go and Do Likewise'?

INDEX

Abraham, 104
Adams, W. S., 212
Afrodite, 218
Akhen-Aten, 42
Aldrin, E. E., 176
Alexander the Great, 173
Alfvén, H., 296f
Algol (β Persei), 103
Altair (α Aquilae), 49, 52, 60
Ambi-plasma, 297
Anders, W. A., 176
Andromeda Nebula (M31), 76, 264ff
Anti-matter, 296
Apollo 8–14 missions to the Moon, 176, 202ff
Archimedes, 140, 307
Aristarchos, 275, 307
Aristoteles, 125f
Armstrong, N. A., 176
Associations, stellar, 251
Asteroids, 117, 192
Astroblemes, 193
Astronomical Unit (A.U.), 24f
Atmosphere, of the Earth, 147ff;
  of the Moon (lack of), 180f;
  of planets, 122, 210, 241;
  of Venus, 212;
  of Mars, 221f
β Aurigae, 71, 102
Australopithecus, 167

Baade, W., 105, 266
Barnard, E. E., 78
Barnard's star, 65, 74, 115
Baum, W. A., 280
Bean, A., 176

Beteigeuze (α Orionis), 49, 53, 55
Big-Bang Universe, theory of, 288, 295ff
Binary stars, 61ff;
  visual, 63ff;
  spectroscopic, 68;
  eclipsing, 69ff
Black holes, 110f
Borman, F., 176
Bouguer, P., 127
Bruno, Giordano, 43, 275

Caesar, Caius Julius, 173
Cambrian period, 162
Canopus (α Carinae), 49, 53
Capella (α Aurigae), 49f
Carboniferous period, 41, 162, 165
Carbon-nitrogen cycle, 91
Cepheid variables, 96f, 253
Cephei, 96f, 253f
Cernan, E. A., 176
Clusters of stars, *see* Open or Globular Clusters
Cluster-type variables, 255
Collins, M., 176
Comets, 117, 228ff;
  impacts on Earth, 167f;
  on the Moon, 182, 193
Conrad, Ch., 176
Continental drift, 140ff, 194
Copernicus, N., 275
Cosmic rays, 296
Cosmic year, 257
Coulomb barrier, 37f
Crab nebula (supernova of), 140ff, 282

Crab pulsar, 105
Cretaceous period, 163, 165
Cromagnon man, 170
Curtis, H. D., 265
Cusa, Nicolas de, 43
SS Cygni, 98
61 Cygni, 45ff, 65
Cygnus A radio source, 282
Cysat, J. B., 76

Dante, Alighieri, 33, 43
Deneb (α Cygni), 49, 53
De Sitter Model of the Universe, 287
Devonian period, 162
Doppler, Chr., 66
Doppler effect, 66ff, 74, 78f, 99, 280f, 292, 294
Doppler broadening (of spectral lines), 99
Duncan, J. C., 265
Dunham, Th., 212

Earth, 124ff;
  mass and size, 126ff;
  age of, 142;
  atmosphere of, 147ff;
  core of, 132ff;
  crust of, 138;
  exosphere of, 150;
  hydrosphere of, 145ff;
  ionosphere of, 149;
  life on, 157ff;
  magnetic field of, 136;
  mantle of, 132;
  stratosphere of, 149;
  troposphere of, 148
Earthquakes, 129f
Eclipsing variables, 69f
Eddington, A. S., 33, 36, 287ff, 294
Einstein, A., 286ff
Eratosthenes, 125f
Ewen, H. I., 80

Faraday rotation, 261
Flammarion, C., 286
Friedmann, A., 287ff

Galaxy (our), 241, 251ff, 301;
  spiral arms of, 259, 267;
  halo of, 255, 260;
  centre of, 255f;
  corona of, 260;
  "windows" in, 264
Galaxies (external), spiral, 265ff;
  spheroidal (elliptical), 266;
  dwarf, 267;
  clusters of, 268
Galilei, Galileo, 24, 126, 195, 275, 285
U Geminorum, 98
Geothermic degree, 134
Giant stars, 93ff, 108
Gilbert, W., 192
Globular clusters, 256, 261, 266, 295
Gordon, R. F., 176
Gravitation constant, 127f

Hadley rille (on the Moon), 176
Halley's comet, 229
Hamlet, Prince of Denmark, 276
Hartmann, J., 78
Helium flash, 94
Helmholtz, H., 35
Herschel, W. F., 62, 76, 104, 264f, 275, 285
Hertzsprung, E., 89
HR-Diagram, 89ff, 252, 261
Hesiod, 124f
Homo Sapiens, 170, 177
Hubble, E. P., 265, 280
Hubble's Law, 281ff, 289, 294
Hubble's Constant, 284, 289, 293
Huggins, W., 67, 76, 279
Humason, M. L., 280
Huyghens, Chr., 44

Ice Ages (on the Earth), 163, 165, 170, 257
Inner Metagalaxy (Local Group), 267ff
Intergalactic Tramps, 273
Irwin, J. B., 176

Jeans, J. H., 243

Index

Jeffreys, H., 243
Jupiter, 116ff
Jurassic period, 163

Kant, I., 242, 276
Kelvin, Lord (William Thomson), 35
Kepler, Johannes, 24, 44, 61, 126, 232, 275, 285
Kepler's Third Law (of periodic times), 25, 61ff
Klein, H., 296f
Koino-plasma, 297
Krüger 60 (star), 64, 92
Kuiper, G. P., 221

Laplace, P. S., 242
Laser, 304
Lemaître, G., 287ff
Leonardo da Vinci, 44
Life on the Earth, 157ff;
  evolution of, 160ff;
  life in the Universe, 300ff
Lindblad, B., 257
Long-period variables, 96
Lovell, J. A., 176
Lynds, R., 283

Magellanic Clouds, 264, 272
Main Sequence, 60, 89, 90ff, 102ff, 108
Mars, 116f, 208ff, 218ff;
  orbit of, 218f;
  size and mass of, 219;
  temperature on, 222f;
  craters on, 223;
  canal (absence of), 223f
Marius (Mayer) S., 76, 264
Maskelyne, N., 127
Mascons (on the Moon), 186, 192
Mass-luminosity relation for the stars, 73, 91
Maxwell's Law, 37
Mercury, 116f, 208ff, 225ff
Mesozoic Era, 163, 257
Metallic A stars, 99
Meteorites, impact on Earth, 165f;
  on the Moon, 189ff
Meteors, 233ff
Minkowski, R., 105
Miocene period, 163
Mira Ceti, 96
Mitchell, E. D., 176
Mizar (ξ UMa), 67
Moon, 175ff;
  orbit of, 178f;
  size and mass, 179;
  interior of, 185;
  craters on, 189ff;
  maria, 186, 189;
  "circular" maria, 192;
  temperature on the surface, 196f;
  in the interior, 187;
  radar contact with, 200f;
  composition of, 203f;
  age of, 205f
Muller, P. M., 186

Napoleon Bonaparte, 41, 173
Neanderthal man, 170
Neptune, 116ff
Neutron stars, 109
Newton, Isaac, 35, 54, 61, 126ff, 285, 290
Nicholson, S. B., 213
Novae, 97f, 265

Olbers, H. W. M., 277
Olber's paradox, 278f, 286, 288
Oligocene period, 163
Oort, J. H., 257
Opposition effect (in lunar light changes), 195
Optical Window (of atmospheric transparence), 26, 151f
Ordovician period, 162
Orion belt, 76, 78, 82
Orion Nebula, (M 42), 76f, 81f
OZMA project, 304

Paleocene period, 163
Paleozoic era, 162
Parallax (stellar) annual, 45f;
  spectroscopic, 252

Parmenides, 125
Parsec, 47
Pease, F. G., 280, 286
Period-luminosity relation, 96, 254
Permian period, 163
Pettit, E. B., 213
Pigafetta, A., 264
Pithecanthropus erectus, 169f
Planck's Law, 30, 55
Pleiades (cluster), 77, 252
Pliocene period, 164
Pluto, 53, 116f, 208ff, 225ff
Population I-II stars, 261ff, 271f, 291, 295;
 disc population, 271
Porphyrines, 79
Primeval Egg Universe, 288
Primeval Fireball, 292
Procyon (α CMi), 52, 100, 103
Proper motions (stellar), 52
Proto-galaxies, 271
Proton-proton reaction, 37, 91
Proto-stars, 84
Prutkov, K., 23
Pulsars, 101, 105f, 109
Purcell, E. M., 80
Pygmy stars, 100

Quasars, 282f, 293
Quaternary Era, 164
Quiesars, 283

Range-Doppler tracking, 217
Radial velocity, 67
Red Dwarfs, 97
Regolith (lunar), 202;
 on Mercury, 227
Relaxation (explosive) variable stars, 97f
Richer, J., 128
Rigel (β Orionis), 49, 52, 55
Roosa, S. A., 176
Rosse, Lord (William Parsons), 265
Russell, H. N., 89

Saari, J. M., 198

Sandage, A., 280, 283
Sargon, King of Sumer and Akkad, 104
Saturn, 116ff
Schmidt, M., 280, 282
Scott, D. R., 176
Seismometer, 130
Shakespeare, W., 147
Shapley, H., 255, 257
Shorthill, R. W., 198
Sinanthropus, 169
Sirius (α CMi), 49, 52, 100, 103
Sirius B, 103
Sjogren, W. L., 186
Slipher, V. M., 279, 286
Spectral classification (stellar), 58
Spectroscopic binaries, 68
Stafford, T. P., 176
Stefan's Law, 59
Stellar magnitudes, 47, 50;
 absolute, 51, 252
Stellar spectra, 54ff
Stonehenge, 41
Strong, J., 213
Subdwarfs, 97
Subgiants, 93, 108
Sun, 23ff;
 size and mass, 25;
 luminosity, 27;
 surface temperature, 27, 31;
 internal temperature and pressure, 29, 32;
 composition of, 32;
 energy sources, 34ff
Supernovae, 97f, 101, 104f;
 Kepler's, 104;
 Tycho's, 104, 282

Tantalos, 100
Temperature scale (stellar), 58
Tertiary Era, 164, 169
Triassic period, 163, 257
Tolstoy, A., 23

Uranus, 116ff
Urey, H. C., 192
Ussher, Archbishop, 35, 285, 290

Vega (α Lyrae), 45f, 47, 49f, 55
Vela pulsar, 105
Venus,, 50, 208ff;
  orbit of, 208;
  size and mass, 211f;
  temperature of, 213f;
  radar contact with, 215f;
  rotation of, 216f

Waves, elastic (longitudinal or transversal), 130
White dwarfs, 59, 99f, 109, 298
Wien's Law, 54

Wills, D., 283
Wind, solar, 29, 86, 94;
  stellar, 86
Wirtz, C., 280
Wolf 359 star, 48, 52
Worden, A. M., 176
Writing, invention of, 176

Young, J. W., 176

Zeeman splitting, 99
Zwicky, F., 104

Astronomy
Science

MAN AND HIS UNIVERSE

"*Man and His Universe* . . . explains in beautiful and simple language the history of the earth: its place in the solar system, and among the stars and galaxies. The story is told with authority. . . ."
—S. Fred Singer

During the past few years the science of astronomy has made enormous progress in unlocking the mysteries of the universe. Radio telescopes probe the depths of space, while spacecraft send back fresh knowledge of our planetary neighbors.

Using the latest methods and results of astronomical research, Professor Kopal, one of the world's leading astronomers and the author of numerous books on astronomy, has written a majestic survey of our universe and man's place in it. It was his aim to produce a book intelligible to the enthusiastic amateur, yet one that would also be of interest to the student of astronomy.

Professor Kopal interprets what is generally known about stars —including our Sun—their origin and evolution. He discusses our planetary system, and suggests how and why life developed only on the Earth. He analyzes what we know about the universe at large and adds some fascinating speculation concerning its past and future. He indicates where astronomical exploration may take man in centuries to come.

ZDENĚK KOPAL is a U.S. citizen who was born in Czechoslovakia in 1914. He has been Professor of Astronomy at the University of Manchester in England since 1951. During the academic year 1971–72 he was on leave with the Lunar Science Institute in Houston. He was a Research Associate at Harvard University from 1940 to 1946, and an Associate Professor at Massachusetts Institute of Technology from 1947 to 1951.

MORROW PAPERBACK EDITIONS
105 Madison Avenue, New York, New York 10016   0-688-05014-X